taste of home
Christmas
2010

taste of home
BOOKS

taste of home

© 2010 Reiman Media Group, Inc.
5400 S. 60th St., Greendale WI 53129
All rights reserved.

Taste of Home and Reader's Digest are registered trademarks of The Reader's Digest Association, Inc.

Editor in Chief: **Catherine Cassidy**

Vice President, Executive Editor/Books:
Heidi Reuter Lloyd

Food Director: **Diane Werner RD**

Senior Editor/Books: **Mark Hagen**

Editor: **Janet Briggs**

Craft Editor: **Jane Craig**

Project Editor: **Julie Schnittka**

Associate Editor: **Amy Glander**

Art Director: **Edwin Robles, Jr.**

Content Production Supervisor: **Julie Wagner**

Design Layout Artists: **Catherine Fletcher, Emma Acevedo**

Proofreader: **Linne Bruskewitz**

Recipe Asset System Manager: **Coleen Martin**

Premedia Supervisor: **Scott Berger**

Food Editors: **Karen Scales, Wendy Stenman**

Recipe Testing & Editing: **Taste of Home Test Kitchen**

Food Photography: **Taste of Home Photo Studio**

Administrative Assistant: **Barb Czysz**

North American Chief Marketing Officer: **Lisa Karpinski**

Vice President, Book Marketing: **Dan Fink**

Creative Director/Creative Marketing: **Jim Palmen**

The Reader's Digest Association, Inc.

President and Chief Executive Officer: **Mary G. Berner**

President, North American Affinities: **Suzanne M. Grimes**

"Cooking, Caring, Sharing" is a registered trademark of Reiman Media Group, Inc.

For other Taste of Home books and products, visit **ShopTasteofHome.com.**

International Standard
Book Number (10): 0-89821-797-0

International Standard
Book Number (13): 978-0-89821-797-1

International Standard Serial Number: 1948-8386

Cover Photography

Photographers: **James Wieland, Dan Roberts**

Food Stylists: **Kaitlyn Besasie, Diane Armstrong**

Craft Stylist: **Jane Craig**

Set Stylist: **Melissa Haberman**

Pictured on front cover (clockwise from top left):
Vanilla Chai Tea (p. 84) Goat Cheese & Pear Stuffed Tenderloin (p. 23) with Elegant Roasted Potatoes (p. 41) and Raspberry Pear Salad with Glazed Walnuts (p. 30), Ribbon Revelry (p. 113), Taco Chili Mix (p. 120) and Best Chocolate Raspberry Torte (p. 57).

Pictured on back cover (from left to right):
Cranberry-White Chocolate Trifle (p. 159), Pasta Puttanesca (p. 98) and Wine Bottle Gift Sack (p. 225).

Printed in U.S.A.

Contents

Party Starters & Beverages.............. 5

Christmas Dinners 21

From Special to Spectacular 45

Carefree Entertaining................. 59

Seasonal Get-Togethers 75

Festive Sides 91

Yuletide Breads 107

Gifts from the Kitchen............... 119

Cookie Exchange..................... 135

Holiday Sweets...................... 153

Deck the Halls 175

Gifts to Give 205

Recipe and Craft Indexes 230

The Most *Wonderful* Time Of the Year *Made Easy!*

"It's the most wonderful time of the year..." Or so the song goes. But when you're in the midst of the holiday hustle and bustle, it's sometimes hard to revel in the joy of the season. That's why we've put together this second edition of Taste of Home Christmas.

From 222 recipes perfect for entertaining and gift-giving to 56 crafting ideas for decking the halls and gifting to family and friends, this timeless treasury offers everything you need to make Christmas merry...without losing your patience and good humor!

Party Starters & Beverages. Bright beginnings to holiday parties start with delicious appetizers and drinks, such as Beef & Roasted Pepper Pinwheels, Chicken Artichoke Pizzas and Pumpkin Pie Martinis.

Christmas Dinners. Sit-down dinners are stress-free when you rely on such stunning selections as Goat Cheese & Pear Stuffed Tenderloin, Golden Roasted Turkey and Grouper with Crabmeat Sauce.

From Special to Spectacular. For this chapter's meal, we offer two versions of each recipe. One is simple yet striking (like Herb-Rubbed Pork Loin or Best Chocolate Cake). With additional ingredients or different cooking techniques, the second version becomes magnificent (such as Brined Pork Roast with Port Wine Sauce or Best Chocolate Raspberry Torte).

Carefree Entertaining. From Pork & Mozzarella Crostini and Sesame Chicken with Ginger Shiitake Cream Sauce to Pumpkin Pecan Sundaes and Cranberry Orange Cream Pie, entertaining can be both elegant and easy!

Seasonal Get-Togethers. *Taste of Home Christmas 2010* provides complete menus for Christmas morning brunch, a holiday high tea and a fun-filled St. Nick celebration.

Festive Sides. Don't forget to round out meals with special side dishes like Garlic Roasted Winter Vegetables, Mushroom Bread Dressing and Apple Sweet Potato Bake.

Yuletide Breads. Poppy Seed Cheese Bread...Almond-Cheese Coffee Cake...Maple Wheat Bread. No matter what you choose, fresh-baked goodies and the holidays just seem to go hand in hand!

Gifts from the Kitchen. You can express your sentiments to the special people in your life by giving a gift made from the heart. From savory to sweet, you'll find a tasty treat to please everyone.

Cookie Exchange. Bite-sized beauties—including Cinnamon Spritz, Coconut Pecan Joys, Peppermint Meringue Clouds and Pistachio Buttons—will liven up your dessert tray.

Holiday Sweets. Caramel Apple Trifle Delight, Chocolate Cran-Raspberry Cheesecake Bars, Heavenly Praline Cake and Mini Pumpkin Custards are just a few of this chapter's fitting finales.

Deck the Halls. From easy ideas (like a Santa Tree Topper) to more advanced crafts (such as a Checkerboard Tree Skirt), it's a snap to trim your home in a joyful way.

Gifts to Give. Don't head to the mall to buy expensive Christmas gifts! With a little time and tenderness, you can make festive presents such as a Skyline Purse, Reindeer Pull Toy, Pretty Painted Soap and Three-Tiered Beaded Necklace.

Making moments to remember during this spectacular season is simple with the stress-free recipes, seasonal decor and great gift ideas in Taste of Home Christmas 2010. Just turn the page and discover why Christmas truly is the most wonderful time of the year.

Party Starters
& BEVERAGES

Place bread on baking sheets; brush with 2 tablespoons oil. Broil 4-6 in. from heat for 1-2 minutes or until bread is lightly toasted.

In a large skillet, saute mushrooms with Italian seasoning in butter and remaining oil until tender. Add garlic; cook 1 minute longer. Remove from the heat and set aside.

Place artichokes in a food processor; cover and process until finely chopped. Add mayonnaise and Parmesan cheese; cover and process until blended. Spread over toast slices; top with mushrooms and sprinkle with Swiss cheese.

Bake at 350° for 4-6 minutes or until cheese is melted.

TO MAKE AHEAD: Prep the toasts earlier in the day and store on baking sheets in the refrigerator. Sprinkle with Swiss cheese just before baking.

Cranberry Chutney Crostini

PREP: 20 MIN.   **COOK:** 20 MIN.   **YIELD:** 2 DOZEN

Cranberry-topped crostinis look very pretty on a Christmas appetizer buffet. Every bite has the perfect balance of sweet, tart and savory flavors.

Cheryl Woodson ★ Liberty, Missouri

1	cup dried cranberries
1/3	cup chopped sweet red pepper
1/3	cup white wine vinegar
1/4	cup packed brown sugar
3	tablespoons chopped shallots
1	garlic clove, minced
1/2	teaspoon crushed red pepper flakes
1/4	teaspoon salt
1/4	teaspoon coarsely ground pepper
1/2	cup water, *divided*
1/4	cup chopped walnuts
24	slices French bread baguette (1/2 inch thick)
1	package (3 ounces) cream cheese, softened
3/4	cup crumbled Gorgonzola cheese

Minced chives, optional

For chutney, in a large saucepan, combine the first nine ingredients. Add 1/4 cup water. Bring to a boil. Reduce heat; simmer, uncovered, for 5 minutes. Add walnuts and remaining water; cover and cook for 10-15 minutes or until berries pop and chutney is thickened.

Meanwhile, place bread on an ungreased baking sheet. Bake at 350° for 8-10 minutes or until lightly browned. Combine cream cheese and Gorgonzola until smooth. Spread 1-1/2 teaspoons over each bread slice; top each with 1 tablespoon chutney. Sprinkle with chives if desired.

Artichoke & Mushroom Toasts

PREP: 30 MIN.   **BAKE:** 5 MIN.   **YIELD:** 3 DOZEN

Our winters can get cold here, so I like to warm up holiday guests with oven-fresh appetizers. Crunchy bread slices are topped with mushrooms, artichokes and a blend of cheeses.

Nancy Mueller ★ Bloomington, Minnesota

36	slices French bread baguette (1/2 inch thick)
3	tablespoons olive oil, *divided*
1/2	pound sliced fresh mushrooms
1/2	pound sliced baby portobello mushrooms
1/2	teaspoon Italian seasoning
2	tablespoons butter
6	garlic cloves, minced
1	jar (7-1/2 ounces) marinated quartered artichoke hearts, drained
1/3	cup mayonnaise
1	tablespoon shredded Parmesan cheese
2	cups (8 ounces) shredded Swiss cheese

Warm Chicken Fiesta Dip

PREP: 25 MIN.   **BAKE:** 25 MIN.   **YIELD:** 8 CUPS

This crowd-pleasing dip is always a success, whether I follow the recipe as is or if I substitute shredded pork and stir in chopped fresh mushrooms.

Shannon Arthur ★ Lucasville, Ohio

- 1   medium green pepper, chopped
- 1   medium onion, chopped
- 1   tablespoon olive oil
- 1/2 teaspoon chili powder
- 1/4 teaspoon salt
- 1/4 teaspoon pepper
- 1/4 teaspoon ground cumin
- 1   package (8 ounces) cream cheese, softened
- 1   can (10-3/4 ounces) condensed cream of chicken soup, undiluted
- 1   can (10 ounces) diced tomatoes and green chilies, undrained
- 1   jalapeno pepper, finely chopped
- 4   cups shredded rotisserie chicken
- 2   cups (8 ounces) shredded Mexican cheese blend, *divided*
- 1   green onion, thinly sliced

Tortilla *or* corn chips

In a large skillet, saute green pepper and onion in oil until tender. Add the chili powder, salt, pepper and cumin; cook 1 minute longer. Remove from the heat and set aside.

In a large bowl, beat cream cheese until smooth. Add the soup, tomatoes and jalapeno; mix well. Stir in the chicken, 1 cup cheese blend and green pepper mixture. Transfer to a greased 11-in. x 7-in. baking dish. Sprinkle with green onion and remaining cheese blend.

Bake, uncovered, at 350° for 25-30 minutes or until bubbly. Let stand for 5 minutes. Serve with chips.

Editor's Note: When cutting hot peppers, disposable gloves are recommended. Avoid touching your face.

Blue Cheese-Stuffed Shrimp

PREP: 20 MIN. + CHILLING   **YIELD:** 2 DOZEN

Cooked shrimp become something extraordinary when stuffed with blue cheese. The mild taste has mass appeal.

Amy Dollimount ★ Glace Bay, Nova Scotia

- 1   package (3 ounces) cream cheese, softened
- 2/3 cup minced fresh parsley, *divided*
- 1/4 cup crumbled blue cheese
- 1   teaspoon chopped shallot
- 1/2 teaspoon Creole mustard
- 24 cooked jumbo shrimp, peeled and deveined

In a small bowl, beat cream cheese until smooth. Beat in 1/3 cup parsley, blue cheese, shallot and mustard. Refrigerate for at least 1 hour.

Starting with the tail end of each shrimp, make a deep slit along the deveining line to within 1/4 to 1/2 in. of the bottom. Stuff with cream cheese mixture; press remaining parsley onto cream cheese mixture.

Poached Pears with Cheddar

(pictured at left)

PREP: 20 MIN.　**BAKE:** 15 MIN.　**YIELD:** 8 SERVINGS

This elegant hors d'oeuvre combines fruit, cheese and bread. I make it often during the Christmas season. You can experiment with different types of cheese.

Mary Ann Dell ★ Phoenixville, Pennsylvania

```
 4     medium Bosc pears
1-1/2  cups cranberry juice
 1/2   cup sugar
 1/4   cup raspberry vinegar
16     slices French bread baguette (1/2 inch thick)
 2     tablespoons butter, melted
 2     cups watercress
 8     ounces sharp cheddar cheese, thinly sliced
```

Core pears from the bottoms, leaving stems intact. Peel pears. Place on their sides in a large saucepan; add the cranberry juice, sugar and vinegar. Bring to a boil. Reduce heat; cover and simmer for 6-8 minutes or until pears are almost tender, turning once.

Remove pears with a slotted spoon; set aside. Bring poaching liquid to a boil; cook until liquid is reduced to about 1/3 cup.

Meanwhile, brush bread with butter. Place on an ungreased baking sheet. Bake at 375° for 8-10 minutes or until lightly browned.

Divide watercress among eight salad plates; top each with a pear half. Drizzle with poaching liquid. Place toast and cheese on plates.

Coring Pears Like a Pro

To core a fresh pear, insert an apple corer into the bottom of the pear to within 1 in. of its top. Twist the corer to cut around the core, then slowly pull the corer out of the pear to remove the core.

If you don't have an apple corer, use a sharp knife or vegetable peeler to cut the core from the bottom of the pear.

Beef & Roasted Pepper Pinwheels

PREP: 30 MIN. + CHILLING　**YIELD:** 2 DOZEN

Colorful basil leaves and roasted sweet red peppers add a delightfully festive touch to roll-ups featuring a garlic-cheese spread and deli meat.

Virginia Anthony ★ Jacksonville, Florida

```
 3     ounces reduced-fat cream cheese
 1/3   cup crumbled farmer or ricotta cheese
 3     tablespoons minced chives
 1     tablespoon minced fresh parsley
 1     small garlic clove, minced
Dash salt
Dash pepper
 3     flour tortillas (8 inches), room temperature
12     fresh basil leaves
 1/2   cup julienned roasted sweet red peppers
 6     slices deli roast beef
 1     tablespoon reduced-fat mayonnaise
```

Combine the first seven ingredients. Cover and refrigerate for at least 4 hours.

Spread 1/4 cup cheese mixture over each tortilla; layer with basil leaves, red peppers and beef. Spread mayonnaise over beef. Roll up tightly; wrap each in plastic wrap. Refrigerate for at least 1 hour. Unwrap and cut each into eight slices.

TO MAKE AHEAD: Prepare the roll-ups the day before; remove plastic wrap and slice as needed.

Pepperoncini Poppers

PREP/TOTAL TIME: 30 MIN.　**YIELD:** ABOUT 2 DOZEN

Guests won't be able to stop from popping these cheese-filled pepperoncinis into their mouths while mingling at your party! Bacon lends a slightly smoky flavor.

Connie Barszcz ★ Elmvale, Ontario

```
1/2   pound bacon strips, chopped
 1    medium onion, chopped
 1    package (8 ounces) cream cheese, softened
2/3   cup shredded cheddar cheese
 1    jar (32 ounces) pepperoncinis, drained
```

In a small skillet, cook bacon over medium heat until crisp. Remove bacon to paper towels with a slotted spoon; drain, reserving 2 tablespoons drippings. Saute the onion in the drippings.

Transfer to a small bowl; add cheeses and bacon. Stir until blended. Stuff pepperoncinis with cheese mixture. Refrigerate until serving.

Italian Cheese Wontons

PREP: 25 MIN. + CHILLING   **COOK:** 5 MIN./BATCH
YIELD: 40 WONTONS

A cheesy filling gives wonton wrappers a taste-tempting Italian twist. The hot and crispy snacks get gobbled up...no matter how many I make!

Barbara Pletzke ★ Herndon, Virginia

- 2   cups (8 ounces) shredded Italian cheese blend
- 1   carton (15 ounces) ricotta cheese
- 1   egg, beaten
- 1   tablespoon minced fresh parsley
- 1   garlic clove, minced
- 1/4   teaspoon salt
- 1/8   teaspoon pepper
- 40   wonton wrappers

Oil for deep-fat frying
Marinara *or* spaghetti sauce, warmed

In a large bowl, combine the first seven ingredients.

Position a wonton wrapper with one point toward you. (Keep remaining wrappers covered with a damp paper towel until ready to use.) Place 1 tablespoon filling in the center of wrapper. Fold bottom corner over filling; fold sides toward center over filling. Roll toward the remaining point. Moisten top corner with water; press to seal. Repeat. Refrigerate for 30 minutes.

In an electric skillet or deep-fat fryer, heat oil to 375°. Fry wontons, a few at a time, for 1-2 minutes on each side or until golden brown. Drain on paper towels. Serve with marinara.

TO MAKE AHEAD: Prepare the wonton filling the day before. Fill the wontons the day of the party, cover with damp paper towels and plastic wrap and store in the refrigerator.

Gourmet Stuffed Mushrooms

PREP: 30 MIN.   **BAKE:** 10 MIN.   **YIELD:** ABOUT 2 DOZEN

The slightly smoky flavor of sun-dried tomatoes comes through beautifully in these stunning "shrooms."

Vicki Moore ★ Little Rock, Arkansas

-   2 pounds large fresh mushrooms
-   2 tablespoons olive oil, *divided*
-   1/2 pound ground pork
-   1 small onion, chopped
-   4 garlic cloves, minced
-   1/2 cup chopped shallots
-   3 tablespoons butter
-   3 tablespoons all-purpose flour
-   1 teaspoon dried basil
-   1/2 teaspoon salt
-   1/4 teaspoon pepper
-   1/4 cup pine nuts, toasted
-   1/4 cup sun-dried tomatoes (not packed in oil), chopped
-   1/4 cup water-packed artichoke hearts, rinsed, drained and chopped
-   1 cup (4 ounces) shredded Gruyere *or* Swiss cheese
-   1/3 cup sour cream
-   1/2 cup grated Parmesan cheese

Remove stems from mushrooms and finely chop; set aside. Place mushroom caps in a large bowl. Drizzle with 1 tablespoon oil; toss to coat. Place caps in an ungreased 15-in. x 10-in. x 1-in. baking pan. Bake at 400° for 8-10 minutes or until tender.

Meanwhile, in a large skillet over medium heat, cook pork and onion until meat is no longer pink. Add garlic; cook 1 minute longer. Drain and set aside.

In the same skillet, saute shallots and mushroom stems in butter until tender. Stir in the flour, basil, salt and pepper until blended. Add the pine nuts, tomatoes, artichokes and pork mixture; cool slightly. Stir in Gruyere and sour cream.

Spoon filling into mushroom caps; sprinkle with Parmesan cheese. Bake for 8-10 minutes or until the filling is bubbly.

Glazed Orange Chicken Wings

PREP: 10 MIN.   **BAKE:** 30 MIN.   **YIELD:** 1-1/2 DOZEN

Frozen juice concentrate is the tasty base for moist and tender chicken wings. They're well-glazed but not too sticky, so the wings are easy to eat while mingling with friends and family.

Marie Brown ★ Carthage, Mississippi

-   2 pounds chicken wingettes and drumettes
-   1 can (6 ounces) frozen orange juice concentrate, thawed
-   2 tablespoons reduced-sodium soy sauce
-   1/2 teaspoon salt
-   1/2 teaspoon celery seed
-   1/2 teaspoon hot pepper sauce
-   1/4 teaspoon ground ginger

Place chicken in a greased 13-in. x 9-in. baking dish. Combine the remaining ingredients; pour over chicken. Bake, uncovered, at 375° for 30-40 minutes or until juices run clear, basting occasionally with glaze.

TO MAKE AHEAD: Prepare the glaze ingredients up to 1 week in advance; store in the refrigerator.

Raspberry Fizz

PREP/TOTAL TIME: 5 MIN.   **YIELD:** 1 SERVING

As a festive, nonalcoholic beverage, this pretty pink drink comes from our Test Kitchen. It has a mild raspberry flavor and isn't overly sweet.

- 2 ounces ruby red grapefruit juice
- 1/2 to 1 ounce raspberry flavoring syrup
- 1/2 to 3/4 cup ice cubes
- 6 ounces club soda, chilled

In a mixing glass or tumbler, combine grapefruit juice and syrup. Place ice in a highball glass; add juice mixture. Top with club soda.

Editor's Note: This recipe was tested with Torani brand flavoring syrup. Look for it in the coffee section of your grocery store.

Hot Crab & Artichoke Dip

PREP: 20 MIN.   **BAKE:** 20 MIN.   **YIELD:** 3-1/2 CUPS

The addition of crabmeat makes this artichoke spread a little more special than most. The recipe proves that great-tasting dishes don't have to take a lot of time to prepare!

Emily Almaguer ★ Fort Worth, Texas

- 1 medium leek (white portion only), thinly sliced
- 2 tablespoons olive oil
- 1 can (14 ounces) water-packed artichoke hearts, rinsed, drained and chopped
- 2 cans (6 ounces *each*) crabmeat, drained, flaked and cartilage removed
- 1 package (8 ounces) cream cheese
- 1 tablespoon lemon juice
- 1/2 teaspoon salt
- 1/4 teaspoon pepper
- 1/8 teaspoon cayenne pepper
- 1 cup (4 ounces) Gruyere cheese, *divided*
- 1/2 cup sour cream
- 1/3 cup plus 2 tablespoons shredded Asiago cheese, *divided*

Cubed French bread

In a large skillet, saute leek in oil until tender. Add the artichokes, crab, cream cheese, lemon juice, salt, pepper and cayenne; heat until cream cheese is melted. Remove from the heat; stir in 3/4 cup Gruyere cheese, sour cream and 1/3 cup Asiago cheese.

Transfer to a greased 9-in. pie plate; sprinkle with remaining cheeses. Bake, uncovered, at 350° for 20-25 minutes or until golden brown. Serve with bread.

Cleaning Leeks

Leeks often contain sand between their many layers. Cut the leeks lengthwise in half. Rinse under cold running water, gently separating the leaves to allow the water to flush out any trapped sand or dirt.

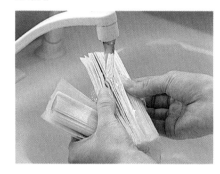

2 tablespoons honey
2 teaspoons ground cinnamon
1 can (14 ounces) whole-berry cranberry sauce
1 cup sliced almonds, toasted
Assorted crackers

In a small bowl, beat the cream cheese, sour cream, honey and cinnamon until smooth. Spread into a shallow bowl or 9-in. pie plate. Top with cranberry sauce. Cover and refrigerate for at least 1 hour. Just before serving, sprinkle with almonds. Serve with crackers.

TO MAKE AHEAD: Prepare the dip up to 2 days ahead. Sprinkle with almonds and let stand at room temperature for 30 minutes before serving.

Eggnog

PREP: 15 MIN.   **COOK:** 20 MIN. + CHILLING
YIELD: 20 SERVINGS (3/4 CUP EACH)

Store-bought eggnog just can't compete with my homemade version. Apricot brandy is my secret ingredient!

Shelia Weimer ★ Bluefield, West Virginia

1-3/4 cups sugar
1/4 cup all-purpose flour
1/2 teaspoon salt
2 quarts 2% milk
6 eggs, beaten
1 cup apricot brandy *or* brandy
1/2 cup rum
2 tablespoons bourbon
2 tablespoons vanilla extract
1 quart half-and-half cream
1/2 teaspoon ground nutmeg

In a Dutch oven, combine the sugar, flour and salt. Gradually whisk in milk until smooth. Cook and stir over medium-high heat until thickened and bubbly. Reduce heat; cook and stir 2 minutes longer. Remove from the heat.

Stir a small amount of hot mixture into eggs; return all to the pan, stirring constantly. Cook and stir over medium heat until mixture is slightly thickened and coats the back of a spoon.

Transfer to a large bowl; cool quickly by placing bowl in ice water and stirring for 2 minutes. Stir in the brandy, rum, bourbon and vanilla. Cool completely. Cover and refrigerate for at least 3 hours. Just before serving, stir in cream and nutmeg.

Greek Veggie Tartlets

PREP/TOTAL TIME: 20 MIN.   **YIELD:** 45 TARTLETS

This recipe started out as a salad, which I re-created after a trip to Greece. When my husband suggested I serve the savory mixture in phyllo cups, it became my most-requested appetizer!

Radelle Knappenberger ★ Oviedo, Florida

3/4 cup *each* finely chopped red onion, seeded peeled cucumber and seeded tomatoes
3/4 cup Greek olives, finely chopped
1/2 cup Greek vinaigrette
3 packages (1.9 ounces *each*) frozen miniature phyllo tart shells
3/4 cup crumbled feta cheese

In a large bowl, combine the vegetables, olives and vinaigrette. Spoon into tart shells, about 1 tablespoon in each. Sprinkle with cheese.

Creamy Cranberry Dip

PREP: 15 MIN. + CHILLING   **YIELD:** 4 CUPS

You can use a variety of salty crackers to scoop up helpings of this slightly sweet cranberry dip. The recipe yields a lot so it's perfect for large gatherings.

Joy McQuaid ★ Darlington, Wisconsin

1 package (8 ounces) cream cheese, softened
1 cup (8 ounces) sour cream

In a large saucepan, bring 1/2 in. of water to a boil. Add spinach; cover and boil for 3-5 minutes or until wilted. Drain well and chop.

In a large skillet, saute onion in oil until tender. Stir in tomatoes and cream cheese until blended. Stir in the spinach, cheese blend, chilies, vinegar and pepper sauce. Transfer to an 8-in. square baking dish. Bake, uncovered, at 350° for 30-35 minutes or until bubbly and lightly browned. Serve warm with chips.

Lemon Fruit Dip

PREP: 10 MIN. + CHILLING **YIELD:** 3 CUPS

I prepare this fluffy dip several times a month to encourage my kids to eat more fruit. Partygoers also appreciate a more nutritious snack option.

Sonja Whitchurch ★ Thomas, Ontario

- 1/2 cup confectioners' sugar
- 3 tablespoons lemon juice
- 1-1/2 teaspoons grated lemon peel
- 1 carton (8 ounces) frozen whipped topping, thawed
- 4 to 5 drops yellow food coloring, optional

Assorted fresh fruit

In a small bowl, combine the confectioners' sugar, lemon juice and peel. Stir in whipped topping and food coloring if desired. Refrigerate for at least 4 hours. Serve with fruit.

TO MAKE AHEAD: Prepare the dip up to 3 days ahead. Cut fruit and arrange on serving trays the day of the party. Refrigerate both until you are ready to serve them.

Southwest Spinach Dip

PREP: 20 MIN. **BAKE:** 30 MIN. **YIELD:** 5-1/2 CUPS

Even people who usually stay away from spinach will indulge in this delicious dip. You can increase the spiciness by adding more hot sauce.

Caula Barley ★ Johnstown, Pennsylvania

- 1 package (6 ounces) fresh baby spinach
- 1 large onion, chopped
- 1 tablespoon canola oil
- 2 cans (14-1/2 ounces *each*) Mexican diced tomatoes, drained
- 1 package (8 ounces) cream cheese
- 2 cups (8 ounces) shredded Mexican cheese blend
- 1 can (4 ounces) chopped green chilies
- 4-1/2 teaspoons red wine vinegar
- 1/8 teaspoon hot pepper sauce

Tortilla chips

Second Life for Tortilla Chips

After a party, do you have leftover tortilla chips that are going stale? Here are some tasty ways to give those chips a second life.

- Finely crush the chips and use in place of dry bread crumbs as a coating for poultry or fish.
- Coarsely crush them and add to spicy Mexican-style soups or chowders.
- Crush them and sprinkle on casseroles before baking as a tasty topping.
- Coarsely crush them and use in place of croutons on a salad.

Herbed Cheesecake

PREP: 35 MIN.   **BAKE:** 45 MIN. + CHILLING
YIELD: 16 SERVINGS

If this large cheesecake is too much for your gathering, cut it into wedges. Enjoy one now and freeze the other wedges for a fast appetizer in the future.

Ann Chan ★ Atlanta, Georgia

CRUST:
- 1 egg yolk, beaten
- 1 cup all-purpose flour
- 1/2 cup butter, softened
- 2 teaspoons grated lemon peel
- 1/2 teaspoon salt

FILLING:
- 3 packages (8 ounces *each*) cream cheese, softened
- 3 tablespoons all-purpose flour
- 4 eggs, lightly beaten
- 1 cup grated Parmesan cheese
- 2/3 cup minced fresh parsley
- 1 small onion, chopped
- 1/2 cup chopped pepperoni
- 2 tablespoons lemon juice
- 1 tablespoon *each* minced fresh basil, tarragon and oregano *or* 1 teaspoon *each* dried basil, tarragon and oregano
- 1-1/2 teaspoons minced fresh rosemary *or* 1/2 teaspoon dried rosemary, crushed
- 2 garlic cloves, minced
- 1 teaspoon salt
- 1/2 teaspoon hot pepper sauce

Assorted crackers

In a small bowl, combine the crust ingredients. Press onto the bottom and 2 in. up the sides of a greased 9-in. springform pan. Place pan on a baking sheet. Bake at 325° for 15-20 minutes or until crust is lightly browned. Cool on a wire rack.

In a large bowl, beat cream cheese and flour until smooth. Add eggs; beat on low speed just until combined. Stir in Parmesan cheese, parsley, onion, pepperoni, lemon juice, herbs, garlic, salt and pepper sauce. Pour into crust.

Bake at 325° for 45-55 minutes or until center is almost set. Cool on a wire rack for 10 minutes. Carefully run a knife around the edge of pan to loosen; cool 1 hour longer. Refrigerate overnight. Remove the sides of the pan. Serve with crackers.

Bake for 6-8 minutes or until golden brown. Cool completely on wire racks.

For topping, in a small saucepan, combine cranberry sauce and 3 tablespoons water. Combine cornstarch and remaining water until smooth; gradually stir into cranberry mixture. Bring to a boil; cook and stir for 1 minute or until thickened. Spoon over tartlets.

Chicken Artichoke Pizzas

PREP/TOTAL TIME: 25 MIN.
YIELD: 2 PIZZAS (12 SLICES EACH)

You'll need a knife and fork to delve into the ooey-gooey goodness of this delectable pizza. Pepper Jack cheese and green chilies give it a little kick.

Paula Gylland ★ Brookfield, Wisconsin

- 1 can (14 ounces) water-packed artichoke hearts, rinsed, drained and chopped
- 3 cups (12 ounces) shredded pepper Jack cheese, *divided*
- 1-1/2 cups cubed cooked chicken breast
- 1 can (4 ounces) chopped green chilies
- 1/4 cup mayonnaise
- 1/4 cup sour cream
- 1 envelope Italian salad dressing mix
- 2 prebaked 12-inch thin pizza crusts

In a large bowl, combine the artichokes, 1 cup cheese, chicken, chilies, mayonnaise, sour cream and salad dressing mix. Place crusts on pizza pans; spread with artichoke mixture. Sprinkle with remaining cheese.

Bake at 450° for 10-14 minutes or until bubbly.

Cranberry-Orange Tartlets

PREP: 25 MIN.   **BAKE:** 15 MIN. + COOLING
YIELD: 6 DOZEN

I like to mix up my offerings at appetizer parties by including some sweeter selections. With Mascarpone cheese and cranberries in puff pastry shells, these bite-sized beauties are always a delight.

Mary Licata ★ Pembroke Pines, Florida

- 1 package (17.3 ounces) frozen puff pastry, thawed
- 3/4 cup Mascarpone cheese
- 1/4 cup sugar
- 3 tablespoons finely chopped dried cranberries
- 3 tablespoons beaten egg
- 2 teaspoons grated orange peel
- 3 tablespoons finely chopped walnuts

TOPPING:
- 1/2 cup whole-berry cranberry sauce
- 3 tablespoons plus 4-1/2 teaspoons water, *divided*
- 2 teaspoons cornstarch

Unfold puff pastry; roll each sheet into a 10-in. square. Cut each into 36 squares. Gently press squares into greased miniature muffin cups. Bake at 375° for 10 minutes. Using the end of a wooden spoon handle, make a 1/2-in. indentation in the center of each.

In a small bowl, combine the cheese, sugar, cranberries, egg and orange peel. Place about 1 teaspoon filling in each muffin cup. Sprinkle with walnuts.

Smoked Sausages with Mustard Sauce

PREP/TOTAL TIME: 30 MIN.   **YIELD:** ABOUT 3-1/2 DOZEN

Miniature sausages are a welcome sight at any party. I keep the ingredients for this always-pleasing appetizer on hand so I can whip it up on a moment's notice.

Doris Heath ★ Franklin, North Carolina

- 1 package (16 ounces) miniature smoked sausages
- 2 teaspoons canola oil
- 1/2 cup sugar
- 3 tablespoons ground mustard
- 2 tablespoons all-purpose flour
- 1/2 teaspoon salt
- 1 cup half-and-half cream
- 2 egg yolks, beaten
- 2 tablespoons white vinegar

In a large skillet, brown the sausages in oil; drain and keep warm.

In a small saucepan, combine the sugar, mustard, flour and salt. Stir in cream until smooth. Cook and stir over medium heat until thickened and bubbly. Reduce heat; cook and stir 2 minutes longer.

Remove from the heat. Stir a small amount of hot mixture into egg yolks; return all to the pan, stirring constantly. Bring mixture to a gentle boil; cook and stir 1 minute longer.

Remove from the heat and gently stir in vinegar. Pour over sausages; serve warm.

Cooked Chicken

If you don't have any leftover chicken for Chicken Artichoke Pizzas, you can poach, bake or microwave some chicken breasts. You'll need about 10 to 12 ounces of boneless, skinless chicken breasts to make 1-1/2 cups of cubes. Another super easy way to have cubed chicken is to buy two fried bone-in chicken breasts at your supermarket. The cooking is done and all you need to do is remove the bones and skin and cube the meat.

Spiced Peanuts

PREP: 10 MIN.   **BAKE:** 20 MIN.   **YIELD:** 3 CUPS

Liven up plain peanuts with a sweet-and-spicy blend of flavors from sugar, cumin and cayenne pepper. You'll want to double—or triple—the recipe!

Holly Kunkle ★ Walton, Kentucky

- 1 jar (16 ounces) unsalted dry roasted peanuts
- 2 tablespoons canola oil
- 2 tablespoons sugar
- 1-1/2 teaspoons ground cumin
- 1 teaspoon salt
- 1/2 teaspoon cayenne pepper
- 1/2 teaspoon garlic powder

Place peanuts in a small bowl; drizzle with oil and toss to coat. Combine sugar and seasonings; sprinkle over nuts and toss to coat. Transfer to an ungreased 15-in. x 10-in. x 1-in. baking pan. Bake at 300° for 20-25 minutes or until lightly browned, stirring occasionally. Spread on waxed paper to cool. Store in an airtight container.

Pumpkin Pie Martinis

PREP/TOTAL TIME: 5 MIN. **YIELD:** 2 SERVINGS

My girlfriends begin requesting this cocktail in fall and continue to ask for it through the holidays. Every sip is like a taste of pumpkin pie!

Cathleen Bushman ★ Geneva, Illinois

  1 vanilla wafer, crushed, optional
Ice cubes
  2 ounces vanilla-flavored vodka
  2 ounces milk
  2 ounces heavy whipping cream
  1 ounce simple syrup (see recipe at right)
  1 ounce hazelnut liqueur
  1/8 teaspoon pumpkin pie spice
Dash ground cinnamon

If a cookie-crumb rim is desired, moisten the rims of two cocktail glasses with water. Place cookie crumbs on a plate; dip rims in crumbs. Set aside.

Fill a mixing glass or tumbler three-fourths full with ice. Add the remaining ingredients; stir until condensation forms on outside of glass. Strain martini into two chilled cocktail glasses.

Editor's Note: You may substitute 1 ounce pumpkin flavoring syrup for the simple syrup and pumpkin pie spice. Look for flavoring syrup in the coffee section of your grocery store.

Enjoy Your Party

So that you can spend more time with guests, look for appetizers that can be made ahead and require little last-minute fuss. Also, supplement homemade nibbles with purchased party fare.

Simple Syrup

PREP: 15 MIN. + COOLING **YIELD:** 1-2/3 CUPS

Sometimes called sugar syrup, this simple syrup is a staple in many beverage recipes.

  2 cups sugar
  1 cup water

In a small saucepan, combine sugar and water. Bring to a boil over medium heat. Reduce heat; simmer, uncovered, for 3-5 minutes or until sugar is dissolved, stirring occasionally. Remove from the heat; cool to room temperature.

Transfer to a container with a tight-fitting lid. Store in the refrigerator for up to 2 weeks.

Felt Christmas Coasters

In the photo at left, glasses of Pumpkin Pie Martinis are sitting on festive felt coasters that you can easily make. Here's how:

Trace tree pattern on page 90. Use pinking shears to cut a 3-1/2-in. square piece of white felt. Glue white square onto a 4-in. square of blue felt. Cut out a tree using the tree pattern from the blue felt. Cut tree on dashed lines to make four sections as shown right. Glue to the white felt, leaving a small gap between each section. With the pinking shears, cut out four small blue felt triangles and glue them to the corners. Glue the bottom of the blue felt square to a 3-3/4-in. square of cork. Let dry completely before using.

Pancetta Scallops on Potato Rounds

PREP: 35 MIN.   **COOK:** 5 MIN./BATCH
YIELD: ABOUT 15 APPETIZERS (PLUS 1/2 CUP
LEFTOVER VINAIGRETTE)

Serving the pancetta-wrapped scallops on red potato slices makes for a pretty presentation. The delicate flavors will appeal to seafood lovers.

Cheryl Perry ★ Hertford, North Carolina

- 5 small red potatoes, cut into 1/4-inch slices
- 1/3 pound sliced pancetta *or* bacon
- 1/2 teaspoon salt
- 1/2 teaspoon onion powder
- 1/2 teaspoon coarsely ground pepper
- 1 pound sea scallops
- 2 tablespoons butter
- 1 tablespoon olive oil

VINAIGRETTE:

- 3 tablespoons white wine vinegar
- 2 tablespoons minced fresh rosemary *or* 1 teaspoon dried rosemary, crushed
- 1 garlic clove, halved
- 1/4 teaspoon salt
- 1/2 cup olive oil

Place potatoes in a large saucepan and cover with water. Bring to a boil. Reduce heat; cover and cook for 8-10 minutes or until tender.

Meanwhile, in a large skillet, cook pancetta over medium heat until partially cooked but not crisp. Remove to paper towels to drain. Combine the salt, onion powder and pepper. Wrap a slice of pancetta around each scallop; sprinkle salt mixture over both sides.

In a large skillet over medium-high heat, cook scallops in butter and oil for 1-1/2 to 2 minutes on each side or until firm and opaque. Remove from the heat and keep warm. Drain potatoes; set aside.

In a blender, combine the vinegar, rosemary, garlic and salt; cover and process until blended. While processing, gradually add oil in a steady stream.

To assemble appetizers, top each potato slice with a scallop; drizzle each with 1/4 teaspoon vinaigrette (save remaining vinaigrette for another use).

Editor's Note: Pancetta is an Italian bacon, which is cured with salt, spices and pepper. Look for it in the packaged gourmet deli section of your grocery store.

Christmas
DINNERS

Beef Dinner

Goat Cheese & Pear
Stuffed Tenderloin
pg. 23

Bacon Caesar Salad
pg. 26

Baked Sweet Onions
pg. 24

Garlic Roasted Broccoli
pg. 25

Cranberry-Champagne
Granita
pg. 27

Goat Cheese & Pear Stuffed Tenderloin

PREP: 40 MIN.   **BAKE:** 40 MIN. + STANDING
YIELD: 8 SERVINGS (3/4 CUP SAUCE)

Fresh pears provide a bit of sweetness to a special stuffing for beef tenderloin and beautifully balances the peppery arugula and tart goat cheese.

Cindie Haras ★ Boca Raton, Florida

- 2 medium pears, peeled and sliced
- 1 tablespoon butter
- 1 beef tenderloin roast (2-1/2 pounds)
- 1 cup fresh arugula *or* baby spinach
- 1/2 cup crumbled goat cheese
- 1 tablespoon plus 1 teaspoon *each* minced fresh parsley, basil and tarragon
- 1 tablespoon olive oil
- 1/8 teaspoon salt
- 1/8 teaspoon pepper

SAUCE:
- 4 shallots, finely chopped
- 2 teaspoons butter
- 1/2 cup sherry
- 1/2 cup reduced-sodium beef broth
- 2 tablespoons minced fresh tarragon
- 2 teaspoons cornstarch
- 2 teaspoons cold water

In a large skillet, saute pears in butter until tender.

Cut a lengthwise slit down the center of the tenderloin to within 1/2 in. of bottom. Open tenderloin so it lies flat. On each half, make another, lengthwise slit down the center to within 1/2 in. of bottom; open roast and cover with plastic wrap. Flatten to 1/2-in. thickness. Remove the plastic wrap.

Spread the pears, arugula, cheese and herbs over meat to within 1 in. of edge. Roll up jelly-roll style, starting with a long side. Tie roast at 1-1/2-in. intervals with kitchen string.

Place on a rack in a shallow roasting pan. Combine the oil, salt and pepper; rub over roast. Bake at 425° for 40-50 minutes or until meat reaches desired doneness (for medium-rare, a meat thermometer should read 145°; medium, 160°; well-done, 170°). Let stand for 15 minutes before slicing.

In a small saucepan, saute shallots in butter until tender. Add sherry; cook over low heat for 4 minutes. Add broth and tarragon. Combine cornstarch and water until smooth; gradually stir into the pan. Bring to a boil; cook and stir for 1 minute or until thickened. Serve with beef.

Snowy Candle Centerpiece

Bring a bit of nature's winter wonderland indoors! Place two sheets of copy paper inside a clear glass vase so that each piece is against the inside of the vase. The papers will overlap and extend from the top. Slip natural or artificial flat greens between the paper and the vase. Pour Epsom salt, canning salt or sugar into vase until it is about two-thirds full. Carefully remove each piece of paper so that the greens remain pressed against the side of the vase. Set small red berries on top of the Epsom salt. Insert a white taper candle in the center, pushing it down to the bottom of the vase.

Baked Sweet Onions

PREP: 25 MIN.   **BAKE:** 40 MIN.   **YIELD:** 8 SERVINGS

Baking enhances the natural sweetness of my family's favorite Vidalia onions. Perfect alongside beef entrees, this side dish has a similar taste to French onion soup.

Ann Yarber ★ Goldsby, Oklahoma

8	large sweet onions, peeled
1/2	cup butter, melted
1/2	cup Burgundy wine *or* beef broth
8	teaspoons beef bouillon granules
1	teaspoon dried thyme
1	teaspoon pepper
1-1/2	cups shredded Swiss cheese

Cut each onion into six wedges to within 1/2 in. of the bottom. Place each onion on a piece of heavy-duty foil (about 12 in. square).

In a small bowl, combine the butter, wine, bouillon, thyme and pepper. Spoon over onions; sprinkle with cheese. Fold foil around each onion and seal tightly. Place on a baking sheet. Bake at 425° for 40-45 minutes or until onions are tender. Open foil carefully to allow the steam to escape.

Garlic Roasted Broccoli

PREP/TOTAL TIME: 30 MIN. **YIELD:** 8 SERVINGS

The sweet-tart flavor of balsamic vinegar enhances roasted broccoli spears seasoned with garlic. You can conveniently pop this dish into the oven while a beef roast or turkey is resting.

Nella Parker ★ Hersey, Michigan

- 2 bunches broccoli, cut into spears
- 1/3 cup olive oil
- 4 garlic cloves, minced
- 1/2 teaspoon salt
- 1/4 teaspoon pepper
- 2 tablespoons balsamic vinegar

Place broccoli in a greased 15-in. x 10-in. x 1-in. baking pan. Combine the oil, garlic, salt and pepper; drizzle over broccoli and toss to coat.

Bake, uncovered, at 425° for 15-20 minutes or until tender, stirring occasionally. Drizzle with vinegar.

Balsamic Vinegar

Over the years balsamic vinegar has gone from an exotic ingredient to a pantry staple. This Italian vinegar is a dark, thick, sweet-smelling liquid. When used in cooking, it adds a rich, dark color to the dish. When a dark color is undesirable, use white balsamic vinegar.

You can find quite a range in price for this vinegar. Just like wine, the grapes, processing and aging method and aging time contribute to the cost of the vinegar. The higher priced balsamic is best drizzled over cooked foods as a finishing touch.

Bacon Caesar Salad

PREP/TOTAL TIME: 20 MIN.
YIELD: 12 SERVINGS (3/4 CUP EACH)

Family and friends always say my Caesar salad rivals any restaurant version. The addition of bacon lends a slightly smoky flavor and makes it unique.

Sharon Tipton ★ Orlando, Florida

- 2 cups cubed day-old bread
- 3 garlic cloves, sliced
- 2 tablespoons olive oil

DRESSING:
- 1/2 cup olive oil
- 1/4 cup lemon juice
- 1 tablespoon Dijon mustard
- 3 garlic cloves, minced
- 1-1/2 teaspoons anchovy paste
- Dash pepper
- 1 large bunch romaine, torn
- 4 bacon strips, cooked and crumbled
- 1/2 cup shredded Parmesan cheese

In a large skillet, cook bread cubes and garlic in oil over medium heat for 4-5 minutes or until golden brown, stirring frequently. Remove to paper towels; cool.

For dressing, in a small bowl, whisk the oil, lemon juice, mustard, garlic, anchovy paste and pepper. In a serving bowl, combine romaine and bacon. Drizzle with dressing; toss to coat. Sprinkle with croutons and cheese.

TO MAKE AHEAD: Prepare the croutons a few days before. Store in an airtight container.

Cranberry-Champagne Granita

PREP: 20 MIN. + FREEZING   **YIELD:** 4 CUPS

After serving a heavy holiday meal, I like to offer a light, refreshing dessert, like this gorgeous granita. Because it is made ahead, there's no last-minute fuss.

Joyce Gemperlein ★ Rockville, Maryland

3-1/2	teaspoons grated lime peel
1-3/4	cups unsweetened cranberry juice
1-1/2	cups sugar
1-3/4	cups Champagne

Place the lime peel in a small saucepan and cover with water. Bring to a boil. Cook for 1 minute. Drain and discard liquid; set the peel aside.

In a small saucepan, bring cranberry juice and sugar to a boil. Cook and stir until sugar is dissolved. Remove from the heat; stir in champagne and lime peel. Transfer to a 13-in. x 9-in. dish; cool to room temperature. Freeze for 1 hour; stir with a fork. Freeze 2-3 hours longer or until completely frozen, stirring every 30 minutes.

Stir granita with a fork just before serving; spoon into dessert dishes.

Editor's Note: This recipe was tested with R.W. Knudsen unsweetened cranberry juice. Look for it in the health food aisle.

A Refreshing Ice

Granita is a low-tech frozen dessert...no ice cream maker is required. A simple mixture of juice or other flavored liquid, water and sugar is frozen, then stirred occasionally. The stirring creates the desirable ice-crystal texture. Serving it in a clear dish, highlights its beautiful color and inviting frosty appearance.

Traditional Turkey Dinner

Golden Roasted Turkey
pg. 29

Curried Sweet Potato Soup
pg. 31

Raspberry Pear Salad
with Glazed Walnuts
pg. 30

Herbed Chestnut Stuffing
(not pictured)
pg. 30

Triple-Tasty Cloverleaf Rolls
pg. 33

Apricot Caramel Tart
pg. 33

Golden Roasted Turkey

PREP: 40 MIN. + MARINATING
BAKE: 2-3/4 HOURS + STANDING   **YIELD:** 14 SERVINGS

Your holiday turkey will never turn out dry again if you reach for this recipe. Brining overnight and stuffing with apples results in moist, tender meat.

Michael Williams ★ Moreno Valley, California

4	cartons (32 ounces *each*) vegetable broth
1	cup kosher salt
1/2	cup packed brown sugar
1	tablespoon whole peppercorns
1-1/2	teaspoons whole allspice
1-1/2	teaspoons minced fresh gingerroot
4	quarts cold water
2	turkey-size oven roasting bags
1	turkey (14 to 16 pounds)
1	cup water
1	medium apple, sliced
1	small onion, sliced
1	cinnamon stick (3 inches)
6	fresh sage leaves
4	fresh rosemary sprigs
1	tablespoon canola oil
1/2	teaspoon pepper

In a stockpot, combine the first six ingredients. Bring to a boil. Cook and stir until salt and brown sugar are dissolved. Remove from the heat. Add the cold water to cool the brine to room temperature.

Place a turkey-size oven roasting bag inside a second roasting bag; add turkey. Carefully pour cooled brine into bag. Squeeze out as much air as possible; seal bags and turn to coat. Place in a roasting pan. Refrigerate for 18-24 hours, turning occasionally.

In a small bowl, combine the water, apple, onion and cinnamon. Microwave on high for 3-4 minutes or until apples are tender; drain water.

Drain and discard brine. Rinse turkey under cold water; pat dry. Place cooked apple mixture, sage and rosemary in turkey cavity. Skewer turkey openings; tie drumsticks together.

Place turkey breast side up on a rack in a roasting pan. Rub with oil and pepper. Bake, uncovered, at 325° for 2-3/4 to 3-1/4 hours or until a meat thermometer reads 180°. (Cover loosely with foil if turkey browns too quickly.) Cover and let stand for 15 minutes before carving; discard apple mixture and herbs.

Bow Place Cards

A cute, bow-topped name card is a fun and festive way to present dinner guests with their places at the table. Begin by folding a 3-1/2-in. x 4-in. piece of card stock in half to form a 3-1/2-in. x 2-in. rectangle. Open the place card; use a craft knife to cut a 1/2-in.-long slit through the center of the fold.

With an embossing pen, write dinner guest's name on the card. Sprinkle with embossing powder; melt powder with a heat gun. You can also write names with a paint pen.

Wrap a 22-in. length of organza (sheer) ribbon around a 1-in.-wide piece of cardboard. Tie ribbon ends in bow. Slip the bow off of the cardboard piece. Thread the bottom loop of the ribbon through the slit in the place card to hold the bow in place.

Herbed Chestnut Stuffing

PREP: 45 MIN. **BAKE:** 20 MIN.
YIELD: 12 SERVINGS (3/4 CUP EACH)

Chestnuts lend a bit of crunch to every bite of this moist, buttery stuffing. One taste and you'll understand why it's a crowd favorite!

Tammy Nordberg ★ Caledonia, Illinois

2-1/2 cups chestnuts
1 celery rib, chopped
2 tablespoons finely chopped onion
1 cup butter, cubed
1 package (12 ounces) unseasoned stuffing cubes
2 cups chicken broth, *divided*
2 tablespoons dried parsley flakes
1/2 teaspoon salt
1/2 teaspoon dried rosemary, crushed
1/2 teaspoon rubbed sage
1/2 teaspoon pepper
1/8 teaspoon ground nutmeg

With a small sharp knife, score an "X" on the rounded side of each chestnut, being careful not to cut through the nutmeat.

In a Dutch oven, bring 8 cups water to a boil. Add chestnuts. Return to a boil; cook, uncovered, for 15 minutes. Drain and return chestnuts to the pan; cover and keep warm. With a kitchen towel or pot holder, remove one or two chestnuts at a time. Peel and discard outer shell and inner skin. Slice nutmeats.

In a large saucepan, saute celery and onion in butter until crisp-tender. Add chestnuts; saute 5 minutes longer. Stir in the stuffing cubes, 1-1/2 cups broth and seasonings.

Transfer to a greased 13-in. x 9-in. baking dish; pour remaining broth over top. Cover and bake at 350° for 20-25 minutes or until heated through.

TO MAKE AHEAD: One to two days before, boil, peel and slice the chestnuts; cover and refrigerate.

Raspberry Pear Salad With Glazed Walnuts

PREP/TOTAL TIME: 30 MIN. **YIELD:** 12 SERVINGS

The sweet and tart tastes of this spectacular salad both surprise and please the palate. A raspberry vinaigrette ties everything together.

Diana Neve ★ Lafayette, California

2 tablespoons honey
1/4 teaspoon sugar
1/2 cup walnut halves
2 packages (5 ounces *each*) spring mix salad greens
3 medium pears, peeled and sliced
1/2 cup fresh raspberries
2 ounces Cambozola cheese, cubed
1/4 cup olive oil
3 tablespoons raspberry vinaigrette
1 shallot, minced
2 teaspoons Dijon mustard
1/4 teaspoon salt
1/4 teaspoon pepper

In a small heavy skillet over low heat, stir honey and sugar until sugar is melted; add walnuts. Transfer to a foil-lined baking sheet. Bake at 350° for 8-10 minutes or until nuts are toasted. Spread on foil to cool.

In a large bowl, combine the salad greens, pears, raspberries, cheese and walnuts. In a small bowl, whisk the vinaigrette ingredients. Pour over salad and toss to coat. Serve immediately.

Editor's Note: You may substitute Brie and/or blue cheese for the Cambozola cheese.

TO MAKE AHEAD: Prepare the glazed walnuts a few days before. Store in an airtight container.

Curried Sweet Potato Soup

PREP: 30 MIN.   **COOK:** 45 MIN.   **YIELD:** 8 SERVINGS

This lovely cream soup makes a fabulous first course at special sit-down dinners. I often double the recipe because family and friends can't stop eating it!

Paula Marchesi ★ Lenhartsville, Pennsylvania

  1   medium onion, chopped
  2   tablespoons butter
  2   teaspoons curry powder
  2   teaspoons minced fresh gingerroot
1/2   teaspoon salt
  2   pounds sweet potatoes, peeled and cubed
  1   can (14-1/2 ounces) vegetable broth
1-1/4 cups water
  1   can (14 ounces) coconut milk
3/4   cup half-and-half cream
1/3   cup minced fresh cilantro
Optional garnishes: minced fresh cilantro, toasted flaked
      coconut and toasted chopped pecans

In a large saucepan, saute onion in butter until tender. Stir in the curry, gingerroot and salt; cook 1 minute longer. Stir in the potatoes, broth and water. Bring to a boil. Reduce heat; cover and simmer for 15-20 minutes or until sweet potatoes are tender. Cool slightly.

In a blender, process soup in batches until smooth. Return all to the pan. Stir in the coconut milk, cream and cilantro; heat through (do not boil). Garnish with cilantro, coconut and pecans if desired.

Apricot Caramel Tart

PREP: 30 MIN. + CHILLING **BAKE:** 35 MIN. + COOLING
YIELD: 12 SERVINGS

A buttery shortbread crust plus a sweet apricot and caramel filling makes for an appealing finish to any holiday meal. Be sure to chill the dough overnight for easier handling.

- 1-1/4 cups slivered almonds
- 2-1/4 cups all-purpose flour
- 1 cup plus 1 teaspoon sugar, *divided*
- 1/4 teaspoon ground cinnamon
- 1/4 teaspoon ground coriander
- 1/8 teaspoon salt
- 1 cup cold butter, cubed
- 4 egg yolks
- 2 tablespoons lemon juice
- 1/2 teaspoon almond extract
- 1 jar (12 ounces) apricot preserves
- 1/2 cup caramel ice cream topping
- 1 egg, lightly beaten
- 1/4 teaspoon water
- 3 tablespoons sliced almonds

Place slivered almonds in a food processor; cover and process until chopped. Add the flour, 1 cup sugar, cinnamon, coriander and salt; cover and pulse to blend. Add butter; cover and pulse until mixture resembles coarse crumbs. Add the egg yolks, lemon juice and almond extract; cover and process until dough forms a ball.

Divide dough in half; wrap in plastic wrap. Cover and refrigerate overnight.

Let dough stand at room temperature for 30 minutes. Press one portion of dough onto the bottom and up the sides of a greased 9-in. fluted tart pan with a removable bottom. Combine preserves with ice cream topping; spread over crust. Roll out remaining pastry; make a lattice crust. Trim and seal edges. Beat egg and water; brush over lattice top. Sprinkle with remaining sugar and sliced almonds. Place on a baking sheet.

Bake at 400° for 10 minutes. Reduce heat to 325°; bake 25-30 minutes longer or until golden brown. Cool on a wire rack.

Triple-Tasty Cloverleaf Rolls

PREP: 40 MIN. + RISING **BAKE:** 15 MIN. **YIELD:** 2 DOZEN

Three types of dough—white, wheat and cornmeal—dress up everyday cloverleaf rolls. Pass a basket for an eye-catching addition to the table.

Kristina Vanni ★ North Hollywood, California

- 1 package (1/4 ounce) active dry yeast
- 1-1/2 cups warm water (110° to 115°)
- 1/2 cup sugar
- 1/4 cup canola oil
- 2 eggs, lightly beaten
- 1-1/2 teaspoons salt
- 4 cups all-purpose flour
- 1 cup whole wheat flour
- 1 cup yellow cornmeal
- 1/4 cup butter, melted

In a large bowl, dissolve yeast in warm water. Add the sugar, oil, eggs, salt and 3 cups all-purpose flour. Beat on medium speed for 3 minutes. Divide dough into three portions; place in separate bowls. Add the remaining all-purpose flour to one bowl, the whole wheat flour to another bowl and the cornmeal to the last bowl.

Turn each portion onto a surface floured with all-purpose flour; knead until smooth and elastic, about 6-8 minutes. Place each portion in a greased bowl, turning once to grease the top. Cover and let rise in a warm place until doubled, about 1 hour.

Divide each portion of dough into 24 pieces. Shape each into a ball. Place one of each of the balls in greased muffin cups; brush with butter. Cover and let rise until doubled, about 30 minutes.

Bake at 375° for 15-18 minutes or until golden brown. Remove from pans to wire racks to cool.

From-the-Sea Fare

Grouper with Crabmeat Sauce
pg. 35

Beet Salad with
Orange Vinaigrette
pg. 37

Herb-Buttered Green Beans
pg. 36

Raspberry Sachertorte
pg. 39

White Sangria
pg. 36

Grouper with Crabmeat Sauce

PREP: 25 MIN.   **BROIL:** 15 MIN.   **YIELD:** 8 SERVINGS

A creamy seafood sauce drapes over mild-flavored grouper for an elegant entree. Whether served to my family or to hundreds of people at a charity event, it's a winner.

Virginia Anthony ★ Jacksonville, Florida

- 8   grouper *or* red snapper fillets (8 ounces *each*), skin removed
- 1/4 cup lemon juice
- 2   tablespoons marinade for chicken
- 1   tablespoon seafood seasoning
- 1   tablespoon olive oil

SAUCE:
- 2   large onions, chopped
- 1   large sweet red pepper, chopped
- 8   green onions, chopped
- 2   garlic cloves, minced
- 1/4 cup butter, cubed
- 3   tablespoons all-purpose flour
- 2   teaspoons seafood seasoning
- 2-1/2 cups half-and-half cream
- 2   cups fresh crabmeat
- 1/4 cup minced fresh parsley

Place fillets on a foil-lined 15-in. x 10-in. x 1-in. baking pan. In a small bowl, combine the lemon juice, marinade for chicken, seafood seasoning and oil; brush over fillets. Broil 4 in. from the heat for 6-7 minutes on each side or until fish flakes easily with a fork.

Meanwhile, for sauce, in a large skillet, saute the onions, red pepper, green onions and garlic in butter until tender. Stir in flour and seafood seasoning until blended; gradually add cream. Bring to a boil; cook and stir for 2 minutes or until thickened. Gently stir in crabmeat; heat through. Serve with fish. Sprinkle with parsley.

Editor's Note: This recipe was tested with Lea & Perrins Marinade for Chicken. This dish is great served with a spinach pasta. Just cook enough for 8 side servings and toss with a little olive oil, minced garlic and shredded Romano.

Testing Fish for Doneness

Overcooked fish loses its flavor and becomes tough. As a general guideline, fish is cooked 10 minutes for every inch of thickness.

For fish fillets, check for doneness by inserting a fork at an angle into the thickest portion of the fish and gently parting the meat. When it is opaque and flakes into sections, it is cooked completely.

Herb-Buttered Green Beans

PREP: 25 MIN. **COOK:** 10 MIN. **YIELD:** 8 SERVINGS

Dishes don't have to be elaborate in order to be delicious. Rosemary, basil, oregano and parsley season green beans for a simple, yet special, dinner accompaniment.

Tamara Trouten ★ Fort Wayne, Indiana

1-1/2	pounds fresh green beans, trimmed
1/3	cup finely chopped onion
1/3	cup finely chopped celery
3	tablespoons sesame seeds
4	garlic cloves, minced
2	tablespoons dried parsley flakes
3/4	teaspoon salt
3/4	teaspoon dried basil
3/4	teaspoon dried oregano
1/4	teaspoon dried rosemary, crushed
1/3	cup butter

Place beans in a steamer basket; place in a Dutch oven over 1 in. of water. Bring to a boil; cover and steam for 7-9 minutes or until crisp-tender.

Meanwhile, in a large skillet, saute the onion, celery, sesame seeds, garlic and seasonings in butter until vegetables are tender. Add the beans; toss to coat.

White Sangria

PREP/TOTAL TIME: 10 MIN. **YIELD:** 8 SERVINGS (2 QUARTS)

Using white instead of red wine makes my version of sangria a little lighter, yet it still has the same wonderful sweetness. Frozen fruit allows me to serve this any time of year.

Sharon Tipton ★ Orlando, Florida

3	cups dry white wine
4	tablespoons sugar
1/4	cup brandy
1	can (12 ounces) lemon-lime soda, chilled
1	cup frozen unsweetened sliced peaches
3/4	cup frozen unsweetened strawberries
1	medium lemon, sliced
1	medium lime, sliced

In a pitcher, stir the wine, sugar and brandy until sugar is dissolved. Add the soda, frozen fruits, lemon and lime. Serve immediately.

Beet Salad with Orange Vinaigrette

PREP: 25 MIN. + CHILLING   **BAKE:** 40 MIN. + COOLING
YIELD: 8 SERVINGS

Special occasions call for extraordinary dishes. Beets are anything but basic when combined with blue cheese, walnuts and orange dressing.

Mary Moskovitz ★ Ventnor, New Jersey

1/2   cup orange juice
1   tablespoon olive oil
2   teaspoons white wine vinegar
1   teaspoon minced fresh rosemary *or* 1/4 teaspoon dried rosemary, crushed
1   teaspoon chopped shallot
1/2   teaspoon grated orange peel
1/8   teaspoon salt
1/8   teaspoon pepper
4   fresh beets (about 1/2 pound)
1   bunch watercress
1/4   cup walnut halves, toasted
1/4   cup crumbled Gorgonzola cheese

For vinaigrette, combine the first eight ingredients in a jar with a tight-fitting lid; shake well. Refrigerate for at least 1 hour.

Place beets in a 13-in. x 9-in. baking dish; add 1 in. of water. Cover and bake at 400° for 40-45 minutes or until tender. Cool; peel and cut into thin slices.

Just before serving, arrange watercress on a platter or individual plates; top with beets. Sprinkle with walnuts and cheese; drizzle with vinaigrette.

Raspberry Sachertorte

PREP: 50 MIN. **BAKE:** 25 MIN. + COOLING
YIELD: 12 SERVINGS

It may look like this torte took hours to make, but it has a surprisingly short list of ingredients. A small slice splendidly satisfies a sweet tooth.

Rosetta Hockett ★ Colorado Springs, Colorado

4	eggs, *separated*
5	tablespoons butter
2/3	cup sugar
9	ounces bittersweet chocolate, melted
3/4	cup ground almonds
1/4	cup all-purpose flour
1/4	cup seedless raspberry jam

GLAZE:

3	ounces bittersweet chocolate
2	tablespoons butter

Place egg whites in a large bowl; let stand at room temperature for 30 minutes. In another large bowl, beat butter and sugar until crumbly, about 2 minutes. Add egg yolks and melted chocolate; beat on low speed just until combined. Combine almonds and flour; stir into the butter mixture.

In another bowl with clean beaters, beat egg whites until stiff peaks form; fold into batter.

Transfer to a greased 9-in. springform pan. Bake at 350° for 25-30 minutes or until a toothpick inserted near the center comes out clean. Cool on a wire rack for 10 minutes. Carefully run a knife around edge of pan to loosen; remove sides of pan. Cool completely.

Spread jam over top of cake. For glaze, in a small saucepan, melt chocolate and butter; stir until smooth. Spread over jam. Let stand at room temperature for 1 hour or until set.

TO MAKE AHEAD: Bake the cake and let cool (do not top with jam); freeze in a heavy-duty resealable plastic bag for up to 3 months. When ready to use, thaw at room temperature overnight. Top with the jam and glaze.

Extra, Extra

The following are additional recipes that you can use to customize the previous dinner menus. You can use these recipes to expand the menus with another fabulous side or entree. Or, mix-and-match by swapping out one of the menu items with one of the extra dishes to create the prefect holiday meal for your family. If you're looking for more sensational dessert ideas, look no further than the Holiday Sweets chapter, starting on page 153.

Pesto Bread

PREP: 20 MIN. **BAKE:** 35 MIN. + COOLING
YIELD: 1 LOAF (12 SLICES)

I like to walk down the grocery aisle thinking of what different ingredients I can incorporate into new recipes. This Italian-inspired quick bread that I created took home a prize at our state fair.

Leigh Doutt ★ Pueblo West, Colorado

1-3/4	cups all-purpose flour
1	teaspoon sugar
1	teaspoon baking powder
1	teaspoon garlic powder
1/2	teaspoon salt
1/4	teaspoon baking soda
2	eggs, beaten
1/2	cup sour cream
1/2	cup 2% milk
3	tablespoons olive oil
1/2	cup pine nuts, toasted and chopped
1/4	cup grated Parmesan cheese
1/4	cup minced fresh parsley *or* 4 teaspoons dried parsley flakes
2	tablespoons minced fresh basil *or* 2 teaspoons dried basil

In a large bowl, combine the first six ingredients. In another bowl, combine the eggs, sour cream, milk and oil. Stir into dry ingredients just until moistened. Fold in the pine nuts, cheese, parsley and basil.

Transfer to a greased 8-in. x 4-in. loaf pan. Bake at 350° for 35-40 minutes or until a toothpick inserted near the center comes out clean. Cool for 10 minutes before removing from pan to a wire rack.

Cranberry-Gorgonzola Stuffed Chicken

PREP: 30 MIN.   **BAKE:** 35 MIN.   **YIELD:** 6 SERVINGS

Chicken breasts go from ordinary to extraordinary when filled with tart cranberries and creamy Gorgonzola. It makes a meal with couscous and a green salad.

Kara Firstenberger ★ Cardiff, California

  6 boneless skinless chicken breast halves (6 ounces *each*)
  1 cup (4 ounces) crumbled Gorgonzola cheese
1/2 cup dried cranberries
2/3 cup chopped walnuts
1/3 cup packed fresh parsley sprigs
2/3 cup dry bread crumbs
1/2 teaspoon salt
1/2 teaspoon pepper
  2 eggs
  1 tablespoon Dijon mustard
1/2 cup all-purpose flour

Flatten chicken to 1/4-in. thickness. In a small bowl, combine cheese and cranberries. Spoon 1/4 cup cheese mixture down the center of each chicken breast. Roll up and secure with toothpicks.

Place walnuts and parsley in a food processor, cover and process until ground. Transfer to a shallow bowl; stir in the bread crumbs, salt and pepper. In another shallow bowl, combine eggs and mustard. Place flour in a third shallow bowl. Coat chicken with flour, then dip in egg mixture and coat with walnut mixture.

Place seam side down in a greased 15-in. x 10-in. x 1-in. baking pan. Bake at 350° for 35-40 minutes or until a meat thermometer reads 170°. Discard toothpicks.

TO MAKE AHEAD: Prepare the roll-ups; cover and refrigerate until ready to bake.

Elegant Roasted Potatoes

PREP: 20 MIN.   **BAKE:** 40 MIN.   **YIELD:** 6 SERVINGS

This is an excellent way to provide an easy, nutrition-packed side dish for any meal. It's a personal favorite since I grow Swiss chard in my garden.

Kathy Rairigh ★ Milford, Indiana

- 1 pound small red potatoes, quartered
- 1-1/2 cups cut fresh green beans (2-inch pieces)
- 1 medium sweet red pepper, julienned
- 1 tablespoon olive oil
- 1 teaspoon garlic powder
- 1 teaspoon minced fresh oregano
- 1 teaspoon minced fresh thyme
- 1/2 teaspoon salt
- 1/4 teaspoon pepper
- 2 cups chopped Swiss chard

In a large bowl, combine the first nine ingredients. Transfer to a greased 15-in. x 10-in. x 1-in. baking pan.

Bake, uncovered, at 425° for 25 minutes, stirring once. Add Swiss chard. Bake 15-20 minutes longer or until potatoes are tender, stirring once.

Editor's Note: You may substitute chopped fresh spinach for Swiss chard. Bake potato mixture 35 minutes. Add spinach and cook 5-10 minutes longer.

Decadent Broccoli Souffle

PREP: 20 MIN.   **BAKE:** 35 MIN. + STANDING   **YIELD:** 10 SERVINGS

I combine fresh broccoli with cheddar cheese for a stunning side dish that appeals to everyone...even kids!

Elaine Luther ★ Homosassa, Florida

- 3 eggs
- 4 tablespoons butter, *divided*
- 2 bunches broccoli
- 2 tablespoons all-purpose flour
- 1/4 teaspoon salt
- 1/4 teaspoon pepper
- 1-1/2 cups 2% milk
- 2 cups (8 ounces) shredded cheddar cheese, *divided*
- 1 teaspoon Dijon mustard
- 2 tablespoons dry bread crumbs

Separate eggs; let stand at room temperature for 30 minutes. Grease a 2-1/2-qt. souffle dish with 1 tablespoon butter; set aside.

Cut broccoli into florets; peel and chop stems. Place broccoli in a steamer basket; place in a Dutch oven over 1 in. of water. Bring to a boil; cover and steam for 4-6 minutes or until crisp-tender.

In a large saucepan, melt remaining butter. Stir in the flour, salt and pepper until smooth. Gradually add milk. Bring to a boil; cook and stir for 2 minutes or until thickened. Add 1-1/2 cups cheese and mustard; stir until cheese is melted.

Remove from the heat. Stir a small amount of hot mixture into egg yolks; return all to the pan, stirring constantly. Stir in broccoli. Allow to cool slightly.

In a large bowl, beat egg whites until stiff peaks form. With a spatula, stir a fourth of the egg whites into broccoli mixture until no white streaks remain. Fold in remaining egg whites until combined. Transfer to prepared dish. Sprinkle with remaining cheese and bread crumbs.

Bake at 350° for 35-40 minutes or until the top is puffed and center appears set. Let souffle stand for 15 minutes before serving.

Fontina-Vegetable Crab Soup

PREP: 30 MIN.   **COOK:** 25 MIN.   **YIELD:** 5 SERVINGS

Cayenne pepper adds a hint of heat to this rich, creamy soup loaded with vegetables and crab. Serve it as a first course or as a meal by itself.

Charlene Chambers ★ Ormond Beach, Florida

1-1/2   cups frozen corn, thawed
1   large onion, chopped
1   cup roasted sweet red peppers, drained and chopped
1   celery rib, chopped
1   garlic clove, minced
1   tablespoon canola oil
2   cans (14-1/2 ounces *each*) chicken broth
1   teaspoon minced fresh thyme *or* 1/4 teaspoon dried thyme
1/4   teaspoon cayenne pepper
1/4   cup all-purpose flour
3/4   cup heavy whipping cream
4   ounces fontina cheese, cut into 1/4-inch cubes
1/2   cup canned lump crabmeat

Pat corn dry; transfer to a greased 15-in. x 10-in. x 1-in. baking pan. Bake at 450° for 12-15 minutes or until lightly browned, stirring once.

Meanwhile, in a Dutch oven, saute the onion, red peppers, celery and garlic in oil until tender. Add the broth, thyme, cayenne and corn. Bring to a boil. Reduce heat; simmer, uncovered, for 15 minutes.

Combine flour and cream until smooth. Gradually stir into broth mixture; add cheese. Bring to a gentle boil; cook and stir for 2 minutes or until thickened and cheese is melted. Top each serving with crab.

Spice-Brined Pork Roast

PREP: 15 MIN. + MARINATING **GRILL:** 1-1/2 HOURS
YIELD: 10 SERVINGS

This brined and barbecued pork roast is unbelievably moist. Adding seasonings to the coals produces an awesome aroma that draws guests to the grill!

Lorraine Schroeder ★ Albany, Oregon

      2 quarts water
      8 orange peel strips (1 to 3 inches)
    1/2 cup sugar
    1/4 cup salt
      3 tablespoons fennel seed, crushed
      2 tablespoons dried thyme
      2 tablespoons whole peppercorns
      1 boneless rolled pork loin roast (4 pounds)

In a large saucepan, combine the first seven ingredients. Bring to a boil; cook and stir until salt and sugar are dissolved. Remove from the heat; cool to room temperature.

Place a large heavy-duty resealable plastic bag inside a second large resealable plastic bag; add the pork. Carefully pour cooled marinade into bag. Squeeze out as much air as possible; seal bags and turn to coat. Place in a roasting pan. Refrigerate for 12-24 hours, turning several times. Strain brine; discard liquid and set aside seasonings.

Using long-handled tongs, dip a paper towel in cooking oil and lightly coat the grill rack. Grill, covered, over indirect medium heat for 1-1/2 to 2 hours or until a meat thermometer reads 160°, adding reserved seasonings to coals. Let stand for 5 minutes before slicing.

Cranberry & Port Wine Chutney

PREP: 15 MIN. **COOK:** 30 MIN. **YIELD:** 5 CUPS

Sweet-tart cranberry chutney complements roasted chicken, pork and duck. I also spread it on cold sandwiches showcasing leftover holiday turkey.

Kristen Weyant ★ York, Pennsylvania

      2 packages (12 ounces *each*) fresh *or* frozen cranberries
  1-1/2 cups packed brown sugar
      1 large onion, chopped
      1 cup port wine *or* cranberry juice
      1 medium tart apple, peeled and finely chopped
    3/4 cup golden raisins
    1/4 cup balsamic vinegar

In a large saucepan, combine all the ingredients. Bring to a boil over medium heat. Reduce heat; simmer, uncovered, for 30-35 minutes or until thickened, stirring occasionally.

Transfer to a serving bowl. Serve warm or cover and refrigerate until chilled. Refrigerate leftovers.

TO MAKE AHEAD: Chutney can be made a week in advance and stored in the refrigerator.

Vegetable Couscous

PREP/TOTAL TIME: 30 MIN. **YIELD:** 9 SERVINGS

Couscous is a nice change from rice and potatoes, and the vegetables make it a colorful addition to your plate. The quick-cooking convenience is also a plus!

Kim Wenzel ★ Jefferson, Oregon

      2 medium carrots, julienned
      1 celery rib, chopped
    1/2 cup julienned sweet red pepper
      2 tablespoons finely chopped onion
      1 tablespoon butter
      1 small zucchini, chopped
      1 teaspoon dried basil
      1 teaspoon dried parsley flakes
    1/4 teaspoon salt
      2 cups chicken broth
      1 package (10 ounces) uncooked couscous

In a large skillet, saute the carrots, celery, red pepper and onion in butter until crisp-tender. Stir in the zucchini, basil, parsley and salt; saute 2 minutes longer. Add broth; bring to a boil. Stir in couscous. Remove from the heat; cover and let stand for 5-10 minutes or until liquid is absorbed. Fluff with a fork.

Veal Saltimbocca

PREP: 25 MIN.　**COOK:** 10 MIN.　**YIELD:** 8 SERVINGS

A delicious wine sauce makes this hearty entree even more special. You can assemble the veal rolls ahead of time and chill until ready to cook.

Vance Werner Jr. ★ Franklin, Wisconsin

2	ounces fontina cheese
8	thin slices prosciutto *or* deli ham
16	fresh sage leaves
8	veal cutlets
1/2	cup all-purpose flour
1/2	teaspoon salt
1/4	teaspoon pepper
2	tablespoons butter
2	tablespoons olive oil
1	cup chicken broth
1/4	cup white wine *or* chicken broth
1/2	cup minced fresh parsley
1	tablespoon lemon juice

Cut cheese into 1/4-in. strips. Place a prosciutto slice, 2 sage leaves and cheese down center of each cutlet. Roll up and secure with toothpicks.

In a large resealable plastic bag, combine the flour, salt and pepper. Add veal, a few rolls at a time, and shake to coat. In a large skillet, brown veal in butter and oil on all sides; remove and keep warm.

Add broth and wine, stirring to loosen browned bits from pan. Return rolls to the pan; cook for 8-10 minutes or until a meat thermometer reads 160° and sauce is thickened. Stir in parsley and lemon juice; heat through. Discard toothpicks; serve with sauce.

From Special to
SPECTACULAR

From Special to Spectacular

This unique chapter features two versions of each recipe. One is simple yet special enough for holiday entertaining. With a few additional ingredients or different cooking techniques, the other recipe dresses things up to create a second spectacular dish. Either prepare all of the special or all of the spectacular recipes...or mix and match dishes to suit your time and tastes. Either way, dinner guests are sure to be impressed!

SPECIAL

Apple & Walnut Salad

(pictured at left)

PREP/TOTAL TIME: 20 MIN.
YIELD: 12 SERVINGS (1 CUP EACH)

Simple greens get a sweet and tangy flavor with dried cranberries and Gorgonzola cheese. Then the salad is drizzled with a quick and lively cider vinaigrette.

5	cups torn romaine
5	cups torn red leaf lettuce
1	large red apple, chopped
1	large green apple, chopped
1	cup (4 ounces) crumbled Gorgonzola cheese
1/2	cup chopped walnuts, toasted
1/3	cup thinly sliced red onion
1/3	cup dried cranberries

CIDER VINAIGRETTE:

3/4	cup apple cider *or* juice
3	tablespoons cider vinegar
2	teaspoons honey
1/4	teaspoon salt
1/4	teaspoon pepper
1/4	cup walnut oil *or* canola oil

In a salad bowl, combine the first eight ingredients.

In a small bowl, whisk the cider, vinegar, honey, salt and pepper; gradually whisk in oil. Drizzle over salad; toss to coat. Serve immediately.

Roasted Apple & Candied Walnut Salad

PREP: 20 MIN.   **BAKE:** 20 MIN.   **YIELD:** 12 SERVINGS

To add even more visual interest and tasty texture to a green salad, top plated servings with roasted apple fans and crunchy sugared walnuts. You can use the nuts to liven up any salad you serve.

2	teaspoons butter
1/2	cup chopped walnuts
1	tablespoon brown sugar
3	large apples, peeled
3/4	cup apple cider *or* juice
3	tablespoons cider vinegar
2	teaspoons honey
1/4	teaspoon salt
1/4	teaspoon pepper
1/4	cup walnut oil *or* canola oil
5	cups torn romaine
5	cups torn red leaf lettuce
1/3	cup thinly sliced red onion
1/3	cup dried cranberries
1	cup (4 ounces) crumbled Gorgonzola cheese

In a small heavy skillet, melt butter. Add walnuts and cook over medium heat until toasted, about 4 minutes. Sprinkle with brown sugar. Cook and stir for 2-4 minutes or until sugar is melted. Spread on foil to cool.

Core apples and cut into quarters. Slice apples, but not all the way through, leaving slices attached at the stem end. Place apple quarters in a greased 15-in. x 10-in. x 1-in. baking pan; fan slightly.

In a small bowl, whisk the cider, vinegar, honey, salt and pepper; gradually whisk in oil. Set aside 1 cup for dressing; brush remaining mixture over apples. Bake, uncovered, at 425° for 18-22 minutes or until tender.

Meanwhile, arrange the romaine, leaf lettuce, onion and cranberries on 12 salad plates. Top each with a roasted apple fan; sprinkle with cheese and candied nuts. Drizzle with reserved dressing.

TO MAKE AHEAD: Prepare the sugared walnuts and the dressing a few days before. Store the nuts in a covered container at room temperature. Cover and chill dressing. The apple fans can be prepared a day ahead, then refrigerated. Rewarm them in the oven or microwave when ready to use.

SPECIAL

Creamy Garlic & Mushroom Soup

PREP: 15 MIN.   **COOK:** 30 MIN.
YIELD: 13 SERVINGS (1 CUP EACH)

Cool, crisp winter evenings call for comforting bowls of rich, creamy soup featuring three kinds of mushrooms. It's a terrific first course at holiday meals.

Mandy Howison ★ Glenshaw, Pennsylvania

1	pound medium fresh mushrooms, halved
1	pound sliced baby portobello mushrooms
1/2	pound sliced fresh shiitake mushrooms
7	tablespoons butter
12	garlic cloves, minced
2	green onions, chopped
1/2	cup all-purpose flour
2	cans (14-1/2 ounces *each*) chicken broth
3-1/3	cups whole milk
1-2/3	cups heavy whipping cream
4	teaspoons minced fresh thyme *or* 1-1/2 teaspoons dried thyme
2	teaspoons minced fresh basil *or* 3/4 teaspoon dried basil
1	teaspoon salt
1	teaspoon pepper

Minced fresh parsley

In a Dutch oven, saute mushrooms in butter in batches until tender. Return all to the pan; add garlic and onions. Cook and stir for 2 minutes. Sprinkle with flour; stir until blended.

Gradually stir in broth and milk. Bring to a boil; cook and stir for 2 minutes or until thickened. Stir in the cream, thyme, basil, salt and pepper; heat through. Sprinkle each serving with parsley.

Creamy Garlic & Mushroom Soup with Pastry Caps

PREP: 50 MIN.   **BAKE:** 15 MIN.   **YIELD:** 12 SERVINGS

Surprise Christmas dinner guests with puff pastry "packages" that blanket bowls of Creamy Garlic & Mushroom Soup. Stir in a splash of sherry to heighten the soup's wonderful flavor.

- 1 pound medium fresh mushrooms, halved
- 1 pound sliced baby portobello mushrooms
- 1/2 pound sliced fresh shiitake mushrooms
- 7 tablespoons butter
- 12 garlic cloves, minced
- 2 green onions, chopped
- 1/2 cup all-purpose flour
- 2 cans (14-1/2 ounces *each*) chicken broth
- 3-1/3 cups whole milk
- 1-2/3 cups heavy whipping cream
- 2 tablespoons sherry
- 4 teaspoons minced fresh thyme *or* 1-1/2 teaspoons dried thyme
- 2 teaspoons minced fresh basil *or* 3/4 teaspoon dried basil
- 1 teaspoon salt
- 1 teaspoon pepper
- 3 sheets frozen puff pastry, thawed
- 1 egg, beaten
- 1 teaspoon water

In a Dutch oven, saute mushrooms in butter in batches until tender. Return all to the pan; add garlic and onions. Cook and stir for 2 minutes. Sprinkle with flour; stir until blended.

Gradually stir in broth and milk. Bring to a boil; cook and stir for 2 minutes or until thickened. Stir in the cream, sherry and seasonings; heat through.

On a lightly floured surface, roll out each sheet of puff pastry into a 12-in. square. Using a 10-oz. ramekin for a pattern, cut out four pastry circles 1 in. larger than the ramekin's diameter from each square.

Fill twelve 10-ounce ramekins with soup, about 1 cup in each. In a small bowl, combine egg and water. Brush edges of pastry circles with egg mixture; seal circles to edges of ramekins. Place on baking sheets. Bake at 400° for 12-15 minutes or until golden brown.

TO MAKE AHEAD: A day before, make the soup up to the point of adding the cream, sherry and seasonings; cover and refrigerate. Reheat when ready to use; continue with the recipe as directed.

Spectacular

SPECIAL

Hurricane Vase Centerpieces

To find out how you can create these lovely centerpieces, turn to page 58.

SPECIAL

Spectacular

Herb-Rubbed Pork Loin

PREP: 15 MIN. **BAKE:** 1 HOUR + STANDING
YIELD: 12 SERVINGS

A savory herb rub—and a mere 15 minutes of prep time—turns plain pork roast into an easy, elegant entree. It's a fast and pleasing way to feed a large group.

Robin Schloesser ★ Chester, New Jersey

- 1 tablespoon olive oil
- 2 teaspoons *each* minced fresh marjoram, rosemary, sage and thyme
- 1 teaspoon salt
- 1/2 teaspoon pepper
- 1 boneless whole pork loin roast (4 pounds)
- 1 cup water

In a small bowl, combine the oil, herbs, salt and pepper; rub over pork. Place roast on a rack in a large shallow roasting pan. Pour water into pan.

Bake, uncovered, at 350° for 1 to 1-1/2 hours or until a meat thermometer reads 160°. Transfer to a serving platter. Let stand for 10 minutes before slicing.

Brined Pork Roast with Port Wine Sauce

PREP: 50 MIN. + CHILLING   **BAKE:** 1 HOUR + STANDING
YIELD: 12 SERVINGS (2 CUPS SAUCE)

For extra-special occasions, I enhance my basic Herb-Rubbed Pork Loin (recipe at left) by first brining the roast, which results in extremely tender meat. At the table, I pass around a robust wine sauce that makes each slice even more savory.

Robin Schloesser ★ Chester, New Jersey

8	cups water
1/2	cup kosher salt
1/2	cup packed brown sugar
6	fresh thyme sprigs
3	fresh rosemary sprigs
3	fresh sage sprigs
3	bay leaves
1	tablespoon fennel seed
1	tablespoon coriander seeds
1	tablespoon whole peppercorns

PORK:

1	boneless whole pork loin roast (4 pounds)
1	tablespoon olive oil
2	teaspoons *each* minced fresh marjoram, rosemary, sage and thyme
1/2	teaspoon pepper
1	cup water

SAUCE:

1/4	cup butter, cubed
3	shallots, thinly sliced
1-1/2	cups port wine
1	bay leaf
1	can (14-1/2 ounces) reduced-sodium chicken broth
2	tablespoons white wine vinegar
4	teaspoons sugar
1/4	cup heavy whipping cream
1-1/2	teaspoons minced fresh thyme
1/8	teaspoon salt
1/8	teaspoon pepper
1/2	teaspoon browning sauce, optional
2	teaspoons cornstarch
2	teaspoons cold water

In a Dutch oven, combine the first 10 ingredients. Bring to a boil. Cook and stir until salt and sugar are dissolved. Remove from the heat; cool brine to room temperature.

Place a 2-gallon resealable plastic bag inside a second resealable bag; add roast. Carefully pour cooled brine into bag. Squeeze out as much air as possible; seal bags and turn to coat. Place in a large bowl. Refrigerate for 18-24 hours, turning occasionally.

Spectacular

Drain and discard brine; pat roast dry. In a small bowl, combine the oil, herbs and pepper; rub over pork. Place roast on a rack in a large shallow roasting pan. Pour water into pan. Bake at 350° for 1 to 1-1/2 hours or until a meat thermometer reads 160°.

For sauce, melt butter in a large saucepan. Add shallots; cook and stir until tender. Stir in wine and bay leaf. Bring to a boil; cook until liquid is reduced by half. Stir in the broth, vinegar and sugar. Cook, uncovered, for 20-25 minutes or until slightly thickened.

Stir in the cream, thyme, salt, pepper and browning sauce if desired. Discard bay leaf. Combine cornstarch and water until smooth; gradually stir into the pan. Bring to a boil; cook and stir for 2 minutes or until thickened.

Transfer roast to a serving platter. Let stand for 10 minutes before slicing. Serve with sauce.

TO MAKE AHEAD: The port wine sauce can be made a day before; cover and refrigerate. Reheat over low when ready to serve.

SPECIAL

Spicy Garlic Broccoli Rabe

PREP/TOTAL TIME: 30 MIN.
YIELD: 12 SERVINGS (2/3 CUP EACH)

When it comes to carefree entertaining, you can't beat a four-ingredient recipe like this! Red pepper flakes add just the right amount of spice to colorful broccoli rabe. Substitute broccoli florets if you prefer.

Clara Coulston ★ Washington Court House, Ohio

3-1/2	pounds broccoli rabe
6	garlic cloves, thinly sliced
2	tablespoons olive oil
1/2	teaspoon crushed red pepper flakes
1	teaspoon salt

Fill a Dutch oven two-thirds full with water; bring to a boil. Trim 1/2 in. from broccoli rabe stems; discard any coarse or damaged leaves. Rinse broccoli rabe in cold water and cut into 2-in. pieces. Add to boiling water. Reduce heat; simmer, uncovered, for 1-2 minutes or until crisp-tender. Drain.

In a large skillet over medium heat, cook garlic in oil for 1 minute. Add pepper flakes; cook and stir 30 seconds longer. Add broccoli rabe and salt; heat through.

Broccoli Rabe with Tuscan Crumbs

PREP: 25 MIN.　**COOK:** 10 MIN.
YIELD: 12 SERVINGS (2/3 CUP EACH)

With seasoned bread crumbs, cheese and currants, you can turn basic broccoli rabe into a more special side. Serve it with a variety of entrees or try the topping on any of your favorite vegetables for a festive touch.

2	slices day-old Italian bread, cubed
1	teaspoon butter
1	teaspoon plus 1 tablespoon olive oil, *divided*
1	tablespoon minced fresh parsley
1	teaspoon dried thyme
1	teaspoon grated lemon peel
3-1/2	pounds broccoli rabe
6	garlic cloves, thinly sliced
1/2	teaspoon crushed red pepper flakes
1/3	cup shredded Romano cheese
1/4	cup dried currants
1	teaspoon salt

Place bread in a food processor; cover and process until coarse crumbs are formed. In a large skillet, heat butter and 1 teaspoon oil. Add the crumbs, parsley, thyme and lemon peel; cook until toasted. Set aside.

Fill a Dutch oven two-thirds full with water; bring to a boil. Trim 1/2 in. from broccoli rabe stems; discard any coarse or damaged leaves. Rinse broccoli rabe in cold water and cut into 2-in. pieces. Add to boiling water. Reduce heat; simmer, uncovered, for 1-2 minutes or until crisp-tender. Drain.

In a large skillet over medium heat, cook garlic in remaining oil for 1 minute. Add pepper flakes; cook and stir 30 seconds longer. Add the broccoli rabe, cheese, currants and salt; heat through. Transfer to a serving dish; sprinkle with toasted crumbs.

Spectacular

SPECIAL

Dinner Rolls

PREP: 30 MIN. + RISING   **BAKE:** 20 MIN.   **YIELD:** 2 DOZEN

Although they may be basic, oven-fresh rolls are always a welcome sight at everyday suppers and holiday dinners alike. You'll turn to this classic recipe and set baskets brimming with golden treats on the table year after year.

Anna Baker ★ Blaine, Washington

> 2 packages (1/4 ounce *each*) active dry yeast
> 1/2 cup warm water (110° to 115°)
> 1 teaspoon plus 1/3 cup sugar, *divided*
> 1-1/4 cups warm 2% milk (110° to 115°)
> 1/2 cup butter, melted
> 2 eggs
> 1-1/2 teaspoons salt
> 6 to 6-1/2 cups all-purpose flour
> Additional melted butter, optional

In a large bowl, dissolve yeast in warm water with 1 teaspoon sugar. Add the milk, butter, eggs, salt, 3 cups flour and remaining sugar; beat until smooth. Stir in enough remaining flour to form a soft dough.

Turn onto a floured surface; knead until smooth and elastic, about 6-8 minutes. Place in a greased bowl, turning once to grease the top. Cover and let rise in a warm place until doubled, about 1 hour.

Punch dough down; turn onto a lightly floured surface. Divide in half; shape each portion into 12 balls. Place rolls in two greased 13-in. x 9-in. baking pans; cover and let rise until doubled, about 30 minutes.

Bake at 375° for 20-25 minutes or until golden brown. Lightly brush with melted butter if desired. Place pans on wire racks. Serve warm.

Forming Fan Rolls

1. Score each of the rectangles widthwise at 2-in. intervals. Carefully fold the dough accordion-style back and forth along the score lines until you reach the end.

2. Cut the folded dough into 1-in. pieces. Place cut side down in the greased muffin cups.

Herbed Dinner Rolls

PREP: 40 MIN. + CHILLING   **BAKE:** 20 MIN.
YIELD: 2 DOZEN

To dress up plain Dinner Rolls, brush herbed butter over the dough, and then formed fan rolls. The aroma while baking is so incredible, guests will likely grab them as soon as they come out of the oven!

2	packages (1/4 ounce *each*) active dry yeast
1/2	cup warm water (110° to 115°)
1	teaspoon plus 1/3 cup sugar, *divided*
1-1/4	cups warm 2% milk (110° to 115°)
1/2	cup butter, melted
2	eggs
1-1/2	teaspoons salt
6	to 6-1/2 cups all-purpose flour
3	tablespoons butter, softened
1	teaspoon Italian seasoning
1	egg white, beaten

In a large bowl, dissolve yeast in warm water with 1 teaspoon sugar. Add the milk, melted butter, eggs, salt, 3 cups flour and remaining sugar; beat until smooth. Stir in enough remaining flour to form a soft dough.

Turn onto a floured surface; knead until smooth and elastic, about 6-8 minutes. Place in a greased bowl, turning once to grease the top. Cover and let rise in a warm place until doubled, about 1 hour.

Punch dough down; place on a lightly floured surface. Divide into four portions. Roll each portion into a 14-in. x 6-in. rectangle. Combine softened butter and Italian seasoning; spread over dough.

Score each rectangle widthwise at 2-in. intervals. Using marks as a guide, fold dough accordion-style back and forth along score lines. Cut folded dough into six 1-in. pieces. Place pieces cut side down in greased muffin cups. Cover loosely with plastic wrap. Refrigerate for 8 hours or overnight.

Uncover and let stand at room temperature for 10 minutes before baking. Brush with egg white. Bake at 375° for 18-22 minutes or until golden brown. Remove from pans to wire racks. Serve warm.

Basil & Oregano Dinner Rolls: Substitute 1/2 teaspoon each dried oregano and basil for Italian seasoning.

Fresh Herb Dinner Rolls: Substitute 1-1/2 teaspoons minced fresh parsley and 1/2 teaspoon minced fresh thyme for Italian seasoning.

Best Chocolate Cake

PREP: 20 MIN.   **BAKE:** 20 MIN. + COOLING
YIELD: 16 SERVINGS

With a tender crumb and rich frosting, a layered chocolate cake always impresses...no matter the occasion. Tangy sour cream balances the sweetness in the fantastic frosting. One bite and you'll agree this cake is awesome!

Elvi Kaukinen ★ Horseheads, New York

- 3/4   cup butter, softened
- 2   cups sugar
- 3   eggs
- 2   teaspoons vanilla extract
- 2   cups all-purpose flour
- 3/4   cup baking cocoa
- 1   teaspoon baking soda
- 1/2   teaspoon salt
- 1/4   teaspoon baking powder
- 1-1/2   cups 2% milk

CHOCOLATE FROSTING:

- 2   cups (12 ounces) semisweet chocolate chips
- 1/2   cup butter, cubed
- 1   cup (8 ounces) sour cream
- 4-1/2   cups confectioners' sugar

Chocolate curls, optional

Line three 9-in. round baking pans with waxed paper; grease and flour the pans and paper. Set aside.

In a large bowl, cream butter and sugar until light and fluffy. Add eggs, one at a time, beating well after each addition. Beat in vanilla. Combine the flour, cocoa, baking soda, salt and baking powder; add to the creamed mixture alternately with milk, beating well after each addition.

Transfer to prepared pans. Bake at 350° for 20-25 minutes or until a toothpick inserted near the center comes out clean. Cool for 10 minutes before removing from pans to wire racks to cool completely.

For frosting, in a small heavy saucepan, melt chips and butter over low heat. Transfer to a large bowl; cool for 5 minutes. Stir in sour cream. Gradually beat in confectioners' sugar until smooth. Spread between layers and over top and sides of cake. Garnish with chocolate curls if desired. Refrigerate leftovers.

Splitting Cakes Into Layers

Thin layers of cake add to the elegance of Best Chocolate Raspberry Torte (recipe at right). Using a ruler, mark the center of the side of the cake with a toothpick. Continue inserting toothpicks around the cake. Using the toothpicks as a guide, cut the cake horizontally in half with a long serrated knife. Carefully remove the top half. Repeat with remaining cakes.

Best Chocolate Raspberry Torte

PREP: 40 MIN. **BAKE:** 20 MIN. + COOLING
YIELD: 16 SERVINGS

How can you make already delicious chocolate cake even more decadent? By adding a heavenly raspberry filling and a lovely chocolate drizzle! If you prefer, skip the step of cutting each cake layer in half and make a three-layer torte.

- 3/4 cup butter, softened
- 2 cups sugar
- 3 eggs
- 2 teaspoons vanilla extract
- 2 cups all-purpose flour
- 3/4 cup baking cocoa
- 1 teaspoon baking soda
- 1/2 teaspoon salt
- 1/4 teaspoon baking powder
- 1-1/2 cups 2% milk

CHOCOLATE FROSTING:
- 2 cups (12 ounces) semisweet chocolate chips
- 1/2 cup butter, cubed
- 1 cup (8 ounces) sour cream
- 4-1/2 cups confectioners' sugar

RASPBERRY FILLING:
- 1/2 cup heavy whipping cream
- 1/4 cup red raspberry preserves
- 1-1/2 teaspoons sugar
- 1 teaspoon raspberry liqueur

CHOCOLATE DRIZZLE:
- 1/4 cup semisweet chocolate chips
- 1 tablespoon butter
- 1/4 cup heavy whipping cream

Chocolate curls and fresh raspberries

Line three 9-in. round baking pans with waxed paper; grease and flour the pans and paper. Set aside.

In a large bowl, cream butter and sugar until light and fluffy. Add eggs, one at a time, beating well after each addition. Beat in vanilla. Combine the flour, cocoa, baking soda, salt and baking powder; add to the creamed mixture alternately with milk, beating well after each addition.

Transfer to prepared pans. Bake at 350° for 20-25 minutes or until a toothpick inserted near the center comes out clean. Cool for 10 minutes before removing from pans to wire racks to cool completely.

For frosting, in a small heavy saucepan, melt chips and butter over low heat. Transfer to a large bowl; cool for 5 minutes. Stir in sour cream. Gradually beat in confectioners' sugar until smooth.

For filling, in a small bowl, beat cream until it begins to thicken. Add the preserves, sugar and liqueur; beat until stiff peaks form.

Cut each cake horizontally into two layers. Place bottom layer on a serving plate; spread with 1/2 cup filling. Top with another cake layer and spread with 1/2 cup frosting. Repeat layers. Top with another cake layer, 1/2 cup filling and remaining cake layer. Spread remaining frosting over top and sides of cake.

For drizzle, place chips and butter in a small bowl. In a small saucepan, bring cream just to a boil. Pour over chocolate; whisk until smooth. Place mixture in a heavy-duty resealable plastic bag; cut a small hole in a corner of bag. Pipe a lattice design over top of cake, allowing some drizzle to drape down the sides. Decorate with chocolate curls and raspberries as desired. Refrigerate leftovers.

TO MAKE AHEAD: Bake and assemble the torte one day in advance. Garnish just before serving.

Simply Stunning Hurricane Vase

Hurricane vases are handy to keep on hand for in-a-dash decorating. With four items you can assemble a fast yet attractive holiday centerpiece.

Taste of Home Craft Editor

MATERIALS:

Tall clear glass hurricane vase

Purchased evergreen candle wreath

Tall white pillar candle

Shiny red berry sprigs

DIRECTIONS:

Place a hurricane vase in the center of a candle wreath. Add a few red berry sprigs to the candle wreath for accents. Place a candle inside the vase. With remaining red berry sprigs, form a wreath around the base of the candle.

Classy Frosted Hurricane Vase

Store-bought tights are the surprisingly simple way to frost the outside of a hurricane vase with an eye-catching lacy design. Add a candle and surround with sparkling acrylic pieces and shiny lights, and you'll have a centerpiece that is sure to impress your guests.

Taste of Home Craft Editor

MATERIALS:

Tall clear glass hurricane vase

Frosted glass finish

Open-patterned tights

Tall turquoise pillar candle

Clear acrylic ice pieces

String of white battery-operated mini or rice lights

Clear bead garland

DIRECTIONS:

1. Turn the hurricane vase upside down on a protected surface. Slip one leg of the patterned tights over the vase. Tie the end of the leg in a knot to secure. Tuck the other tights leg inside the vase.

2. Spray the outside of the vase with frosted glass finish following manufacturer's instructions. Let dry. Remove tights; discard.

3. Place a pillar candle inside the vase. Place clear ice pieces around the base of the candle.

4. Place battery operated lights around outside of vase.

5. Form bead garland into a circle and set on top of lights. Arrange lights so that they can be seen. Use the garland to hide the light's battery case.

Clever Way to Color a Vase

Turn the vase upside down; slip one leg of a pair of patterned tights over the vase. Tie the end of the leg in a knot. Tuck the remaining tights leg inside the vase. Spray with frosted glass finish; let dry before removing and discarding tights.

Carefree
ENTERTAINING

In a small bowl, combine the butter, cheese, basil, 2 tablespoons pesto, pepper and garlic salt. Shape into a 4-in. disk; wrap in plastic wrap. Refrigerate until serving.

Rub remaining pesto over both sides of steaks. Grill, covered, over medium heat or broil 4 in. from the heat for 7-9 minutes on each side or until meat reaches desired doneness (for medium-rare, a meat thermometer should read 145°; medium, 160°; well-done, 170°).

Unwrap tomato butter; cut into four wedges. Place one wedge on each steak.

TO MAKE AHEAD: Prepare the butter up to a week in advance; store in the refrigerator.

T-Bones with Sun-Dried Tomato Butter

PREP/TOTAL TIME: 30 MIN.   **YIELD:** 4 SERVINGS

I like to take T-bone steaks to a new level by topping individual servings with a dollop of savory butter seasoned with sun-dried tomato pesto.

Agnes Ward ★ Stratford, Ontario

- 1/3 cup butter, softened
- 1/4 cup grated Parmesan cheese
- 3 tablespoons minced fresh basil *or* 1 tablespoon dried basil
- 5 tablespoons sun-dried tomato pesto, *divided*
- 1/2 teaspoon pepper
- 1/4 teaspoon garlic salt
- 4 beef T-bone steaks (1 inch thick and 16 ounces *each*)

Gift Bag Flower Centerpiece

With so many pretty patterns and colors to fit any decor, paper gift bags are a great way to dress up purchased potted plants or silk flowers (like the red nosegays, below)...and they're less expensive than glass vases. Use all of the same bag or mix and match. If the plant is too short for the bag, add something to raise it, such as crumbled newspaper or a small cardboard box. For a fun party favor at a sit-down dinner, place a number under a few of the chairs. After eating, have guests look under their chair. Whoever has a number gets to take home a centerpiece.

Cut lemon in half lengthwise; cut one half into eight thin wedges. Thread olives and lemon wedges onto toothpicks for garnishes; set aside.

Using the lemon half, moisten the rims of eight large cocktail glasses. Sprinkle salt on a plate; hold glasses upside down and dip rims into salt. Divide the salad greens, tomatoes, onion and sliced olives among prepared glasses. Top each with a prepared toothpick.

In a food processor, combine shallot and olives; cover and process until finely chopped. Add the vinegar, vodka, olive juice and lemon juice; cover and process until blended. While processing, gradually add oil in a steady stream. Divide among eight shot glasses; serve with salads.

TO MAKE AHEAD: Prepare salad dressing up to a week in advance; mix well before serving. Prepare cocktail glasses and garnishes before guests arrive; cover and refrigerate garnishes until serving.

Pickled Shrimp

PREP: 25 MIN. + MARINATING **YIELD:** ABOUT 6 DOZEN

Holiday entertaining is a breeze when I turn to this special appetizer that can be prepared days in advance. A special combination of spices make it stand out from the usual cold shrimp and cocktail sauce.

Inge Schermerhorn ★ Kingston, New Hampshire

- 2 pounds cooked medium shrimp, peeled and deveined
- 2 bay leaves
- 1 cup canola oil
- 1 cup red wine vinegar
- 3 tablespoons capers, drained
- 2 teaspoons celery seed
- 1-1/2 teaspoons seasoned salt
- 1/4 teaspoon hot pepper sauce
- 1 large red onion, thinly sliced
- 2 small lemons, thinly sliced

Place shrimp and bay leaves in an 11-in. x 7-in. dish. In a small bowl, whisk the oil, vinegar, capers, celery seed, seasoned salt and pepper sauce; pour over shrimp. Top with onion and lemons (dish will be full). Cover and refrigerate for 24 hours.

Just before serving, drain and discard marinade and discard bay leaves.

Spectacular Dirty Martini Salad

PREP/TOTAL TIME: 30 MIN. **YIELD:** 8 SERVINGS

I like to dress up simple greens with a unique olive dressing. Serving the salad in martini glasses and the dressing in a shot glass makes for a fun presentation.

Pamela Clark ★ Bonaire, Georgia

- 1 medium lemon
- 8 pimiento-stuffed olives
- 8 frilled toothpicks
- 2 tablespoons kosher salt
- 2 packages (5 ounces *each*) spring mix salad greens
- 2 medium tomatoes, chopped
- 1 small red onion, thinly sliced
- 1/4 cup sliced pimiento-stuffed olives

DRESSING:
- 1 shallot, halved
- 6 pimiento-stuffed olives plus 1/4 cup juice from the jar, *divided*
- 1/4 cup white wine vinegar
- 1/4 cup vodka *or* additional white wine vinegar
- 1 tablespoon lemon juice
- 1 cup olive oil

Northwoods Beef Stew

PREP: 30 MIN.   **COOK:** 8 HOURS
YIELD: 11 SERVINGS (2-3/4 QUARTS)

I live in northern Wisconsin, where we appreciate hot and hearty meals during our cold winters. Conveniently prepared in a slow cooker, this stew is superb for company.

Janice Christofferson ★ Eagle River, Wisconsin

- 3 large carrots, cut into 1-inch pieces
- 3 celery ribs, cut into 1-inch pieces
- 1 large onion, cut into wedges
- 1/4 cup all-purpose flour
- 1/2 teaspoon salt
- 1/4 teaspoon pepper
- 3-1/2 pounds beef stew meat
- 1 can (10-3/4 ounces) condensed tomato soup, undiluted
- 1/2 cup dry red wine *or* beef broth
- 2 tablespoons quick-cooking tapioca
- 1 tablespoon Italian seasoning
- 1 tablespoon paprika
- 1 tablespoon brown sugar
- 1 tablespoon beef bouillon granules
- 1 tablespoon Worcestershire sauce
- 1/2 pound sliced baby portobello mushrooms

Hot cooked egg noodles

Place the carrots, celery and onion in a 5-qt. slow cooker. In a large resealable plastic bag, combine the flour, salt and pepper. Add beef, a few pieces at a time, and shake to coat. Place beef over vegetables.

In a small bowl, combine the soup, wine, tapioca, Italian seasoning, paprika, brown sugar, bouillon and Worcestershire sauce. Pour over the top.

Cover and cook on low for 8-10 hours or until meat and vegetables are tender, adding mushrooms during the last hour. Serve with noodles.

Pork Medallions in Green Peppercorn Sauce

PREP: 15 MIN.   **COOK:** 30 MIN.   **YIELD:** 6 SERVINGS

For birthdays and special occasions, my family requests tender medallions of pork in a flavorful peppercorn sauce. I serve rice pilaf and steamed broccoli on the side.

Karen Hubbs ★ Mahomet, Illinois

- 1-1/2 pounds pork tenderloin
- 1/4 teaspoon salt
- 1/4 teaspoon pepper
- 3 tablespoons butter, *divided*
- 3 shallots, finely chopped
- 1/2 cup dry vermouth
- 1-1/2 cups reduced-sodium chicken broth
- 1 tablespoon whole green peppercorns, crushed
- 1/2 teaspoon dried thyme
- 1/3 cup heavy whipping cream
- 2 teaspoons Dijon mustard

Cut pork into 2-in. slices; flatten slices slightly. Sprinkle with salt and pepper. In a large skillet, brown pork in 2 tablespoons butter in batches; remove and set aside.

In the same skillet, saute shallots in remaining butter until tender. Add the vermouth; cook until liquid is reduced by half.

Stir in the broth, peppercorns and thyme. Bring to a boil over medium heat; cook for 8-10 minutes or until liquid is reduced to about 1 cup. Stir in cream and mustard.

Return pork to the pan and bring to a boil. Reduce heat; simmer, uncovered, for 8-10 minutes or until a meat thermometer reads 160°, turning pork occasionally.

Editor's Note: Look for green peppercorns in spice shops. You may substitute a small amount of coarsely ground black peppercorns if desired.

Romaine Salad with Vanilla Bean Dressing

PREP/TOTAL TIME: 30 MIN.   **YIELD:** 8 SERVINGS

Vanilla bean adds a mellow flavor to a tangy, white-wine-vinegar dressing. Dried apricots in the salad bring a sweet twist, while toasted pine nuts supply some crunch.

Virginia Crowell ★ Stayton, Oregon

1/4	cup water
3	tablespoons white wine vinegar
2	tablespoons sugar
1	tablespoon finely chopped onion
1/4	teaspoon pepper
1/8	teaspoon salt
1	vanilla bean
2/3	cup canola oil
8	cups torn romaine
1	cup dried apricots, sliced
1/2	cup pine nuts, toasted
1	cup (4 ounces) crumbled Gorgonzola cheese

In small saucepan, combine the water, vinegar, sugar, onion, pepper and salt. Split vanilla bean and scrape seeds; add bean and seeds to water mixture. Bring to a boil. Reduce heat; simmer, uncovered, for 5 minutes. Cool.

Discard vanilla bean; pour mixture into a blender. Cover and process until smooth. While processing, gradually add oil in a steady stream.

Divide romaine among eight salad plates; top with apricots, pine nuts and cheese. Drizzle each serving with 2 tablespoons dressing.

TO MAKE AHEAD: Prepare salad dressing up to 3 days in advance; cover and store in the refrigerator. Stir well before using.

Portobello Pizzas

PREP/TOTAL TIME: 30 MIN.   **YIELD:** 6 SERVINGS

Portobello mushroom caps are the creative "crust" in this upscale spin on pizza. I also cut the caps into wedges and serve them as appetizers.

Lisa Scheevel ★ LeRoy, Minnesota

6	large portobello mushrooms (4 to 4-1/2 inches), stems removed
1	tablespoon olive oil
1	pound bulk Italian sausage
1	can (15 ounces) pizza sauce
1	medium green pepper, chopped
1	medium onion, chopped
1/2	cup chopped fresh mushrooms
1/4	cup grated Parmesan cheese
2	garlic cloves, minced
1	cup (4 ounces) shredded part-skim mozzarella cheese

Thinly sliced fresh basil leaves, optional

Place mushrooms, stem side down, on a greased baking sheet; drizzle with oil. Bake at 350° for 20-25 minutes or until tender, turning once.

Meanwhile, cook sausage over medium heat until no longer pink; drain. Stir in the pizza sauce, pepper, onion, mushrooms, Parmesan cheese and garlic. Divide among mushrooms; sprinkle with mozzarella cheese. Broil 2-3 in. from the heat for 1-2 minutes or until cheese is melted. Sprinkle with basil if desired.

Sesame Chicken with Ginger Shiitake Cream Sauce

(pictured at left)

PREP: 15 MIN. **COOK:** 30 MIN. **YIELD:** 4 SERVINGS

The sauce on this skillet chicken dish is so addictive that guests practically lick their plates clean! I often rely on the recipe for last-minute entertaining.

Pamela Gelsomini ★ Wrentham, Massachusetts

    4   boneless skinless chicken breast halves (6 ounces *each*)
  1/8   teaspoon salt
  1/8   teaspoon pepper
  2/3   cup sesame seeds
    2   tablespoons peanut oil
  1/2   pound sliced fresh shiitake mushrooms
4-1/2   teaspoons minced fresh gingerroot
    2   garlic cloves, minced
4-1/2   teaspoons soy sauce
1-1/2   teaspoons butter
    1   cup heavy whipping cream
1-1/2   teaspoons wasabi mustard
Hot cooked rice

Flatten chicken to 1/2-in. thickness; sprinkle with salt and pepper. Place sesame seeds in a shallow bowl; dip chicken in sesame seeds.

In a large skillet, cook chicken in oil over medium heat for 6-8 minutes on each side or until a meat thermometer reads 170°. Remove and keep warm.

In the same skillet, cook and stir the mushrooms, ginger and garlic in soy sauce and butter for 3 minutes. Add cream and mustard; cook and stir for 6-8 minutes or until thickened. Serve sauce with chicken and rice.

Flattening Chicken Breasts

When flattening chicken breasts, place them inside a heavy-duty resealable plastic bag or between two sheets of heavy plastic wrap to prevent messy splatters. Pound with the flat side of a meat mallet. The spiky side will tear the meat. Use a lighter touch than you would for tenderizing a beef round steak; if pounded too hard, the chicken will fall apart and be mushy.

Seafood Brochettes

PREP: 30 MIN. **GRILL:** 5 MIN. **YIELD:** 1 DOZEN

Flavorful seafood shines in these easy-to-grill kabobs. Mild chive butter is an awesome accompaniment.

Nella Parker ★ Hersey, Michigan

   24   medium fresh mushrooms
   24   cherry tomatoes
    8   bacon strips, cut into thirds
    1   pound halibut, cut into 1-inch pieces
    1   pound uncooked large shrimp, peeled and deveined
    1   pound sea scallops
  1/2   cup butter, melted
CHIVE BUTTER:
    1   cup butter, melted
    2   to 3 tablespoons minced chives

On 12 metal or soaked wooden skewers, alternately thread two mushrooms, two tomatoes and two pieces of bacon with four pieces of fish or seafood. Brush kabobs with the melted butter.

Grill, covered, over medium-hot heat for 5-7 minutes or until shrimp turn pink and scallops are opaque, turning once. Combine butter and chives; serve with brochettes.

Spearmint Thins

PREP: 30 MIN. + CHILLING **YIELD:** 4 DOZEN

No time to bake cookies from scratch? Create a tasty treat in little more than half an hour by doctoring butter-flavored crackers with vanilla chips and mint candies.

Kathleen Felton ★ Fairfax, Iowa

    1   package (10 ounces) mint Andes baking chips *or*
         2 packages (4.67 ounces *each*) mint Andes candies, chopped
   48   butter-flavored crackers
  1/2   cup white baking chips
    2   candy canes, crushed

In a microwave, melt baking chips; stir until smooth. Dip crackers in melted chips; allow excess to drip off. Place on a waxed paper-lined baking sheet. Chill for 10 minutes or until set.

In a microwave, melt white chips; stir until smooth. Drizzle over crackers; sprinkle with candy. Chill for 5 minutes or until set. Store in an airtight container.

Crab Dip in a Bread Bowl

PREP/TOTAL TIME: 30 MIN. **YIELD:** 2-1/2 CUPS

I whipped up this recipe for a get-together when my husband had no interest in the spinach dip I had prepared. Ranch salad dressing mix is the fantastic, fast flavoring.

Sharon Monroe ★ Littleton, Colorado

    1   loaf (1 pound) loaf sourdough bread
    2   cups (16 ounces) sour cream
    2   cans (6 ounces *each*) crabmeat, drained, flaked and cartilage removed *or* 2 cups imitation crabmeat
    1   can (8 ounces) water chestnuts, drained and chopped
    1   envelope ranch salad dressing mix
Assorted fresh vegetables

Cut top fourth off of the loaf of bread; carefully hollow out bottom, leaving a 1-in. shell. Cube removed bread; set aside.

In a small bowl, combine the sour cream, crab, water chestnuts and salad dressing mix.

Fill bread shell with crab dip. Serve with vegetables and reserved bread cubes.

In a microwave, melt butter and chocolate; stir until smooth. Cool slightly. In a large bowl, beat the eggs, sugar and vanilla. Stir in chocolate mixture. Combine flour and salt; gradually add to chocolate mixture. Fold in pecans.

Transfer to a greased 13-in. x 9-in. baking pan. Bake at 350° for 35-40 minutes or until a toothpick inserted near the center comes out clean. Cool on a wire rack.

For frosting, in a microwave, melt baking chips; stir until smooth. Cool slightly. In a large bowl, beat cream cheese and butter until fluffy. Add the melted chips, sugars, vanilla and salt; beat until smooth. Stir in coconut and pecans. Spread over brownies. Store in the refrigerator.

French Onion Casserole

PREP/TOTAL TIME: 30 MIN.   **YIELD:** 8 SERVINGS

Fans of French onion soup will be delighted with this comforting casserole. The 30-minute dish is always a nice side to serve along with beef entrees.

Margaret McClatchey ★ Loveland, Colorado

8	medium onions, sliced
5	tablespoons butter, *divided*
2	tablespoons all-purpose flour

Dash pepper

3/4	cup beef broth
1/4	cup sherry *or* additional beef broth
1-1/2	cups salad croutons
1/2	cup shredded Swiss cheese
3	tablespoons grated Parmesan cheese

In a large skillet, saute onions in 3 tablespoons butter until tender. Stir in flour and pepper until blended; gradually add broth and sherry. Bring to a boil; cook and stir for 2 minutes or until thickened. Transfer to an ungreased 9-in. square baking pan.

In a microwave, melt the remaining butter. Add the croutons; toss to coat. Spoon over the onion mixture. Sprinkle with cheeses.

Broil 3-4 in. from the heat for 1-2 minutes or until cheese is melted.

Coconut-Pecan Brownies

PREP: 25 MIN.   **BAKE:** 35 MIN. + COOLING
YIELD: 2 DOZEN

These moist, bakery-style brownies are made even better with a cream cheese frosting featuring coconut and pecans.

Lesley Pew ★ Lynn, Massachusetts

1	cup butter, cubed
4	ounces bittersweet chocolate, chopped
4	eggs
2-1/2	cups sugar
2	teaspoons vanilla extract
2	cups all-purpose flour
1/2	teaspoon salt
2	cups chopped pecans

FROSTING:

3/4	cup white baking chips
2	packages (3 ounces *each*) cream cheese, softened
1/2	cup butter, softened
1-1/2	cups confectioners' sugar
3	tablespoons brown sugar
3/4	teaspoon vanilla extract
1/8	teaspoon salt
3/4	cup flaked coconut
3/4	cup chopped pecans

Maple Peanut Mix

PREP: 15 MIN.   **BAKE:** 15 MIN. + STANDING   **YIELD:** 10 CUPS

Maple syrup and butter combine to coat a combination of nuts, pretzels, dried cranberries and chocolate chips. I like adding some crushed red pepper flakes for a bit of heat.

Sharlene Heatwole ★ McDowell, Virginia

  1   cup maple syrup
  2   tablespoons butter, melted
  6   cups unsalted peanuts
  1   to 1-1/2 teaspoons crushed red pepper flakes, optional
  2   cups pretzel sticks
  1   cup dried cranberries
  1   cup milk chocolate chips

Line a 15-in. x 10-in. x 1-in. baking pan with foil and grease the foil; set aside. In a large bowl, combine syrup and butter. Stir in peanuts and pepper flakes if desired. Spread mixture into prepared pan. Bake at 350° for 15 minutes or until bubbly, stirring occasionally.

Transfer to a large bowl; stir in pretzels and cranberries. Spread mixture onto waxed paper; sprinkle with chips. Let stand until dry. Store in an airtight container.

TO MAKE AHEAD: Prepare the mix up to a week in advance.

Cranberry-Orange Cream Pie

PREP: 30 MIN. + CHILLING   **YIELD:** 8 SERVINGS

Here's an easy dessert that can be chilling while you tend to other meal preparations.

Marjorie Carey ★ Alamosa, Colorado

Pastry for single-crust pie (9 inches)
  1   cup whole-berry cranberry sauce
  1/2 cup packed brown sugar
  1   package (3 ounces) orange gelatin
  1   cup heavy whipping cream
  1/2 cup finely chopped pecans
Additional whipped cream

Line a 9-in. pie plate with pastry; trim and flute edges. Line unpricked pastry with a double thickness of heavy-duty foil. Bake at 450° for 8 minutes. Remove foil; bake 5-7 minutes longer or until lightly browned. Cool on a wire rack.

In a small saucepan, bring cranberry sauce and brown sugar to a boil. Remove from the heat; stir in gelatin until dissolved. Transfer to a large bowl. Cover and refrigerate for 45 minutes or until partially set.

In a small bowl, beat cream until stiff peaks form. Fold whipped cream and pecans into gelatin mixture. Spread into pie crust. Cover and refrigerate for at least 4 hours. Garnish with additional whipped cream.

Ginger Apritinis

PREP: 25 MIN. + CHILLING
YIELD: 16 SERVINGS (3 QUARTS)

Our home economists developed this refreshing beverage for folks who want to offer guests an adult-style sipper without the alcohol. The simple syrup is enhanced with gingerroot and vanilla bean.

  4   cups sugar
  4   cups water
  1/2 cup chopped fresh gingerroot
  1   vanilla bean
  4   cups apricot nectar, chilled
  3   cups white cranberry juice, chilled
  1/2 cup lemon juice
  1   teaspoon vanilla extract
  1/4 teaspoon ground cloves

In a large saucepan, combine the sugar, water and ginger. Split vanilla bean and scrape seeds; add bean and seeds to sugar mixture. Bring to a boil over medium heat. Cook and stir for 1 minute. Remove from the heat; cover and let stand for 20 minutes. Strain mixture, discarding ginger and vanilla bean. Refrigerate until chilled.

In a large pitcher, combine the remaining ingredients; stir in sugar mixture. Serve in cocktail glasses.

Toasted Beer Bread With Asiago Dip

PREP: 30 MIN.   **BAKE:** 50 MIN. + COOLING
YIELD: 4 MINI LOAVES (6 SLICES EACH AND 3 CUPS DIP)

Beer lends robust flavor to a fast-to-fix quick bread. Toasted slices pair perfectly with a rich, cheesy dip that guests can't stop digging into.

Michelle Zupan ★ Augusta, Georgia

- 3 cups all-purpose flour
- 3 tablespoons sugar
- 3 teaspoons baking powder
- 1 teaspoon salt
- 1/2 teaspoon pepper
- 1 bottle (12 ounces) beer
- 1/2 cup shredded cheddar cheese
- 3 tablespoons chopped green onions
- 1/4 cup butter, melted, *divided*

ASIAGO DIP:
- 2 tablespoons chopped sun-dried tomatoes (not packed in oil)
- 1/2 cup boiling water
- 1 cup sour cream
- 1 cup mayonnaise
- 3/4 cup shredded Asiago cheese
- 1/4 cup sliced fresh mushrooms
- 1/4 cup chopped green onions
- 1/4 teaspoon crushed red pepper flakes

In a large bowl, combine the flour, sugar, baking powder, salt and pepper. Stir in beer just until moistened. Fold in cheese and onions. Transfer to four greased 5-3/4-in. x 3-in. x 2-in. loaf pans. Brush with 2 tablespoons butter.

Bake at 350° for 25-30 minutes or until a toothpick inserted near the center comes out clean. Cool for 10 minutes before removing from pans to wire racks. Brush tops with remaining butter.

Remove loaves to a cutting board; cut each into six slices. Place cut side down on ungreased baking sheets. Broil 4 in. from the heat for 2-3 minutes on each side or until toasted. Remove to wire racks to cool.

In small bowl, combine tomatoes and water. Let stand for 5 minutes; drain. In a large bowl, combine the sour cream, mayonnaise, cheese, mushrooms, onions, pepper flakes and tomatoes. Transfer to a greased 1-qt. baking dish. Bake at 350° for 20-25 minutes or until heated through. Serve warm with toast.

TO MAKE AHEAD: Bake the bread 1 day in advance; store in resealable plastic bags. Slice and toast the bread the following day.

Pumpkin Pecan Sundaes

PREP/TOTAL TIME: 20 MIN.   **YIELD:** 6 SERVINGS

My family enjoys anything with pumpkin so I knew this recipe would be well-received. Butter pecan ice cream is a perfect partner for the spiced pumpkin sauce.

Fancheon Resler ★ Bluffton, Indiana

- 1/3 cup sugar
- 2 teaspoons cornstarch
- 1/4 teaspoon *each* ground ginger, cinnamon and nutmeg
- 1 cup canned pumpkin
- 2/3 cup 2% milk
- 1-1/2 teaspoons vanilla extract, *divided*
- 1 cup heavy whipping cream
- 3 tablespoons confectioners' sugar
- 3 cups butter pecan ice cream
- 6 tablespoons chopped pecans, toasted

In a small saucepan, combine the sugar, cornstarch and spices. Stir in pumpkin and milk until smooth. Bring to a boil; cook and stir for 2 minutes or until thickened. Remove from the heat; stir in 1 teaspoon vanilla.

In a small bowl, beat cream until it begins to thicken. Add confectioners' sugar and remaining vanilla; beat until stiff peaks form.

Scoop ice cream into six dessert dishes. Top each with 1/4 cup pumpkin sauce and 1/3 cup whipped cream. Sprinkle with pecans.

Peachy Navel

(pictured at left)

PREP/TOTAL TIME: 5 MIN. **YIELD:** 1 SERVING

With a refreshing blend of peach nectar, orange juice and lemonade, this thirst-quenching beverage will be popular throughout the year.

- 2/3 cup orange juice
- 1/2 cup peach nectar, chilled
-   1 tablespoon thawed lemonade concentrate
- 1/3 cup club soda, chilled

GARNISH:
Orange slice and twist

In a highball glass, combine orange juice, peach nectar and lemonade concentrate. Stir in club soda. Garnish as desired.

Vodka Peachy Navel: Add 2 ounces of vodka.

Horseradish-Celery Deviled Eggs

PREP/TOTAL TIME: 20 MIN. **YIELD:** 1 DOZEN

Ordinary deviled eggs can't compare to this version. Sun-dried tomatoes, horseradish and hot pepper sauce infuse each bite with incredible taste.

Cathy Justus ★ Taylor, Michigan

-    6 hard-cooked eggs
- 1/4 cup mayonnaise
-    2 tablespoons finely chopped celery, *divided*
- 4-1/2 teaspoons finely chopped oil-packed sun-dried tomatoes
-    1 tablespoon prepared horseradish
-    1 teaspoon Worcestershire sauce
- 1/2 teaspoon celery seed
- 1/2 teaspoon Dijon mustard
- 1/2 teaspoon hot pepper sauce
- 1/8 teaspoon salt
- 1/8 teaspoon coarsely ground pepper

Cut eggs in half lengthwise. Remove yolks; set whites aside. In a small bowl, mash yolks. Add the mayonnaise, 1 tablespoon celery, tomatoes, horseradish, Worcestershire sauce, celery seed, mustard, pepper sauce, salt and pepper; mix well.

Stuff or pipe into egg whites. Sprinkle with remaining celery. Refrigerate until serving.

TO MAKE AHEAD: Prepare the eggs up to 1 day in advance.

Pineapple Orange Trifle

PREP: 20 MIN. + CHILLING **YIELD:** 12 SERVINGS

Guests are pleasantly surprised to see this lovely trifle on my holiday table. Coconut, pineapple and mandarin oranges bring a tropical taste to every spoonful.

Renee Schwebach ★ Dumont, Minnesota

-   1 can (14 ounces) pineapple tidbits
-   2 cups cold 2% milk
-   2 packages (3.4 ounces *each*) instant vanilla pudding mix
-   1 cup (8 ounces) sour cream
-   1 can (11 ounces) mandarin oranges, drained
-   1 prepared angel food cake (8 to 10 ounces), cut into 1-inch cubes
-   1 carton (8 ounces) frozen whipped topping, thawed
- 1/2 teaspoon orange extract
- 1/3 cup flaked coconut, toasted

Drain pineapple, reserving 2/3 cup juice; set pineapple aside. In a large bowl, whisk the milk, pineapple juice and pudding mixes for 2 minutes. Let stand for 2 minutes or until soft-set. Whisk in sour cream; fold in oranges and pineapple.

Place a third of the cake cubes in a 3-qt. trifle bowl; top with a third of the pudding mixture. Repeat layers twice. Cover and refrigerate for 3 hours. Combine whipped topping and extract; spread over the top. Sprinkle with coconut.

Chocolate Mousse Cakes

PREP: 30 MIN. **BAKE:** 20 MIN. + COOLING
YIELD: 2 CAKES (8 SERVINGS EACH)

Fans of chocolate will fall head over heels for this decadent dessert. The recipe makes two cakes, so it's a wonderful choice for entertaining.

Lisa Angalich ★ Wheeling, West Virginia

- 3/4 cup butter, softened
- 1-2/3 cups sugar
- 3 eggs
- 1 teaspoon vanilla extract
- 2 cups all-purpose flour
- 2/3 cup baking cocoa
- 1-1/4 teaspoons baking soda
- 1 teaspoon salt
- 1/4 teaspoon baking powder
- 1-1/3 cups water

FROSTING/FINISHING:
- 4 ounces cream cheese, softened
- 1/2 cup confectioners' sugar
- 1/4 cup baking cocoa
- 3/4 teaspoon vanilla extract
- 1 cup heavy whipping cream, whipped
- 1 ounce semisweet chocolate, grated

In a large bowl, cream butter and sugar until light and fluffy. Add eggs, one at a time, beating well after each addition. Beat in vanilla. Combine the flour, cocoa, baking soda, salt and baking powder; add to the creamed mixture alternately with water, beating well after each addition.

Transfer to two greased 9-in. tart pans with removable bottoms. Bake at 350° for 20-25 minutes or until a toothpick inserted near the center comes out clean. Cool for 10 minutes before removing from pans to wire racks to cool completely.

In a large bowl, beat the cream cheese, confectioners' sugar, cocoa and vanilla until smooth. Fold in whipped cream. Pipe frosting over tops of cakes; sprinkle with grated chocolate. Refrigerate leftovers.

Pork & Mozzarella Crostini

PREP: 30 MIN. **BAKE:** 20 MIN. **YIELD:** 2-1/2 DOZEN

When hosting an appetizer party, it's a good idea to offer a few heartier options like this meaty crostini. You can make the pork a day ahead, then assemble and broil as guests arrive.

Elizabeth Dumont ★ Boulder, Colorado

- 1 pork tenderloin (1 pound)
- 2 teaspoons plus 2 tablespoons olive oil, *divided*
- 1/8 teaspoon salt
- 1/8 teaspoon pepper
- 1 French bread baguette (10-1/2 ounces), sliced
- 2 garlic cloves, halved
- 1 package (8 ounces) cream cheese, softened
- 1 shallot, finely chopped
- 2 tablespoons prepared horseradish
- 2 teaspoons Worcestershire sauce
- 1/4 teaspoon cayenne pepper
- 4 plum tomatoes
- 8 ounces fresh mozzarella cheese

Minced fresh parsley, optional

Place pork on a rack in a shallow roasting pan. Rub with 2 teaspoons oil; sprinkle with salt and pepper. Bake at 450° for 20-30 minutes or until a meat thermometer reads 160°. Let stand for 10 minutes.

Place bread on ungreased baking sheets; brush with remaining oil. Bake at 350° for 8-10 minutes or until toasted. Rub toast with garlic.

Combine the cream cheese, shallot, horseradish, Worcestershire sauce and cayenne; spread over toast. Thinly slice the pork, tomatoes and mozzarella cheese; arrange on toast. Broil 4-6 in. from the heat for 2-3 minutes or until the cheese is melted. Sprinkle with the parsley if desired.

Beef Fondue with Mustard-Mayonnaise Sauce

(pictured at left)

PREP: 10 MIN. + CHILLING   **COOK:** 5 MIN./BATCH
YIELD: 6 SERVINGS (ABOUT 1 CUP SAUCE)

Fondue is fun, but for me, the accompanying sauces are what make them even more delicious. This creamy, zippy sauce enhances the flavor of beef.

Ruth Peterson ★ Jenison, Michigan

- 1 cup mayonnaise
- 2 teaspoons finely chopped onion
- 2 teaspoons lemon juice
- 2 tablespoons horseradish mustard *or* spicy brown mustard
- 1-1/2 pounds beef tenderloin, cut into 3/4-inch cubes

Oil for deep-fat frying

In a small bowl, combine the mayonnaise, onion, lemon juice and mustard; cover and refrigerate for 30 minutes.

Pat meat dry with paper towels. Heat oil in a fondue pot to 375°. Use fondue forks to cook meat in oil until it reaches desired doneness. Serve with sauce.

TO MAKE AHEAD: Prepare sauce the day before serving.

Citrus Fennel Salad

PREP/TOTAL TIME: 20 MIN.   **YIELD:** 5 SERVINGS

My family really enjoys crunchy fennel, which pairs well with citrus vinaigrette. The salad is a nice addition to any meal.

Denise Elder ★ Hanover, Ontario

- 1 large fennel bulb, thinly sliced
- 1 small apple, thinly sliced
- 1/4 cup sliced sweet onion

DRESSING:

- 1/3 cup olive oil
- 2 tablespoons lemon juice
- 2 tablespoons orange juice
- 1/2 teaspoon grated lemon peel
- 1/2 teaspoon grated orange peel
- 1/2 teaspoon Dijon mustard
- 1/2 teaspoon salt
- 1/8 teaspoon pepper

In a large bowl, combine the fennel, apple and onion. In a small bowl, whisk the dressing ingredients; pour over salad and toss to coat. Chill until serving.

TO MAKE AHEAD: Prepare dressing up to 3 days before serving.

Cranberry Lime Sparkler

PREP: 20 MIN. + CHILLING   **YIELD:** 9 SERVINGS

You just can't beat a reliable punch recipe that has mass appeal. The crimson color of this beverage is well-suited for the Christmas season.

Kari Scilley ★ Perham, Minnesota

- 2-1/2 cups water
- 1 can (14 ounces) jellied cranberry sauce
- 1/2 cup sugar
- 1/2 cup lemon juice
- 1 teaspoon vanilla extract
- 1 cup club soda, chilled
- 1 cup ginger ale, chilled
- 2 medium limes, sliced
- 1 cup maraschino cherries

In a large saucepan, combine water and cranberry sauce; cook and stir over low heat until smooth. Stir in sugar; cool to room temperature.

Transfer to a pitcher; stir in lemon juice and vanilla. Refrigerate until chilled.

Just before serving, add the club soda, ginger ale, limes and cherries.

TO MAKE AHEAD: Prepare cranberry mixture up to 2 days in advance; store, ready to mix in batches, in the refrigerator.

Cheese Tortellini Salad

PREP: 25 MIN. + CHILLING
YIELD: 16 SERVINGS (3/4 CUP EACH)

This chilled toss will add color and variety to your holiday spread. Red and yellow peppers provide a delightful crunch, and an easy homemade dressing lends a lively flavor that will tingle taste buds.

Jennifer Kunz ★ Troy, Michigan

- 1 package (19 ounces) frozen cheese tortellini
- 4 cups fresh arugula *or* baby spinach
- 1 can (14 ounces) water-packed artichoke hearts, rinsed, drained and chopped
- 1 medium red onion, sliced
- 1 medium sweet red pepper, julienned
- 1 medium sweet yellow pepper, julienned
- 3 tablespoons shredded Parmesan cheese

DRESSING:
- 1/2 cup olive oil
- 1/4 cup red wine vinegar
- 3 tablespoons lemon juice
- 1 tablespoon *each* minced fresh basil, mint and parsley
- 1/2 teaspoon salt
- 1/2 teaspoon garlic powder
- 1/4 teaspoon pepper
- 1/4 teaspoon hot pepper sauce

Cook tortellini according to package directions.

Meanwhile, in a large bowl, combine the arugula, artichokes, onion, peppers and cheese. Drain tortellini; add to arugula mixture.

In a bowl, whisk the remaining ingredients. Drizzle over salad; toss to coat. Cover and refrigerate for at least 4 hours.

Seasonal
GET-TOGETHERS

Seasonal Get-Togethers

A Magical Morning Breakfast. . .a Holiday Tea Party. . .a joyful gathering of friends at a Festive St. Nick's Day Party. . .there are countless reasons to gather with loved ones during the Christmas season. Make each occasion merry with these mainstay Yuletide menus.

Magical Morning Breakfast

The sweet scent of a merry breakfast wafting from the kitchen on Christmas morning makes this magical day even more exciting. Quench your thirst with a cool glass of Sunrise Sipper while Bacon & Cheddar Strata warms in the oven. The kids will go crazy over Gingerbread Waffles with Cream Cheese Topping. And you can't go wrong with refreshing Fabulous Fruit Salad. . .made with seven fruits, it's sure to be the hit of the party!

Gingerbread Waffles with Cream Cheese Topping

PREP: 30 MIN.   **COOK:** 5 MIN./BATCH
YIELD: 16 WAFFLES (1-1/3 CUPS TOPPING)

Fans of gingerbread cookies will love these waffles! The breakfast treat features a delicious blend of molasses and spices with a dollop of cream cheese topping.

Jannine Fisk ★ Malden, Massachusetts

- 2 cups all-purpose flour
- 3 teaspoons baking powder
- 1-1/2 teaspoons ground ginger
- 1 teaspoon baking soda
- 1 teaspoon ground cinnamon
- 1/2 teaspoon salt
- 1/4 teaspoon ground nutmeg
- 1/4 cup packed brown sugar
- 2 eggs, *separated*
- 1-1/2 cups buttermilk
- 1/2 cup butter, melted
- 1/2 cup molasses
- 2 teaspoons vanilla extract

TOPPING:
- 1/2 cup butter, softened
- 1/4 cup cream cheese, softened
- 1-1/2 cups confectioners' sugar
- 1/4 cup 2% milk
- 1/2 teaspoon vanilla extract
- 1/8 teaspoon salt

Maple syrup

In a large bowl, combine the first seven ingredients. In a small bowl, beat brown sugar and egg yolks until blended; beat in the buttermilk, butter, molasses and vanilla. Stir into dry ingredients just until combined.

In a small bowl with clean beaters, beat egg whites until stiff peaks form. Fold into batter. Bake in a preheated waffle iron according to manufacturer's directions.

For topping, in a small bowl, beat butter and cream cheese until fluffy. Beat in the confectioners' sugar, milk, vanilla and salt. Serve waffles with topping and maple syrup.

TO MAKE AHEAD: The topping can be made a day in advance. Let stand at room temperature for 30 minutes before serving.

Easy Cheese Danish

PREP/TOTAL TIME: 25 MIN.   **YIELD:** 1-1/2 DOZEN

These cream cheese pastries are baked to flaky perfection and made to shine with a simple egg wash. They taste just as decadent as any breakfast sensation you'd find in a bakery.

Carole Sepstead ★ Grafton, Wisconsin

- 1 package (8 ounces) cream cheese, softened
- 1/3 cup sugar
- 2 egg yolks
- 1 tablespoon grated lemon peel
- 1 teaspoon vanilla extract
- 1/4 teaspoon salt
- 1 package (17.3 ounces) frozen puff pastry, thawed
- 1 egg
- 1 tablespoon water

In a large bowl, beat cream cheese and sugar until fluffy. Add the egg yolks, lemon peel, vanilla and salt; beat on low speed until blended.

On a lightly floured surface, roll out each sheet of puff pastry into a 12-in. square. Cut each into nine squares. Spoon 2-1/2 teaspoons of cheese mixture into the center of each square.

Whisk egg and water; lightly brush over edges. Bring two opposite corners of pastry over filling; pinch to seal. Place on a greased baking sheet; brush with remaining egg mixture. Bake at 400° for 10-12 minutes or until golden brown.

Fabulous Fruit Salad

PREP: 30 MIN. + CHILLING   **YIELD:** 10 SERVINGS

This refreshing fruit salad bursts with a delightful citrus flavor. The recipe makes a big batch so it's perfect for a holiday potluck.

Mary Louise Fash ★ Walterboro, South Carolina

- 1/2 cup sugar
- 1/4 cup orange juice
- 2 tablespoons lemon juice
- 1 egg yolk, lightly beaten
- 1-1/2 teaspoons lime juice
- 1/2 fresh pineapple, peeled and cubed
- 1 small cantaloupe, peeled, seeded and cubed
- 1 large grapefruit, peeled and sectioned
- 1 large navel orange, peeled and sectioned
- 1 small red apple, diced
- 1 small banana, sliced
- 1 cup fresh blueberries

In a small heavy saucepan, combine the first five ingredients. Cook and stir over medium heat until mixture reaches 160° and is thick enough to coat the back of a spoon.

Remove from the heat. Cool quickly by placing pan in a bowl of ice water; stir for 2 minutes.

In a large bowl, combine the pineapple, cantaloupe, grapefruit, orange, apple and banana. Pour dressing over fruit. Cover and refrigerate for 2 hours.

Just before serving, stir salad. Sprinkle with blueberries.

TO MAKE AHEAD: Dressing can be made a day in advance; cover and refrigerate.

Bacon & Cheddar Strata

PREP: 20 MIN. + CHILLING   **BAKE:** 45 MIN.
YIELD: 10 SERVINGS

I prepare this sunrise specialty the day before Christmas so we have something tasty and hearty to warm our tummies while we open gifts the next morning. The key to its perfection is to let it set overnight.

Deb Healey ★ Cold Lake, Alberta

- 1 pound sliced bacon
- 1 medium sweet red pepper, finely chopped
- 8 green onions, thinly sliced
- 1/2 cup chopped oil-packed sun-dried tomatoes
- 8 slices white bread, cubed
- 2 cups (8 ounces) shredded cheddar cheese
- 6 eggs, beaten
- 1-1/2 cups 2% milk
- 1/4 cup mayonnaise
- 1/2 teaspoon salt
- 1/4 teaspoon ground mustard
- 1/8 teaspoon pepper

In a large skillet, cook bacon in batches until crisp; drain on paper towels. Crumble into a large bowl. Add the red pepper, onions and tomatoes. In a greased 13-in. x 9-in. baking dish, layer half of the bread, bacon mixture and cheese. Top with remaining bread and bacon mixture.

In a small bowl, combine the eggs, milk, mayonnaise and seasonings. Pour over the top. Sprinkle with remaining cheese. Cover and refrigerate overnight.

Remove from the refrigerator 30 minutes before baking. Bake, covered, at 350° for 40 minutes. Uncover the dish and bake 5-10 minutes longer or until a knife inserted near the center comes out clean. Let stand for 5 minutes before cutting.

Sunrise Sipper

PREP/TOTAL TIME: 5 MIN.　**YIELD:** 1 SERVING

You'll be surprised to discover how easy it is to stir together this delicious beverage. Its beautiful swirls of pink and orange make it a colorful addition to any holiday brunch menu.

Ice cubes

2	tablespoons grenadine syrup
1-1/2	ounces vodka
1/2	cup orange juice

Fill a tall glass with ice. Add grenadine and vodka. Top with orange juice.

Virgin Sunrise Sipper: Omit Vodka, add 1/3 cup tonic water to grenadine.

Charming Napkin Bows

These beautiful napkin bows will add a touch of elegance to a tabletop. As fancy as they look, the bows are actually quite easy to create. Square napkins that are soft and silky work best.

1. Place napkin wrong side up on a flat surface and fold two opposite corners in to the center, overlapping the corners a bit. Then fold the opposite straight edges in as shown.
2. To form the two loops of the bow, fold the remaining corners over and overlap them.
3. Slide napkin ring over one end of napkin.
4. Arrange loops and ends of napkin as shown.

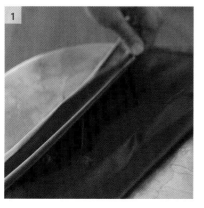

No matter how cold it is outside, a hot cup of tea makes it easy to enjoy the warmth of the season. Guests will appreciate the quick warm-up from a cup of comforting Chai or tangy Cranberry Tea. Fill hungry tummies with tasty Turkey, Gouda & Apple Tea Sandwiches, scrumptious Lobster-Shrimp Salad Croissants and sweet Petite Apricot Pastries. Include Poppy Seed-Filled Scones and Vienna Triangles to add a traditional touch to a memorable and merry tea party!

Vienna Triangles

PREP: 1 HOUR   **BAKE:** 15 MIN. + COOLING
YIELD: 9 DOZEN

Bring these delicate pastry triangles to a holiday tea party, and you're guaranteed to hear praises for the treat. They feature a luscious almond filling and a rich chocolate glaze.

Joanne Wright ★ Niles, Michigan

3	cups all-purpose flour
3/4	cup confectioners' sugar
1/2	teaspoon salt
1-1/2	cups cold butter

FILLING:

3	cups sliced almonds
1-1/2	cups sugar
5	egg whites
3	tablespoons all-purpose flour
1	tablespoon corn syrup
1	teaspoon ground cinnamon
1/2	teaspoon almond extract
1/4	teaspoon baking powder
2/3	cup seedless raspberry jam

COATING:

8	ounces semisweet chocolate, chopped
1	tablespoon shortening

In a large bowl, combine the flour, confectioners' sugar and salt; cut in butter until crumbly. Pat into a greased 15-in. x 10-in. x 1-in. baking pan. Bake at 350° for 15-18 minutes or until lightly browned. Cool on a wire rack.

Meanwhile, in a large saucepan, combine the almonds, sugar, egg whites, flour, corn syrup and cinnamon; cook over low heat until a thermometer reads 200°, stirring constantly. Remove from the heat; stir in extract and baking powder. Spread jam over crust; spread almond mixture over top.

Bake at 350° for 15-20 minutes or until golden brown. Cool completely on a wire rack. Cut into 54 squares; cut each diagonally into two triangles.

In a microwave, melt chocolate and shortening; stir until smooth. Dip half of each triangle in chocolate; allow excess to drip off. Place on waxed paper; let stand until set.

TO MAKE AHEAD: Can be made 2 days in advance. Store in an airtight container at room temperature.

Lobster-Shrimp Salad Croissants

PREP/TOTAL TIME: 25 MIN.   **YIELD:** 10 SERVINGS

This seafood salad has a hint of lemon and dill. The recipe calls for imitation lobster, but feel free to use fresh if you like.

Athena Russell ★ Florence, South Carolina

1/2	cup mayonnaise
1	tablespoon snipped fresh dill
1	tablespoon minced chives
1	tablespoon lemon juice
1/2	teaspoon salt
1/4	teaspoon pepper
1/2	pound imitation lobster
1/2	pound frozen cooked small shrimp, thawed and coarsely chopped
10	miniature croissants, split

In a large bowl, combine the mayonnaise, dill, chives, lemon juice, salt and pepper. Stir in lobster and shrimp. Cover and refrigerate until serving. Serve on croissants.

dough. Combine walnuts and remaining sugar; set aside.

Divide dough into thirds. Between waxed paper, roll one portion into a 15-in. x 10-in. rectangle. Transfer to a greased 15-in. x 10-in. baking pan. Sprinkle with 1-1/2 cups walnut mixture. Roll out second portion of dough; place over walnut layer. Spread apricot filling to within 1 in. of edges. Roll out remaining portion; place over filling.

Bake at 325° for 45-50 minutes or until golden brown. Cool completely on a wire rack. Beat the confectioners' sugar, butter, vanilla and enough milk to achieve desired consistency. Spread over top; sprinkle with remaining walnut mixture. Cut into 1-in. squares. Refrigerate leftovers.

TO MAKE AHEAD: Dough can be made a day in advance; cover and refrigerate each portion.

Cranberry Tea

PREP/TOTAL TIME: 30 MIN.   **YIELD:** 3 QUARTS

On cold winter afternoons, my friends and I like to sip this tangy cranberry tea while sitting next to a glowing fire and enjoying good conversation.

Polly Holbrook ★ Greeley, Colorado

3	cinnamon sticks (3 inches)
6	whole cloves
6	cups water
3	cups fresh *or* frozen cranberries
9	slices peeled fresh gingerroot
6	individual tea bags
6	cups unsweetened apple juice
1/3	cup honey

Place cinnamon and cloves on a double thickness of cheesecloth. Bring up corners of cloth; tie with a string to form a bag.

In a large saucepan, combine the water, cranberries and ginger; add spice bag. Bring to a boil. Reduce heat; cover and simmer for 15-20 minutes or until berries have popped, stirring occasionally. Remove from the heat. Add tea bags; cover and steep for 5 minutes.

Discard tea bags and spice bag. Strain cranberry mixture through a cheesecloth lined colander. Return to saucepan. Stir in juice and honey; heat through. Serve warm.

Petite Apricot Pastries

(pictured above)

PREP: 45 MIN.   **BAKE:** 45 MIN. + COOLING
YIELD: 12-1/2 DOZEN

Looking for a little, decadent treat to serve at your next tea party? Then try these tender, flaky pastries.

Melissa Rose Lundin ★ Kersey, Pennsylvania

1	package (1/4 ounce) active dry yeast
1/2	cup warm 2% milk (110° to 115°)
4	cups all-purpose flour
1	teaspoon plus 2/3 cup sugar, *divided*
1/2	teaspoon salt
1-1/2	cups cold butter
4	egg yolks, beaten
2	cups ground walnuts
2	cans (12 ounces *each*) apricot cake and pastry filling

FROSTING:

4	cups confectioners' sugar
2/3	cup butter, softened
1	teaspoon vanilla extract
2	to 4 tablespoons 2% milk

In a small bowl, dissolve yeast in warm milk. In a large bowl, combine 3 cups flour, 1 teaspoon sugar and salt. Cut in butter until crumbly. Add yeast mixture and egg yolks; mix well. Stir in enough remaining flour to form a soft

Petite Chocolate-Hazelnut Cakes

(pictured on page 82, top right)

PREP: 35 MIN. **BAKE:** 20 MIN. + COOLING
YIELD: 8 DOZEN

Add these sweet treats to a dessert platter featuring other small confections. The cake is moist and extra special with a rich, creamy filling and tempting chocolate ganache.

- 1/2 cup butter, softened
- 2/3 cup sugar
- 2 eggs
- 1-1/2 teaspoons vanilla extract
- 1-1/3 cups all-purpose flour
- 1/2 cup baking cocoa
- 1-1/2 teaspoons baking soda
- 1/4 teaspoon baking powder
- 1/4 teaspoon salt
- 3/4 cup plus 2 tablespoons buttermilk

FILLING:
- 1 teaspoon unflavored gelatin
- 1-1/4 cups heavy whipping cream, *divided*
- 1/4 cup chocolate hazelnut spread

GANACHE:
- 6 ounces semisweet chocolate, chopped
- 2/3 cup heavy whipping cream
- 1 teaspoon instant espresso granules
- 1-1/4 cups hazelnuts, toasted

In a bowl, cream butter and sugar until light and fluffy. Add eggs, one at a time, beating well after each addition. Beat in vanilla. Combine the flour, cocoa, baking soda, baking powder and salt; gradually add to the creamed mixture alternately with buttermilk, beating well after each addition.

Pour into a greased and floured 13-in. x 9-in. baking pan. Bake at 350° for 18-22 minutes or until a toothpick inserted near the center comes out clean.

Cool for 10 minutes before inverting onto a wire rack to cool completely. Trim 1/2 in. from edges of cake. Cut cake horizontally into two layers; set aside.

In a small saucepan, sprinkle gelatin over 1/4 cup cream; let stand for 1 minute. Heat over low heat, stirring until gelatin is completely dissolved. Remove from the heat; cool to room temperature.

In a large bowl, beat gelatin mixture and remaining cream until it begins to thicken. Add hazelnut spread; beat until stiff peaks form.

Place bottom cake layer on a cutting board; spread with whipped cream mixture. Top with remaining cake layer.

Place chocolate in a small bowl. In a small saucepan, bring cream and espresso granules just to a boil. Pour over chocolate; whisk until smooth.

Cool, stirring occasionally, to room temperature or until ganache reaches a spreading consistency, about 30 minutes. Spread over top of cake. Cut cake into 1-in. squares; top each with a hazelnut.

TO MAKE AHEAD: Cakes can be made a day in advance. Place each cake in a miniature muffin cup liner. Store in an airtight container in the refrigerator.

Editor's Note: Look for chocolate hazelnut spread in the peanut butter section of your grocery store.

Turkey, Gouda & Apple Tea Sandwiches

PREP/TOTAL TIME: 25 MIN. **YIELD:** 4 DOZEN

These fun mini sandwiches are a tasty addition to an afternoon tea gathering. The cranberry mayo lends a unique flavor twist, and the apples add a pleasant crunch.

- 2/3 cup reduced-fat mayonnaise
- 2 tablespoons whole-berry cranberry sauce
- 24 very thin slices white bread, crusts removed
- 12 slices deli turkey
- 2 medium apples, thinly sliced
- 12 thin slices smoked Gouda cheese
- 4 cups fresh baby spinach

Place mayonnaise and cranberry sauce in a small food processor. Cover and process until blended. Spread over each bread slice. Layer the turkey, apples, cheese and spinach over each of 12 bread slices; top with remaining bread. Cut each sandwich into quarters.

Vanilla Chai Tea

PREP/TOTAL TIME: 25 MIN.   **YIELD:** 6 SERVINGS

This warm chai is pure comfort in a cup. It's extra special with a dollop of fresh whipped cream and a sprinkling of ground allspice on top.

8	whole peppercorns
1/2	teaspoon whole allspice
1/4	teaspoon cardamom seeds
1	cinnamon stick (3 inches)
4	whole cloves
8	individual tea bags
1	tablespoon honey
4	cups boiling water
2	cups 2% milk
1	tablespoon vanilla extract
1/2	cup heavy whipping cream
1-1/2	teaspoons confectioners' sugar

Ground allspice

Place the first five ingredients in a large bowl; with the end of a wooden spoon handle, crush spices until aroma is released. Add the tea bags, honey and boiling water. Cover and steep for 6 minutes.

Meanwhile, in a small saucepan, heat the milk. Strain tea into a heatproof pitcher; stir in milk and vanilla.

In a small bowl, beat whipping cream and confectioners' sugar until soft peaks form. Serve individual servings of tea with whipped cream; garnish with ground allspice.

TO MAKE AHEAD: Whipped cream can be made a couple of hours in advance; cover and refrigerate.

Making the Perfect Cup

Brewing the perfect cup is easy to do, just following these steps. Begin by heating fresh, cold water to a boil. For black and oolong teas, pour the boiling water over a tea bag, tea infuser or pot containing 1 teaspoon of loose tea for each cup of water. Steep (stand) for 3 to 5 minutes, depending on the blend of tea and your preferred tea strength. Remove the bag or infuser and serve. Leaving the tea in the water will cause the beverage to become bitter. For green and white tea, allow the boiling water to cool slightly (180° to 190°), then pour over tea and steep 1 to 3 minutes.

When using a teapot, warm it just before you make the tea. Pour warm water into the pot, swish the water around and discard. Then add the tea, the water and steep.

Poppy Seed-Filled
Scones with Lemon Curd

PREP: 25 MIN. + CHILLING   **BAKE:** 15 MIN.
YIELD: 16 SCONES (1-1/2 CUPS LEMON CURD)

These scones are lovely when cut into wedges and draped with lemon curd. I often mix up the batter the night before and pop them into the oven the next morning to bake up fresh and golden brown.

Shannon Koene ★ Blacksburg, Virginia

    3   eggs
  1/2   cup sugar
  1/2   cup lemon juice
    2   tablespoons grated lemon peel
  1/4   cup butter, cubed

SCONES:
  3-1/3   cups all-purpose flour
   3/4   cup sugar
   1/3   cup poppy seeds
  1-1/2   teaspoons cream of tartar
  1-1/4   teaspoons baking soda
   3/4   teaspoon salt
   3/4   cup cold butter
   1/2   cup plus 2 tablespoons orange juice
    1   egg
    1   egg, *separated*
    1   teaspoon grated orange peel
    1   can (12-1/2 ounces) poppy seed cake and pastry filling
    1   teaspoon water

In a small heavy saucepan over medium heat, whisk the eggs, sugar, lemon juice and peel until blended. Add butter; cook, whisking constantly, until mixture is thickened and coats the back of a spoon. Transfer to a small bowl; cool for 10 minutes. Cover and refrigerate until chilled.

For scones, in a large bowl, combine the flour, sugar, poppy seeds, cream of tarter, baking soda and salt. Cut in butter until mixture resembles coarse crumbs. In a small bowl, whisk the orange juice, egg, egg yolk and orange peel; stir into crumb mixture just until moistened. Turn onto a floured surface; knead 10 times.

Divide dough into four portions. Pat each portion into a 7-in. circle. Spread poppy seed filling over two circles. Top with remaining circles; pinch edges to seal.

Transfer to two greased baking sheets. Combine egg white and water; brush over scones. Cut each into eight wedges, but do not separate. Bake at 375° for 15-20 minutes or until golden brown. Serve warm with lemon curd.

TO MAKE AHEAD: Lemon curd can be made up to 1 week in advance; cover and store in the refrigerator.

Festive St. Nick's Day Party

For centuries, children around the world have hung their stockings or set out their wooden shoes on the eve of December 6th in hopes that St. Nick would stop by to fill them with sweets, coins and trinkets. This year celebrate the day for all that it is with a festive party in honor of the revered old man himself!

You'll love the tender, slow-cooked flavor of Hearty Chicago-Style Beef Sandwiches. Bowls filled with Apple-Cinnamon Gelatin and Layered Spinach & Orange Salad will add bursts of color to holiday spreads. And traditional Dutch Speculaas and tastefully sinful Lump of Coal Candy will satisfy the most serious sweet tooth. No matter what St. Nick nibbles on this year, these tantalizing Yuletide treats are guaranteed to please!

Chicago-Style Beef Sandwiches

PREP: 30 MIN.   **COOK:** 8 HOURS   **YIELD:** 12 SERVINGS

I'm originally from the Windy City so I love Chicago-style beef. These tender sandwiches lend an authentic flavor, and they're so easy to prepare using a slow cooker.

Lois Szydlowski ★ Tampa, Florida

- 1 boneless beef chuck roast (4 pounds)
- 1 teaspoon salt
- 3/4 teaspoon pepper
- 2 tablespoons olive oil
- 1/2 pound fresh mushrooms
- 2 medium carrots, cut into chunks
- 1 medium onion, cut into wedges
- 6 garlic cloves, halved
- 2 teaspoons dried oregano
- 1 carton (32 ounces) beef broth
- 1 tablespoon beef base
- 12 Italian rolls, split
- 1 jar (16 ounces) giardiniera, drained

Cut roast in half; sprinkle with salt and pepper. In a large skillet, brown meat in oil on all sides; drain. Transfer to a 5-qt. slow cooker.

In a food processor, combine the mushrooms, carrots, onion, garlic and oregano. Cover and process until finely chopped. Transfer to slow cooker. Combine beef broth and base; pour over top. Cover and cook on low for 8-10 hours or until tender.

Remove meat and shred with two forks. Skim fat from cooking juices. Return meat to slow cooker; heat through. Using a slotted spoon, serve beef on buns; top with giardiniera.

Editor's Note: Look for beef base near the broth and bouillon in your grocery store.

Layered Spinach & Orange Salad
(pictured at left)

PREP/TOTAL TIME: 25 MIN.   **YIELD:** 10 SERVINGS

A simple homemade vinaigrette coats this colorful salad sprinkled with mandarin oranges and shavings of Parmesan cheese. If you like salads with the refreshing taste of citrus, you'll love this festive toss.

Jim Gales ★ Glendale, Wisconsin

- 6 cups fresh baby spinach
- 1 can (15 ounces) mandarin oranges, drained
- 1/2 cup chopped red onion

VINAIGRETTE:
- 1/3 cup olive oil
- 2 tablespoons red wine vinegar
- 4 teaspoons orange marmalade
- 1/4 teaspoon salt
- 1/8 teaspoon pepper
- 3/4 cup shaved Parmesan cheese

Arrange the spinach, oranges and onion on a serving plate. In a small bowl, whisk the oil, vinegar, marmalade, salt and pepper. Pour over salad. Top with cheese.

Salad Add-Ins

If you like to add a little more pizzazz to the Layered Spinach & Orange Salad (above), try one of these tasty add-ins: fresh sliced strawberries, blueberries, dried cherries, sliced mushrooms or crumbled bacon. For a touch of crunchiness, you can sprinkle toasted sliced almonds, honey-roasted peanuts or croutons over the salad.

Stocking Utensil Holders

You're sure to elicit oohs and ahhs from guests when you serve your Christmas cutlery in these whimsical handmade stockings.

1. Begin by tracing the stocking onto tracing paper. (see template on page 90). Pin the pattern to a double layer of quilt batting and cut out stocking with a straight-edge scissors.

2. Remove the pattern and pin the batting pieces together with edges matching. With a long running stitch, hand-stitch through both layers about 1/2 in. from the outer edges (leave about 1 inch of the top of the stocking unstitched). Use pinking sheers to cut outside the stitched edge of stocking leaving a narrow seam allowance.

3. Fold each layer of the top of the stocking to the outside to form a cuff. Make a small stitch in the center through both layers of cuff, leaving thread ends on the outside. Tie the thread in a small bow and trim ends as desired.

Lump of Coal Candy

PREP: 20 MIN. **COOK:** 25 MIN. + COOLING
YIELD: ABOUT 5 DOZEN

This dark caramel may look like coal, but it tastes like pure heaven! One bite and you'll beg Santa to stuff your stocking with this sinful delight.

1	teaspoon plus 1 cup butter, *divided*
2	cups sugar
1-1/2	cups corn syrup
1	can (14 ounces) sweetened condensed milk
1/2	teaspoon salt
1	cup chopped walnuts, toasted
2	teaspoons vanilla extract
1/2	teaspoon black food coloring, optional
1	package (12 ounces) dark chocolate chips
2	teaspoons shortening

Line an 8-in. square dish with heavy-duty foil; butter foil with 1 teaspoon butter; set aside. In a large heavy saucepan, combine the sugar, corn syrup, milk, salt and remaining butter; bring to a boil over medium heat. Cook and stir until a candy thermometer reads 244° (firm-ball stage).

Remove from the heat; stir in the walnuts, vanilla and food coloring if desired. Pour into prepared pan (do not scrape saucepan). Cool completely before cutting. Lift foil and candy out of pan; remove foil. Cut into 1-in. squares.

In a microwave, melt chocolate and shortening; stir until smooth. Dip caramels in chocolate; allow excess to drip off. Place on waxed paper; let stand until set. Store in an airtight container at room temperature.

Dutch Speculaas

(pictured at right)

PREP: 40 MIN. + CHILLING   **BAKE:** 10 MIN./BATCH
YIELD: ABOUT 2-1/2 DOZEN

These crispy Dutch spice cookies taste similar to windmill cookies. In Holland, it's tradition to mold the dough into the shape of St. Nicholas and serve the baked cookies on Sinterklaas (St. Nicholas Day).

Template on page 90
Waxed paper

1	cup butter, softened
1	cup packed dark brown sugar
2	eggs
1	tablespoon molasses
2	teaspoons grated orange peel
3-1/2	cups all-purpose flour
1/2	cup finely ground almonds
3	teaspoons ground cinnamon
1	teaspoon baking powder
1/2	teaspoon ground nutmeg
1/2	teaspoon ground cloves
1/4	teaspoon white pepper
1/4	teaspoon ground ginger
1/4	teaspoon ground cardamom

Milk and sliced *or* chopped almonds

Trace template onto waxed paper; cut out. In a large bowl, cream butter and brown sugar until light and fluffy. Beat in the eggs, molasses and orange peel. Combine the flour, ground almonds, cinnamon, baking powder, nutmeg, cloves, pepper, ginger and cardamom. Gradually add to creamed mixture and mix well. Cover and refrigerate for at least 4 hours or until easy to handle.

On a parchment paper-lined surface, roll a small amount of dough to 1/8-in. thickness. Trace around template or cut with floured 3-in. holiday-shaped cookie cutters, leaving 1 in. between cookies. Remove excess dough and reroll scraps if desired.

Slide a baking sheet under the parchment paper and dough. If using template, trace decorative details with a toothpick. Brush cookies with milk and decorate with sliced almonds or sprinkle with chopped almonds as desired. Repeat with remaining dough.

Bake at 350° for 8-10 minutes or until edges are lightly browned. Remove to wire racks to cool.

TO MAKE AHEAD: Dough can be made 2 days in advance. Let stand at room temperature for 30 minutes before rolling out. Cookies can be baked 1 week ahead of time and stored in an airtight container at room temperature or frozen for up to 1 month.

Apple-Cinnamon Gelatin

PREP: 30 MIN. + CHILLING   **YIELD:** 8 SERVINGS

This ruby-red gelatin is a festive addition to your holiday spread. Cinnamon red-hot candies add a surprising flavor that will tingle taste buds.

Suzy Horvath ★ Gladstone, Oregon

2	packages (3 ounces *each*) cranberry gelatin
1-1/2	cups water
3	tablespoons red-hot candies
1-1/2	cups cold water
2	medium tart apples, peeled and chopped
1	package (8 ounces) cream cheese, softened

Place gelatin in a large bowl. In a small saucepan, combine water and candies. Cook and stir until candies are dissolved and mixture comes to a boil. Stir into the gelatin. Stir in the cold water.

Set aside 1 cup gelatin mixture; let stand at room temperature. Refrigerate remaining gelatin until set but not firm. Fold in apples; pour into a 6-cup mold coated with cooking spray. Refrigerate for 30 minutes or until firm.

In a small bowl, beat cream cheese until smooth. Gradually beat in reserved gelatin; carefully spoon over apple layer. Cover and refrigerate for at least 6 hours. Unmold onto a serving platter.

TO MAKE AHEAD: Gelatin can be made a day in advance and unmolded a few hours before serving.

TEMPLATES

Stocking Utensil Holder
PG. 88

KEY
———	**Outline/cutting line**
– – –	**Stitching line**
———	**Trim line**

— Fold —

FIG. 1
Running Stitch

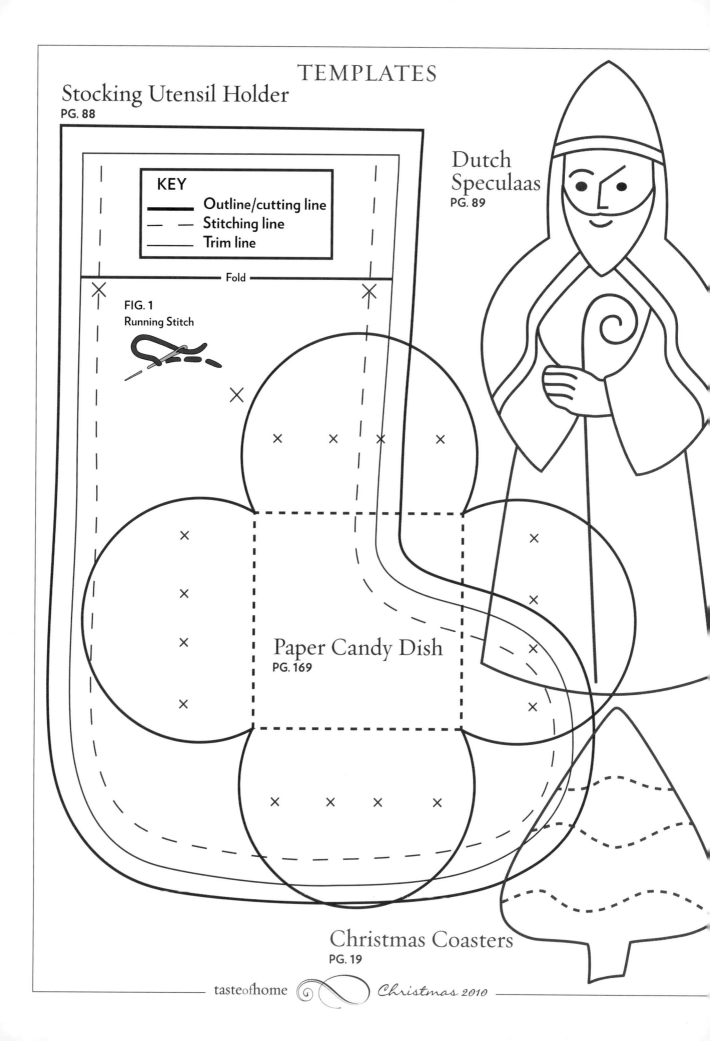

Dutch Speculaas
PG. 89

Paper Candy Dish
PG. 169

Christmas Coasters
PG. 19

tasteofhome *Christmas 2010*

Festive SIDES

Maple-Dijon Glazed Brussels Sprouts

PREP: 20 MIN.   **COOK:** 20 MIN.   **YIELD:** 6 SERVINGS

Ordinary brussels sprouts get jazzed up with a sweet, tangy sauce in this festive side. Even those who normally steer clear of sprouts will ask for seconds of these!

Holly Scarborough ★ Melbourne, Florida

  2   pounds fresh brussels sprouts, trimmed
  2   tablespoons butter
1/2   cup chicken broth
1/4   cup Dijon mustard
1/4   cup maple syrup
1/4   teaspoon pepper

Cut an "X" in the core of each brussels sprout. In a large skillet, saute brussels sprouts in butter for 4-5 minutes or until lightly browned.

Stir in the broth, mustard, syrup and pepper. Bring to a boil. Reduce heat; cover and simmer for 5 minutes. Uncover, cook and stir 8-10 minutes longer or until brussels sprouts are tender.

Creamy Corn Casserole

PREP: 15 MIN.   **BAKE:** 25 MIN.   **YIELD:** 8 SERVINGS

This comforting side dish makes a rich accompaniment to almost any main entree. Kids and adults alike will ask for this dish time and again.

Gail Bigford ★ Glendale, Arizona

  2   tablespoons butter
  2   tablespoons all-purpose flour
  1   cup whole milk
  1   cup heavy whipping cream
  5   cups frozen gold and white corn, thawed
1/2   cup grated Parmesan cheese, *divided*
1/4   cup grated Romano cheese
  2   ounces cream cheese, cubed
  5   teaspoons sugar
  1   teaspoon salt
1/4   teaspoon white pepper

In a large saucepan, melt butter. Stir in flour until smooth; gradually add milk and cream. Bring to a boil; cook and stir for 1 minute or until thickened.

Remove from the heat. Stir in the corn, 1/4 cup Parmesan, Romano, cream cheese, sugar, salt and pepper.

Transfer to an ungreased 1-1/2-qt. baking dish; sprinkle with remaining Parmesan.

Bake, uncovered, at 350° for 25-30 minutes or until cheese is melted and top is golden brown.

Cranberry-Orange Relish

PREP/TOTAL TIME: 25 MIN.   **YIELD:** 4 CUPS

Fresh rosemary adds an unique, but special flavor twist to this homemade cranberry relish. It would be great alongside most roasted meats or poultry.

Nancy Mueller ★ Bloomington, Minnesota

  1   package (12 ounces) fresh *or* frozen cranberries
3/4   cup sugar
  2   teaspoons grated orange peel
  3   medium oranges, peeled and sectioned
  2   tablespoons orange liqueur *or* orange juice
1/2   to 1 teaspoon minced fresh rosemary *or* 1/8 to 1/4 teaspoon dried rosemary, crushed

In a large saucepan, combine the cranberries, sugar and orange peel. Cook over medium heat until the berries pop, about 15 minutes.

Remove from the heat; stir in the oranges, liqueur and rosemary. Transfer to a small bowl. Cover and store in the refrigerator.

TO MAKE AHEAD: You can make this up to 1 week before serving. Store in an airtight container in the refrigerator.

Savory Mediterranean Orzo

PREP: 25 MIN. **BAKE:** 20 MIN.
YIELD: 12 SERVINGS (2/3 CUP EACH)

If you like to celebrate the season by sampling flavors from around the world, you'll love this Mediterranean side. The yellow summer squash, roasted red peppers and spinach yield specks of eye-popping color that make this dish festive.

Kristi Silk ★ Ferndale, Washington

4	cups reduced-sodium chicken broth
1	package (16 ounces) orzo pasta
1	medium onion, finely chopped
4	garlic cloves, minced
2	tablespoons olive oil
2	cups (8 ounces) crumbled feta cheese, *divided*
1	package (10 ounces) frozen chopped spinach, thawed and squeezed dry
1	jar (7-1/2 ounces) roasted sweet red peppers, drained and chopped
1	small yellow summer squash, finely chopped
1/2	teaspoon salt
1/2	teaspoon pepper

In a large saucepan, bring broth to a boil. Stir in orzo; cook over medium heat for 6-8 minutes. Remove from the heat.

In a small skillet, saute onion and garlic in oil until tender; add to orzo mixture. Stir in 1 cup cheese, spinach, red peppers, squash, salt and pepper.

Transfer to a greased 13-in. x 9-in. baking dish; sprinkle with remaining cheese. Bake at 350° for 20-25 minutes or until heated through.

Ribboned Serving Dish

Here's a simple and inexpensive way to dress up your holiday table. Choose a ribbon that coordinates with your dishes or your tablecloth. You can use this idea for any special occasion.

Place a band of double-sided transparent tape around a straight-sided serving dish.

Wrap ribbon around serving dish over tape and tie ribbon ends in a knot. Trim ends.

Rustic Autumn Soup

PREP: 30 MIN.   **COOK:** 25 MIN.   **YIELD:** 13 SERVINGS

This recipe is a great way to use the fall harvest. The rich, velvety soup makes a special first course, and the flavors of root vegetables shine with a subtle sweetness from apple.

Denice Hageli ★ Elmhurst, Illinois

  5   medium parsnips, chopped
  5   medium carrots, chopped
  2   medium onions, chopped
  1   medium sweet potato, peeled and chopped
  1   medium turnip, peeled and chopped
1/2   medium tart apple, peeled and chopped
  2   tablespoons chopped roasted sweet red pepper
  2   celery ribs, chopped
  3   cans (14-1/2 ounces *each*) reduced-sodium chicken broth
  2   bay leaves
  1   garlic clove, minced
  1   teaspoon dried tarragon
1/2   teaspoon salt
1/2   teaspoon pepper
  2   cups half-and-half cream
Optional Garnish: additional cooked finely chopped carrots, parsnips *and/or* apples, fresh chives

In a Dutch oven, combine the first 14 ingredients. Bring to a boil. Reduce heat; cover and simmer for 20-25 minutes or until tender. Discard bay leaves. Cool slightly.

In a blender, process soup in batches until smooth. Return all to the pan; add cream and heat through (do not boil). Garnish with additional cooked vegetables and/or apples and chives.

Onion-Stuffed Portobellos

PREP: 25 MIN.   **COOK:** 15 MIN.   **YIELD:** 4 SERVINGS

These stuffed mushrooms make a pretty visual with burgundy-colored onions and deep green spinach. To serve as appetizers, use small baby Portobello mushrooms and serve over shredded lettuce.

Marie Rizzio ★ Interlochen, Michigan

1	large onion, sliced
3	garlic cloves, minced
1	tablespoon minced fresh thyme *or* 1 teaspoon dried thyme
1/4	teaspoon salt, *divided*
1/4	teaspoon pepper, *divided*
1/4	cup olive oil, *divided*
1	cup port wine
2-1/2	cups coarsely chopped fresh spinach
4	medium portobello mushrooms
1/2	cup crumbled blue cheese

In a large skillet, cook the onion, garlic, thyme and 1/8 teaspoon salt and pepper in 2 tablespoons oil over medium heat for 15-20 minutes or until onion is golden brown, stirring occasionally. Stir in wine. Bring to a boil; cook until liquid is reduced by two-thirds, about 8-10 minutes. Add spinach; cook until wilted.

Remove and discard stems and gills from mushrooms. In a large skillet, cook mushrooms in remaining oil over medium heat for 2 minutes on each side. Sprinkle with remaining salt and pepper.

Fill mushrooms with onion mixture; cover and cook for 5-7 minutes or just until mushrooms are tender. Sprinkle with cheese; cover and cook 2 minutes longer or until cheese is melted.

Creamy Rosemary Potatoes

PREP: 15 MIN.   **BAKE:** 50 MIN.   **YIELD:** 9 SERVINGS

I love making potato dishes during the holidays. Everyone will fall in love with these tender, savory spuds that bake in a Parmesan sauce and are perfectly seasoned with rosemary and garlic.

Tamra Duncan ★ Castle, Oklahoma

2	pounds small red potatoes, quartered
4-1/2	teaspoons butter
4-1/2	teaspoons all-purpose flour
1-1/2	cups whole milk
1/2	cup grated Parmesan cheese
1	tablespoon minced fresh rosemary *or* 1 teaspoon dried rosemary, crushed
1	garlic clove, minced
1/4	teaspoon salt
1/4	teaspoon pepper

Place potatoes in a greased 13-in. x 9-in. baking dish. Bake, uncovered, at 400° for 40 minutes.

Meanwhile, in a small saucepan, melt butter. Stir in flour until smooth; gradually add milk. Bring to a boil; cook and stir for 2 minutes or until thickened. Stir in the cheese, rosemary, garlic, salt and pepper.

Pour over potatoes and stir to coat. Bake 8-12 minutes longer or until sauce is bubbly and potatoes are tender.

Cranberry-Orange Spinach Salad

PREP/TOTAL TIME: 25 MIN.   **YIELD:** 8 SERVINGS

Mandarin oranges, spinach and cranberries give this festive salad a wonderful burst of flavor. The homemade dressing is easy to stir together and gets a unique taste from nutmeg.

Preci D'Silva ★ Dubai, United Arab Emirates

2	cans (11 ounces *each*) mandarin oranges, undrained
2	tablespoons olive oil
4	teaspoons white wine vinegar
1/4	teaspoon salt
1/4	teaspoon ground nutmeg
Dash pepper	
1	package (6 ounces) fresh baby spinach
1/2	cup dried cranberries
1/2	cup coarsely chopped cashews

Drain oranges, reserving 2 tablespoons juice. In a small bowl, whisk the oil, vinegar, salt, nutmeg, pepper and reserved juice. In a serving bowl, combine the spinach, oranges and cranberries. Add dressing; toss to coat. Sprinkle with cashews.

Broccoli Romano Pasta

(pictured at left)

PREP/TOTAL TIME: 30 MIN.   **YIELD:** 10 SERVINGS

This comforting pasta dish is so easy to put together. Try Pecorino Romano cheese for a sharper, tangier flavor, or toss in some frozen peas to add extra nutrition.

Geri Distefano ★ Nepean, Ontario

- 1 package (16 ounces) bow tie pasta
- 6 cups fresh broccoli florets
- 4 green onions, thinly sliced
- 1/4 cup olive oil
- 1/2 cup water
- 1/2 teaspoon salt
- 1/4 teaspoon pepper
- 1/2 cup grated Romano cheese

Cook pasta according to package directions.

Meanwhile, in a Dutch oven, saute broccoli and green onions in oil for 3 minutes. Stir in the water, salt and pepper. Bring to a boil. Reduce heat; cover and simmer for 6-8 minutes or until broccoli is crisp-tender.

Drain the pasta and add to broccoli mixture; toss with the cheese.

Spicy Peppers & Corn

PREP: 15 MIN.   **BAKE:** 20 MIN.   **YIELD:** 6 SERVINGS

Try this crowd-pleasing corn casserole the next time you're looking for a side dish that's colorful, delicious and has a little zip. It's an easy combination everyone will love.

Jeaune Hadl Van Meter ★ Lexington, Kentucky

- 4 cups fresh *or* frozen yellow, white *or* shoepeg corn, thawed
- 2 medium sweet red peppers, chopped
- 1 can (10-3/4 ounces) condensed cream of celery soup, undiluted
- 1/2 cup evaporated milk
- 1 to 2 hot chili peppers, seeded and chopped
- 1 teaspoon garlic salt
- 1/2 teaspoon pepper
- 1/2 teaspoon ground mustard
- 1 cup dry bread crumbs
- 1/4 cup butter, melted

In a large bowl, combine the first eight ingredients. In a small bowl, combine the bread crumbs and butter.

Spoon half of the crumb mixture into an ungreased 2-qt. baking dish. Top with corn mixture and remaining crumb mixture. Bake, uncovered, at 375° for 20-25 minutes or until golden brown and bubbly.

Editor's Note: When cutting hot peppers, disposable gloves are recommended. Avoid touching your face.

Christmas Cauliflower Casserole

PREP: 20 MIN.   **BAKE:** 20 MIN.
YIELD: 12 SERVINGS (3/4 CUP EACH)

Tender cauliflower fills this creamy bake that's topped with a sprinkling of stuffing mixture. The classic-style casserole will appeal to kids and adults.

Carol Rex ★ Ocala, Florida

- 3 packages (16 ounces *each*) frozen cauliflower
- 1/4 cup butter, cubed
- 1 cup stuffing mix
- 3/4 cup chopped walnuts
- 2 cups (16 ounces) sour cream
- 2 cups (8 ounces) shredded cheddar cheese
- 3 teaspoons chicken bouillon granules
- 1-1/2 teaspoons ground mustard

Boil cauliflower according to package directions.

In a large skillet, melt butter; add stuffing mix and walnuts. Cook for 2-3 minutes or until butter is absorbed.

Drain cauliflower; place in a large bowl. Stir in the sour cream, cheese, bouillon and mustard until blended. Transfer to a greased 13-in. x 9-in. baking dish; sprinkle with stuffing mixture.

Bake, uncovered, at 375° for 18-22 minutes or until heated through.

Cook pasta according to package directions.

Meanwhile, in a Dutch oven, saute carrot and anchovy fillets in oil until carrot is tender. Stir in the olives, sun-dried tomatoes, garlic, capers, oregano, thyme, fennel and pepper flakes; cook 1 minute longer. Stir in the diced tomatoes, tomato paste and sugar. Bring to a boil. Reduce heat; simmer, uncovered, for 10-15 minutes or until thickened.

Drain pasta. Add pasta and basil to sauce mixture; toss to coat. Sprinkle with cheese.

Crumb-Topped Carrot Casserole

PREP: 40 MIN. + COOLING   **BAKE:** 30 MIN.
YIELD: 6 SERVINGS

I'm the one that brings the vegetables to my relatives' holiday parties. This one was handed down from my mother and is a family classic.

Lana Buelow ★ Reedsburg, Wisconsin

- 2 pounds carrots, cut into 1/4-inch slices
- 1/2 cup water
- 1/2 teaspoon salt
- 1/4 cup butter, cubed
- 3/4 cup graham cracker crumbs
- Dash ground ginger
- 2 eggs, *separated*

TOPPING:
- 3 tablespoons crushed saltines (about 5 crackers)
- 2 tablespoons brown sugar
- 1 tablespoon butter, melted

Place the carrots, water and salt in a skillet; bring to a boil. Reduce heat; cover and simmer for 25-30 minutes or until tender. Do not drain. Mash carrots. Stir in butter until melted. Add graham cracker crumbs and ginger. Lightly beat the egg yolks; add to carrot mixture. Transfer to a large bowl.

In a small bowl, beat egg whites until stiff peaks form. Gently fold into carrot mixture. Transfer to a greased 1-1/2-qt. baking dish. Combine the topping ingredients; sprinkle over top. Bake, uncovered, at 375° for 30-35 minutes or until a knife inserted near the center comes out clean.

Pasta Puttanesca

PREP: 25 MIN.   **COOK:** 15 MIN.   **YIELD:** 8 SERVINGS

This pasta is great for a big gathering. It works well as a starter dish or as a main dish for a smaller group. One peeled, diced carrot may be used in place of the sugar for a milder, sweeter and healthier substitute.

Kathryn White ★ Pinehurst, North Carolina

- 1 package (16 ounces) penne pasta
- 1 medium carrot, finely chopped
- 3 anchovy fillets
- 1 tablespoon olive oil
- 1/4 cup pitted Greek olives, chopped
- 1/4 cup oil-packed sun-dried tomatoes, drained
- 5 garlic cloves, minced
- 2 tablespoons capers, drained
- 2 teaspoons dried oregano
- 2 teaspoons dried thyme
- 2 teaspoons fennel seed, crushed
- 1 to 1-1/2 teaspoons crushed red pepper flakes
- 1 can (28 ounces) diced tomatoes, undrained
- 1 tablespoon tomato paste
- 1/2 teaspoon sugar
- 6 fresh basil leaves, thinly sliced
- 3 tablespoons grated Parmesan cheese

Mushroom-Swiss Mac & Cheese

PREP: 40 MIN.   **BAKE:** 25 MIN.   **YIELD:** 8 SERVINGS

Portobello mushrooms and three kinds of cheese give an upscale spin to a classic casserole. To make this more of an entree, I add 2 cups of cubed cooked chicken.

Dawn Moore ★ Warren, Pennsylvania

- 1   package (16 ounces) mini penne pasta
- 1/2   pound baby portobello mushrooms, chopped
- 1   small onion, finely chopped
- 2   tablespoons butter
- 1   tablespoon olive oil
- 1   garlic clove, minced

SAUCE:

- 5   tablespoons butter
- 1   package (8 ounces) cream cheese, cubed
- 1-1/4   cups whole milk
- 1-1/4   cups half-and-half cream
- 2-1/2   cups (10 ounces) shredded Swiss cheese
- 1-1/4   cups grated Parmesan and Romano cheese blend
- 1/4   teaspoon salt
- 1/4   teaspoon pepper
- 6   bacon strips, cooked and crumbled

TOPPING:

- 1/3   cup panko (Japanese) bread crumbs
- 2   tablespoons minced fresh parsley
- 2   tablespoons butter, melted

Cook pasta according to package directions. Meanwhile, in a large skillet, saute mushrooms and onion in butter and oil until tender. Add garlic; cook 1 minute longer. Set aside.

For sauce, in a large saucepan, melt butter. Stir in cream cheese until smooth. Gradually add milk and cream; heat through. Stir in the cheeses, salt and pepper until blended. Stir in bacon.

Drain pasta; toss with mushroom mixture and sauce. Transfer to a greased 13-in. x 9-in. baking dish. Combine the bread crumbs, parsley and melted butter; sprinkle over mixture. Bake, uncovered, at 375° for 25-30 minutes or until golden brown.

Garlic Roasted Winter Vegetables

(pictured at left)

PREP: 20 MIN.   **BAKE:** 45 MIN.   **YIELD:** 6 SERVINGS

You'll notice a subtle herb flavor with these colorful vegetables. Roasted to perfection, they are guaranteed to become a holiday favorite.

Donna Lamano ★ Olathe, Kansas

- 2   medium carrots
- 1   medium turnip
- 1   medium parsnip
- 1   cup cubed red potatoes
- 1   cup cubed peeled butternut squash
- 3   whole garlic bulbs, cloves separated and peeled
- 3   shallots, quartered
- 4-1/2   teaspoons olive oil
- 1/4   teaspoon salt
- 1/4   teaspoon dried thyme
- 1/4   teaspoon pepper

Peel the carrots, turnip and parsnip; cut into 1-in. pieces. Place in a large bowl; add the potatoes, squash, garlic, shallots, oil, salt, thyme and pepper. Toss to coat. Transfer to a greased 15-in. x 10-in. x 1-in. baking pan.

Bake, uncovered, at 400° for 45-50 minutes or until tender, stirring once.

Apple Sweet Potato Bake

PREP: 10 MIN.   **BAKE:** 30 MIN.   **YIELD:** 6 SERVINGS

This easy-to-make side bakes up bubbly and golden brown. It comes together in a flash with canned sweet potatoes and apple pie filling, making it the perfect comfort food to serve during the busy Yuletide season.

Cheryl Priano ★ Pittsburgh, Pennsylvania

- 1   can (29 ounces) sweet potatoes, drained
- 1   can (21 ounces) apple pie filling
- 2   tablespoons butter, melted
- 1/2   teaspoon ground cinnamon

TOPPING:
- 1/3   cup packed brown sugar
- 1/3   cup chopped pecans
- 3   tablespoons all-purpose flour
- 2   tablespoons butter, melted

Cut sweet potatoes into thin slices. In a large bowl, combine the sweet potatoes, pie filling, butter and cinnamon. Transfer to a greased 1-1/2-qt. baking dish.

In a small bowl, combine the topping ingredients; sprinkle over top. Bake, uncovered, at 350° for 30-35 minutes or until bubbly.

Orange-Scented Leeks & Mushrooms

PREP: 20 MIN.   **COOK:** 40 MIN.   **YIELD:** 7 SERVINGS

This simple side is great for any festive occasion. The sherry and orange juice add a unique taste twist that makes this dish special.

Carole Bess White ★ Portland, Oregon

- 4   pounds medium leeks (white and light green portions only), thinly sliced (about 8 cups)
- 1   pound sliced fresh mushrooms
- 2   tablespoons olive oil
- 1/4   cup sherry *or* reduced-sodium chicken broth
- 1/2   cup reduced-sodium chicken broth
- 1   tablespoon balsamic vinegar
- 1   teaspoon orange juice
- 1/2   teaspoon grated orange peel
- 1/4   teaspoon salt
- 1/4   teaspoon minced fresh thyme *or* dash dried thyme
- 1/8   teaspoon pepper

In a Dutch oven, cook leeks and mushrooms in oil in batches over medium heat for 15-20 minutes or until tender, stirring occasionally. Return all to the pan. Add sherry, stirring to loosen browned bits from pan.

Stir in the remaining ingredients; cook and stir for 10-15 minutes or until liquid is almost evaporated.

In a small bowl, beat cream until stiff peaks form. Fold cream and walnuts into gelatin mixture. Transfer to an 8-cup ring mold coated with cooking spray; refrigerate for 2 hours or until firm.

Mash and strain raspberries, reserving juice. Discard seeds. Transfer to a small saucepan; stir in jelly. Bring to a boil. Combine cornstarch and water until smooth. Gradually stir into the pan. Bring to a boil; cook and stir for 1 minute or until thickened. Cool to room temperature. Serve with gelatin.

Editor's Note: This recipe was tested with commercially prepared eggnog.

Spinach Amandine Stuffing

PREP: 25 MIN.   **BAKE:** 35 MIN.   **YIELD:** 14 SERVINGS

I received this recipe from a good friend. I think it bakes up perfectly...not too dry or too soggy. It makes a lot, so I often bring it to potlucks where it is always a welcome addition to the food table.

Caryn Hasbrouck ★ South Portland, Maine

2/3 cup sliced almonds
1/2 cup butter, *divided*
1/2 cup chopped onion
1/2 cup chopped celery
1 cup sliced fresh mushrooms
1 package (10 ounces) frozen chopped spinach, thawed and squeezed dry
1 package (14 ounces) crushed seasoned stuffing
1 can (14-1/2 ounces) chicken broth

In a large skillet, saute almonds in 1 tablespoon butter until golden brown; remove from the pan and set aside. In the same skillet, saute onion and celery in remaining butter for 2 minutes. Add mushrooms; saute for 1 minute. Add spinach and heat through.

In a large bowl, combine stuffing with vegetables. Add half the almonds. Gradually add broth, tossing well. Transfer to a greased 3-qt. baking dish; sprinkle with remaining almonds. Cover and bake at 350° for 30 minutes. Uncover; bake 5 minutes longer.

Turkey Spinach Amandine Stuffing: Add 2 to 3 cups cubed cooked turkey or chicken to the stuffing mixture. Bake as directed.

Eggnog Bavarian

PREP: 35 MIN. + CHILLING
YIELD: 12 SERVINGS (1 CUP SAUCE)

This gelatin tastes scrumptious with the classic flavor of eggnog. The pretty bright red color of the raspberry sauce makes this treat a festive addition to any special meal.

Shirley Goering ★ New Ulm, Minnesota

3 envelopes unflavored gelatin
4 cups eggnog, *divided*
1/2 cup 2% milk
1 tablespoon rum extract
1/8 teaspoon salt
2 cups heavy whipping cream
1 cup finely chopped walnuts
RASPBERRY-CURRANT SAUCE:
1 package (10 ounces) frozen sweetened raspberries, thawed
1/2 cup red currant jelly
1 tablespoon cornstarch
2 tablespoons cold water

In a small saucepan, sprinkle gelatin over 1 cup eggnog and milk; let stand for 1 minute. Heat over low heat, stirring until gelatin is completely dissolved. Transfer to a large bowl; stir in the extract, salt and remaining eggnog. Let stand for 10 minutes.

Spiced Cranberry-Chutney Gelatin Salad

PREP: 25 MIN. **COOK:** 30 MIN. + CHILLING
YIELD: 12 SERVINGS

I combined my mother-in-law's famous cranberry chutney with my raspberry gelatin recipe to come up with this nicely spiced salad.

Barbara Estabrook ★ Rhinelander, Wisconsin

1 cup sugar
1 cup water
2 cups fresh *or* frozen cranberries
1/2 cup golden raisins
1/4 cup red wine vinegar
1 tablespoon molasses
1-1/2 teaspoons Worcestershire sauce
1 teaspoon ground ginger
1/2 teaspoon curry powder
1/4 teaspoon salt
1/4 teaspoon ground nutmeg
1/4 cup chopped salted roasted almonds

GELATIN:
1 package (6 ounces) raspberry gelatin
1-1/2 cups boiling water
1/2 cup cold water
12 red lettuce leaves
3/4 cup sour cream
1/4 cup chopped salted roasted almonds

In a large saucepan, combine sugar and water. Bring to a boil over medium heat. Reduce heat; simmer, uncovered, for 5 minutes. Stir in cranberries; cook over medium heat until the berries pop, about 15 minutes.

Stir in the raisins, vinegar, molasses, Worcestershire sauce, ginger, curry, salt and nutmeg. Reduce heat; simmer, uncovered, for 15 minutes, stirring occasionally. Transfer to a large bowl; cool to room temperature. Stir in almonds.

Meanwhile, for gelatin, in a large bowl, dissolve gelatin in boiling water. Stir in cold water. Add cranberry mixture. Transfer to an 11-in. x 7-in. dish coated with cooking spray. Cover and refrigerate for at least 4 hours or until set.

Serve on lettuce leaves. Top with sour cream and nuts.

TO MAKE AHEAD: Prepare the recipe the day before; cover and refrigerate overnight.

Alfredo Rice Casserole

(pictured at left)

PREP/TOTAL TIME: 30 MIN.   **YIELD:** 5 SERVINGS

Rice lovers won't be able to get enough of this creamy, comforting casserole. Substitute a mushroom Alfredo or three-cheese sauce for equally delicious results.

Aysha Schurman ★ Ammon, Idaho

1-1/3 cups refrigerated Alfredo sauce
1 cup cooked brown rice
1 cup cooked wild rice
1 cup marinated quartered artichoke hearts, chopped
8 bacon strips, cooked and crumbled
2 green onions, thinly sliced
1/4 cup grated Parmesan cheese
1/4 cup chopped sun-dried tomatoes (not packed in oil)
1/4 cup chicken broth
1 garlic clove, minced
1/2 teaspoon pepper

In a large bowl, combine all the ingredients. Transfer to a greased 8-in. square baking dish. Bake, uncovered, at 350° for 20-25 minutes or until bubbly.

TO MAKE AHEAD: Cook rice and bacon ahead of time and refrigerate for up to 3 days.

Mushroom Bread Dressing

PREP: 25 MIN.   **BAKE:** 40 MIN.   **YIELD:** 7 SERVINGS

This is a mushroom lover's delight! It's become a tradition in our house to enjoy this rich, flavorful stuffing as part of our Christmas dinner.

Lynn Owen ★ Rochester, Washington

4 to 5 small onions, chopped
1-1/2 pounds fresh mushrooms, chopped
1/2 cup butter, cubed
1-1/2 teaspoons rubbed sage
1/2 teaspoon dried thyme
6 cups cubed day-old whole wheat bread
1 envelope onion soup mix
1/2 cup boiling water

In a large skillet, saute onions and mushrooms in butter until tender. Sprinkle with sage and thyme. Transfer to a large bowl; stir in bread cubes.

In a bowl, combine soup mix and water. Gradually stir into bread mixture. Transfer to a greased 2-qt. baking dish. Cover and bake at 350° for 40-45 minutes or until bubbly.

TO MAKE AHEAD: Saute onions and mushrooms ahead of time. Transfer to a small bowl; sprinkle with herbs and refrigerate. When ready to bake, reheat mixture in the microwave to room temperature and proceed with recipe.

Winter Squash Casserole

PREP: 20 MIN.   **BAKE:** 25 MIN.   **YIELD:** 5 SERVINGS

I can't imagine celebrating the holidays without including this comforting casserole on my menu. You can use any sweet variety of winter squash, but delicata is my personal favorite.

Gloria Jarrett ★ Loveland, Ohio

1 small onion, chopped
1 teaspoon canola oil
3 cups mashed cooked delicata *or* butternut squash
12 bacon strips, cooked and crumbled
1 cup (4 ounces) shredded cheddar cheese
1 teaspoon sugar
1/4 teaspoon salt
1/4 teaspoon pepper
1/2 cup soft bread crumbs
1 tablespoon butter, melted

In a large skillet, saute onion in oil until tender. Remove from the heat. Stir in the squash, bacon, cheese, sugar, salt and pepper. Transfer to a greased 8-in. square baking dish. Combine bread crumbs and butter; sprinkle over top.

Bake, uncovered, at 350° for 20-25 minutes or until heated through and top is lightly browned.

TO MAKE AHEAD: Cook, mash and measure the squash the day before. Cover and refrigerate overnight. Remove from the refrigerator 30 minutes before using and proceed with recipe.

Apple Rice Salad

PREP: 20 MIN. + CHILLING   **YIELD:** 8 SERVINGS

With the classic combination of apples, celery and walnuts, this side tastes like a jazzed up version of Waldorf salad.

Linda Bankauskas ★ Ann Arbor, Michigan

3 cups cooked wild rice
2 cups chopped apples
1 cup chopped walnuts
2 celery ribs, chopped
1/2 cup dried cranberries
1/4 cup unsweetened apple juice
3/4 cup (6 ounces) plain yogurt
3/4 cup mayonnaise
4 teaspoons honey
1/2 teaspoon salt
1/4 teaspoon ground cinnamon

In a bowl, combine the first six ingredients. In a bowl, combine the remaining ingredients. Add to rice mixture and toss to coat. Chill for at least 1 hour before serving.

TO MAKE AHEAD: Cook rice ahead of time and refrigerate for up to 3 days.

Sweet Potatoes with Pecan-Cinnamon Crunch

PREP: 25 MIN.   **BAKE:** 55 MIN.   **YIELD:** 12 SERVINGS

This recipe features tender chunks of sweet potatoes coated with a brown sugar mix and a golden-brown streusel topping. Folks won't be able to get enough of this mouthwatering bake.

Mary Meek ★ Toledo, Ohio

1/2	cup packed brown sugar
2	tablespoons orange juice
2	teaspoons vanilla extract
1/2	teaspoon salt
1/2	teaspoon ground ginger
1/2	teaspoon ground cinnamon
3	pounds medium sweet potatoes, peeled and cut into 1-inch cubes
1	cup dried cranberries
2	tablespoons butter

CRUNCH:

1/2	cup all-purpose flour
1/4	cup packed brown sugar
1	teaspoon ground cinnamon
1/2	teaspoon ground ginger
1/4	cup cold butter
1	cup chopped pecans

In a large bowl, combine the first six ingredients. Add sweet potatoes and cranberries; toss to coat. Transfer to a greased 13-in. x 9-in. baking dish. Dot with butter.

Cover and bake at 400° for 30 minutes; stir. In a small bowl, combine the flour, brown sugar, cinnamon and ginger; cut in butter until mixture resembles coarse crumbs. Stir in pecans.

Sprinkle over sweet potato mixture. Bake, uncovered, for 25-30 minutes or until bubbly and the sweet potatoes are tender.

Yuletide
BREADS

Maple Wheat Bread

PREP: 30 MIN. + RISING **BAKE:** 20 MIN. + COOLING
YIELD: 3 LOAVES (12 SLICES EACH)

This tender loaf is great with honey or maple butter or when used for sandwiches. Since this recipe freezes well, it is a must for my Christmas baking. I can make it up to six weeks before I plan to serve it, which allows me to focus on other last-minute preparations.

Sharlene Heatwole ★ McDowell, Virginia

  2 tablespoons active dry yeast
  2 cups warm water (110° to 115°)
  1 egg
1/2 cup canola oil
1/2 cup maple syrup
  2 teaspoons salt
  3 cups whole wheat flour
2-1/2 to 3 cups all-purpose flour
  2 tablespoons butter, melted

In a large bowl, dissolve yeast in warm water. Add the egg, oil, syrup, salt, whole wheat flour and 1 cup all-purpose flour. Beat on medium speed until smooth. Stir in enough remaining all-purpose flour to form a soft dough (dough will be sticky).

Turn onto a floured surface; knead until smooth and elastic, about 6-8 minutes. Place in a greased bowl, turning once to grease the top. Cover and let rise in a warm place until doubled, about 1 hour.

Punch dough down. Shape into loaves. Place in three greased 8-in. x 4-in. loaf pans. Cover and let rise until nearly doubled, about 40 minutes. Bake at 350° for 18-22 minutes or until golden brown. Remove from pans to wire racks to cool. Brush with melted butter.

Herb Butter Cut-Outs

PREP: 25 MIN. + CHILLING **YIELD:** ABOUT 1 DOZEN

Add this flavorful herb butter to your holiday spread for an adorably festive look. It's easy to make using your favorite holiday cookie cutters, and the unique shapes are sure to spark conversation. You can even mix designs.

1/2 cup butter, softened
  2 teaspoons minced fresh chives
  2 teaspoons minced fresh parsley
  2 teaspoons minced fresh basil
1/8 teaspoon paprika
1/8 teaspoon salt
Dash pepper

In a small bowl, combine all ingredients. Spread butter to 1/4-in. thickness on a waxed paper-lined baking sheet; refrigerate until firm.

Cut out butter using a 1-in. cookie cutter; gently transfer to another waxed paper-lined baking sheet. Refrigerate until firm. Store in an airtight container in the refrigerator or freezer.

Butter Bliss

Who says a little pat of butter has to be square? You'll see just how versatile your favorite Christmas cookie cutters are when you use them to create holiday-themed butter pats.

1. Spread the flavored butter to about 1/4-in. thickness on a waxed paper-lined baking sheet and refrigerate until it is firm. Cut out butter using 1-in. cookie cutters in various festive shapes, such as trees, bells, candy canes, etc.

2. Transfer the cut-outs to another waxed paper-lined baking sheet and refrigerate them till firm. Serve the butter at room temperature for easy spreading.

Jeweled Fruitcake

PREP: 30 MIN.   **BAKE:** 60 MINUTES
YIELD: 4 MINI LOAVES (6 SLICES EACH)

I promise this jeweled fruitcake is simply fantastic. Even my friends and family members who don't normally care for fruitcake say they love it!

Sharon Hoffman ★ Donna, Texas

2	packages (8 ounces *each*) pitted dates, chopped
1/2	pound pecan halves
1/2	pound Brazil nuts
1	jar (10 ounces) red maraschino cherries, well drained
1	jar (10 ounces) green maraschino cherries, well drained
1/2	cup flaked coconut
1-1/2	cups all-purpose flour
1-1/2	cups sugar
1	teaspoon baking powder
1	teaspoon salt
3	eggs
2	teaspoons vanilla extract

Line four greased and floured 5-3/4-in. x 3-in. x 2-in. loaf pans with waxed paper and grease the paper; set aside.

In a large bowl, combine the dates, nuts, cherries and coconut. Combine the flour, sugar, baking powder and salt; stir into fruit mixture until well coated.

In a small bowl, beat eggs and vanilla until foamy. Fold into fruit mixture and mix well. Pour into prepared pans.

Bake at 300° for 60-70 minutes or until a toothpick inserted near the center comes out clean. Cool for 10 minutes before removing from pans to wire racks to cool completely. Wrap tightly and store in a cool dry place. Cut with a serrated knife.

Editor's Note: Fruitcake may be baked in two greased and floured 8-in. x 4-in. loaf pans lined with waxed paper at 300° for 70-80 minutes or until a toothpick inserted near the center comes out clean.

Roasted Red Pepper Bread

PREP: 45 MIN. + RISING   **BAKE:** 20 MIN. + COOLING
YIELD: 2 LOAVES (12 SLICES EACH)

This savory bread is moist and loaded with flavor from grated Parmesan cheese and roasted sweet red peppers.

Cheryl Perry ★ Hertford, North Carolina

1-1/2	cups roasted sweet red peppers, drained
1	package (1/4 ounce) active dry yeast
2	tablespoons warm water (110° to 115°)
1-1/4	cups grated Parmesan cheese, *divided*
1/3	cup warm 2% milk (110° to 115°)
2	tablespoons butter, softened
1-1/4	teaspoons salt
3-1/4	to 3-3/4 cups all-purpose flour
1	egg
1	tablespoon water
1-1/2	teaspoons coarsely ground pepper

Place red peppers in a food processor; cover and process until pureed. In a large bowl, dissolve yeast in warm water. Add the red peppers, 1 cup cheese, milk, butter, salt and 1-1/2 cups flour. Beat until smooth. Stir in enough remaining flour to form a firm dough.

Turn onto a floured surface; knead until smooth and elastic, about 6-8 minutes. Place in a greased bowl, turning once to grease the top. Cover and let rise in a warm place until doubled, about 1 hour.

Punch dough down. Turn onto a lightly floured surface; divide dough into six pieces. Shape each into an 18-in. rope. Place three ropes on a greased baking sheet and braid; pinch ends to seal and tuck under. Repeat with remaining dough. Cover and let rise until doubled, about 1 hour.

In a small bowl, combine egg and water; brush over braids. Sprinkle with pepper and remaining cheese. Bake at 350° for 18-22 minutes or until golden brown.

Almond-Cheese Coffee Cake

PREP: 45 MIN. + CHILLING **BAKE:** 20 MIN. + COOLING
YIELD: 1 LOAF (12 SLICES)

Holiday guests will love the texture of this coffee cake featuring a Mascarpone cheese layer. With a sweet glaze and crunchy almonds on top, it's hard to eat only one piece.

Kristi Overton ★ Meridian, Idaho

1	package (1/4 ounce) active dry yeast
1/4	cup warm water (110° to 115°)
2-1/2	cups all-purpose flour
2	tablespoons sugar
1/2	teaspoon salt
6	tablespoons cold butter
1/2	cup warm 2% milk (110° to 115°)
2	egg yolks, beaten

FILLING:

1	carton (8 ounces) Mascarpone cheese
1/4	cup sugar
3	tablespoons all-purpose flour
1	egg yolk
1	teaspoon grated lemon peel
1	teaspoon almond extract

GLAZE:

1/2	cup confectioners' sugar
1	tablespoon 2% milk
1/2	teaspoon vanilla extract
1/2	cup sliced almonds, toasted

In a small bowl, dissolve yeast in warm water. In a large bowl, combine 2 cups flour, sugar and salt. Cut in butter until crumbly. Stir in the yeast mixture, milk and egg yolks. Add enough remaining flour until mixture forms a soft dough. Cover and refrigerate overnight.

In a small bowl, combine the filling ingredients; set aside. Punch dough down. On a floured surface, roll into a 13-in. x 10-in. rectangle. Transfer to an ungreased baking sheet. Spread filling over dough to within 1 in. of edges.

Starting with a long side, roll just to the center of the rectangle; repeat with remaining side, meeting in the middle. With scissors, cut from outside edges to two-thirds of the way toward center at 1-1/2-in. intervals. Separate strips slightly; twist to allow filling to show. Cover and let rise in a warm place until doubled, about 1 hour.

Bake at 350° for 20-25 minutes or until golden brown. Remove from pan to a wire rack to cool. For glaze, combine the confectioners' sugar, milk and vanilla; drizzle over coffee cake. Sprinkle with almonds.

Reheating Coffee Cakes

A fresh-from-the-oven coffee cake is a real delight. But it's not always possible to make it first thing in the morning. To recapture that comforting flavor, you can warm individual pieces in the microwave at 50% power, checking at 20- to 30-second intervals to see if it is warm. Let it stand before indulging, as the icing may be very hot. To reheat in the oven or toaster oven, wrap an unfrosted coffee cake in foil. Reheat at 350° for a few minutes or until warm to the touch.

Orange-Cheesecake Breakfast Rolls

PREP: 50 MIN. + RISING **BAKE:** 25 MIN. **YIELD:** 2 DOZEN

These yummy rolls are a nice change of pace from the typical brown-sugar and cinnamon kind. They make a great treat for breakfast or brunch.

Hannah Cobb ★ Owings Mills, Maryland

- 2 packages (1/4 ounce *each*) active dry yeast
- 3/4 cup warm water (110° to 115°)
- 1-3/4 cups warm 2% milk (110° to 115°)
- 1 cup sugar
- 2 eggs
- 3 tablespoons butter, melted
- 1-1/2 teaspoons salt
- 7 to 8 cups all-purpose flour

FILLING:
- 1 package (8 ounces) cream cheese, softened
- 1/2 cup sugar
- 1 tablespoon orange juice concentrate
- 1/2 teaspoon vanilla extract

GLAZE:
- 2 cups confectioners' sugar
- 3 tablespoons orange juice
- 1 teaspoon grated orange peel

In a large bowl, dissolve yeast in warm water. Add the milk, sugar, eggs, butter, salt and 5 cups flour. Beat until smooth. Stir in enough remaining flour to form a firm dough.

Turn onto a floured surface; knead until smooth and elastic, about 6-8 minutes. Place in a greased bowl, turning once to grease the top. Cover and let rise in a warm place until doubled, about 1 hour.

In a small bowl, beat the cream cheese, sugar, orange juice concentrate and vanilla until smooth. Punch dough down. Turn onto a lightly floured surface; divide in half. Roll one portion into an 18-in. x 7-in. rectangle. Spread half of the filling to within 1/2 in. of edges.

Roll up jelly-roll style, starting with a long side; pinch seam to seal. Cut into 12 slices; place cut side down in a greased 13-in. x 9-in. baking pan. Repeat with remaining dough and filling. Cover and let rise until doubled, about 30 minutes.

Bake at 350° for 25-30 minutes or until golden brown. Combine the confectioners' sugar, orange juice and peel; drizzle over warm rolls. Refrigerate leftovers.

TO MAKE AHEAD: Prepare, shape and place rolls in baking pans as directed. Cover and refrigerate overnight. Remove rolls from the refrigerator and let stand for 30 minutes. Bake and glaze as directed.

Lemon Bread

PREP: 25 MIN. **BAKE:** 55 MIN. + COOLING
YIELD: 2 LOAVES (12 SLICES EACH)

I love to make this lemon bread around the holidays to give as gifts. The pecans lend a nice crunch, and the glaze adds a wonderfully sweet flavor with a burst of lemon.

Janice Hurd ★ Church Hill, Tennessee

- 1 cup butter, softened
- 2 cups sugar
- 4 eggs
- 3 cups all-purpose flour
- 2 teaspoons baking powder
- 1/2 teaspoon salt
- 1 cup 2% milk
- 1 cup finely chopped pecans
- 4 teaspoons grated lemon peel

GLAZE:
- 1/2 cup sugar
- 1/3 cup lemon juice

In a large bowl, cream butter and sugar. Add eggs, one at a time, beating well after each addition. Combine the flour, baking powder and salt; add to creamed mixture alternately with milk. Fold in pecans and lemon peel.

Spoon into two greased 9-in. x 5-in. loaf pans. Bake at 350° for 55-60 minutes or until a toothpick inserted near the center comes out clean.

For glaze, combine sugar and lemon juice. Immediately spoon over bread. Cool for 10 minutes before removing from pans to a wire rack to cool completely.

Poppy Seed Cheese Bread

PREP: 20 MIN.   **BAKE:** 45 MIN. + COOLING
YIELD: 1 LOAF (16 SLICES)

*The recipe for this moist and delicious bread won me a blue
ribbon at the Los Angeles County Fair. I make several batches
at once and freeze them for later use or to give as gifts.*

Marina Castle ★ North Hollywood, California

- 1/2 cup shortening
- 1/2 cup sugar
- 3 eggs
- 2 cups all-purpose flour
- 2-1/2 teaspoons baking powder
- 1 teaspoon ground mustard
- 3/4 teaspoon salt
- 1 cup 2% milk
- 1-1/4 cups shredded cheddar-Monterey Jack cheese
- 1/2 cup chopped sweet onion
- 1 tablespoon poppy seeds
- 1/8 teaspoon paprika

In a large bowl, cream shortening and sugar until light
and fluffy. Add eggs, one at a time, beating well after each
addition. Combine the flour, baking powder, mustard and
salt; add to creamed mixture alternately with milk. Fold in
the cheese, onion and poppy seeds.

Transfer to a greased 9-in. x 5-in. loaf pan; sprinkle with
paprika. Bake at 375° for 45-55 minutes or until a toothpick
inserted near the center comes out clean. Cool for 10
minutes before removing from pan to a wire rack.

Ribbon Revelry

If you're enchanted with colorful Christmas ribbons or just have a stash you'd like to use up, you'll love this quick and easy holiday tree. Whether featured as a table centerpiece or set out to adorn a mantel or windowsill, these merry trees add timeless Yuletide cheer to any room. They also make lovely handmade gifts that can be assembled in no time.

Begin by glueing a 3-3/4-inch felt circle to the bottom of a 4-inch x 9-inch tall foam cone. Trim coordinating lengths of ribbon into 2- to 5-inch strips. Starting at the bottom of the cone, pin the raw edges of one style of ribbon (starting with the longer 5-inch strips), about 2 inches from the bottom. Repeat with remaining pieces of the same ribbon, overlapping the ribbon as needed to make a complete circle of ribbon around the cone. Repeat this step with the remaining strips of ribbon (using the smaller lengths as you near the top) until you have covered the entire cone. Use double-sided tape to make a loop with a 4-inch length of ribbon, and glue the loop to the top of the ribbon tree.

Let your creativity loose by creating trees in different sizes and in a variety of colors. If you're hosting a crafty Christmas get-together with friends, volunteer to provide the cones and basic supplies and ask each guest to bring a selection of holiday-themed ribbons in a variety of colors and patterns. You'll have fun swapping ribbons to create some truly unique trees!

Apple Cinnamon Rolls

PREP: 25 MIN. **BAKE:** 45 MIN. **YIELD:** 12 SERVINGS

Besides the great flavor, the appeal of these sweet rolls is that they don't need any yeast. They are ready to bake with less than 30 minutes of prep. Serve them as a special treat for breakfast or brunch. I've even used them for dessert.

Pam Hunt ★ Moore, Oklahoma

- 1-1/2 cups sugar
- 3/4 cup water
- 3/4 cup unsweetened apple juice
- 1/4 cup butter, cubed
- 1/4 teaspoon ground cinnamon
- 1/4 teaspoon ground nutmeg
- 2 cups all-purpose flour
- 2 teaspoons baking powder
- 1/2 teaspoon salt
- 3/4 cup butter-flavored shortening
- 2/3 cup buttermilk

FILLING:
- 3 cups shredded peeled tart apples
- 1/4 cup sugar
- 1/2 teaspoon ground cinnamon

In a large saucepan, combine the sugar, water, apple juice, butter, cinnamon and nutmeg. Bring to a boil; cook and stir for 4-6 minutes or until liquid is reduced to about 2 cups. Set sauce aside.

In a large bowl, combine the flour, baking powder and salt. Cut in shortening until mixture resembles coarse crumbs. Stir in buttermilk just until moistened. Turn onto a lightly floured surface; knead 8-10 times. Roll out dough to a 14-in. x 12-in. rectangle.

In a small bowl, combine filling ingredients. Spread evenly over dough. Roll up jelly-roll style, starting from a long side; pinch seam to seal. Cut into 12 slices. Place cut side down in a greased 13-in. x 9-in. baking dish; pour sauce over rolls. Bake at 350° for 45-50 minutes or until a toothpick comes out clean. Serve warm.

Cherry-Cheese Tea Ring

PREP: 40 MIN. + RISING   **BAKE:** 20 MIN. + COOLING
YIELD: 1 RING (12 SLICES)

Cherries and almonds make the perfect pair in this delightful tea ring. It's great for breakfast or brunch, and the cream cheese layer makes it extra-indulgent.

Marie Rizzio ★ Interlochen, Michigan

2-1/2 to 3 cups all-purpose flour
    3 tablespoons sugar
    1 package (1/4 ounce) active dry yeast
  1/2 teaspoon salt
  3/4 cup 2% milk
  1/4 cup butter
    1 egg
    1 teaspoon almond extract

FILLING:
    1 package (8 ounces) cream cheese, softened
  1/2 cup sugar
    1 teaspoon almond extract
    1 jar (10 ounces) maraschino cherries, drained
  3/4 cup chopped almonds

GLAZE:
    1 cup confectioners' sugar
    4 teaspoons 2% milk
  1/2 teaspoon almond extract

In a large bowl, combine 2 cups flour, sugar, yeast and salt. In a small saucepan, heat the milk and butter to 120°-130°. Add to dry ingredients; beat just until moistened. Add egg and extract; beat until smooth. Stir in enough remaining flour to form a soft dough (dough will be sticky).

Turn onto a floured surface; knead until smooth and elastic, about 6-8 minutes. Cover and let rise in a warm place until doubled, about 1 hour.

For filling, in a small bowl, beat the cream cheese, sugar and extract until smooth. Punch dough down and turn onto a lightly floured surface. Roll into a 14-in. x 7-in. rectangle. Spread cream cheese mixture evenly to within 1/2 in. of edges. Sprinkle with cherries and almonds. Roll up jelly-roll style, starting with a long side; pinch seam to seal.

Place seam side down on a greased baking sheet; pinch ends together to form a ring. With scissors, cut from outside edge to two-thirds of the way toward center of ring at 1-in. intervals. Separate strips slightly; twist to allow filling to show.

Bake at 375° for 20-25 minutes or until lightly browned. Remove from pan to a wire rack to cool. Combine glaze ingredients; drizzle over warm tea ring.

Jumbo Banana-Pecan Muffins

PREP: 25 MIN.   **BAKE:** 20 MIN.   **YIELD:** 1 DOZEN

These tender muffins are pretty and flavorful. Topped with a delightful streusel, they go well with fresh fruit.

Pam Ivbuls ★ Omaha, Nebraska

1-1/2 cups all-purpose flour
1-1/2 cups cake flour
1-1/2 cups sugar
1-1/2 teaspoons baking powder
  3/4 teaspoon baking soda
  3/4 teaspoon salt
  1/2 teaspoon ground cinnamon
1-1/2 cups mashed ripe bananas (2 to 3 medium)
1-1/2 cups (12 ounces) sour cream
    3 eggs
    6 tablespoons butter, melted

STREUSEL:
  1/3 cup all-purpose flour
  1/3 cup sugar
    3 tablespoons brown sugar
  1/4 teaspoon ground cinnamon
    3 tablespoons cold butter
  1/2 cup chopped pecans

In a large bowl, combine the first seven ingredients. In another bowl, combine the bananas, sour cream, eggs and butter. Stir into dry ingredients just until moistened.

Fill greased or paper-lined jumbo muffin cups two-thirds full. For streusel, in a small bowl, combine the flour, sugars and cinnamon. Cut in butter until crumbly; stir in pecans. Sprinkle over tops.

Bake at 350° for 20-25 minutes or until a toothpick inserted near the center comes out clean. Cool for 5 minutes before removing muffins from pans to wire racks. Serve warm.

Raspberry Ribbons

PREP: 30 MIN. + CHILLING   **BAKE:** 15 MIN. + COOLING
YIELD: 2 DOZEN

Bake up these lovely raspberry ribbons the next time you're looking for a sweet treat for brunch or a special item to include on your holiday dessert platter.

Jane Ozment ★ Purcell, Oklahoma

4-1/2   cups all-purpose flour
1/3   cup packed brown sugar
1   package (1/4 ounce) quick-rise yeast
1   teaspoon salt
1   cup butter, cubed
1/2   cup water
1/2   cup evaporated milk
2   eggs
1   teaspoon lemon extract

FILLING:
1   cup fresh raspberries
1   cup chopped walnuts
1/4   cup sugar
1   teaspoon grated lemon peel
1/2   cup seedless raspberry jam
Confectioners' sugar

In a large bowl, combine 3 cups flour, brown sugar, yeast and salt. In a small saucepan, heat the butter, water and milk to 120°-130°. Add to dry ingredients; beat just until moistened.

Add eggs and extract; beat until smooth. Stir in enough remaining flour to form a stiff dough. Cover and refrigerate for 2 hours.

For filling, combine the raspberries, walnuts, sugar and lemon peel; set aside. In a microwave, melt jam.

Turn dough onto a lightly floured surface; divide in half. Roll each portion into an 18-in. x 8-in. rectangle; spread each with jam and sprinkle with filling. Fold dough in half lengthwise; cut each rectangle into 12 strips. Twist strips at center; place on greased baking sheets.

Bake at 375° for 15-18 minutes or until golden brown. Remove pastries to wire racks to cool. Dust with confectioners' sugar.

TO MAKE AHEAD: Prepare dough as directed. Cover and refrigerate overnight. Fill and bake as directed.

Cranberry Crunch Coffee Cake

PREP: 30 MIN.   **BAKE:** 45 MIN. + COOLING
YIELD: 12 SERVINGS

This is my all-time favorite coffee cake. The tangy cranberries add a burst of color, and the lemon-flavored streusel adds a unique flavor twist.

Paula Marchesi ★ Lenhartsville, Pennsylvania

- 1 cup sugar
- 2 eggs
- 1/4 cup canola oil
- 2 tablespoons butter, melted
- 3 teaspoons vanilla extract
- 2 cups all-purpose flour
- 2 teaspoons baking powder
- 1/2 teaspoon salt
- 1 cup (8 ounces) lemon yogurt
- 2 cups fresh *or* frozen cranberries, coarsely chopped
- 1/2 teaspoon grated lemon peel

TOPPING:
- 1/2 cup whole wheat flour
- 1/2 cup old-fashioned oats
- 1/2 cup packed brown sugar
- 1/4 cup chopped walnuts
- 1 teaspoon ground cinnamon
- 2 tablespoons thawed lemonade concentrate
- 1 tablespoon canola oil

In a large bowl, beat the sugar, eggs, oil, butter and vanilla until well blended. Combine the flour, baking powder and salt; add to the sugar mixture alternately with yogurt, beating well after each addition. Stir in cranberries and lemon peel.

Pour half of the batter into a greased 10-in. fluted tube pan. Combine the topping ingredients; sprinkle half of topping over the batter. Repeat layers.

Bake at 350° for 45-50 minutes or until a toothpick inserted near the center comes out clean. Cool for 15 minutes before removing from pan to a wire rack to cool.

Olive Bread

PREP: 25 MIN. + RISING   **BAKE:** 20 MIN. + COOLING
YIELD: 1 LOAF (30 SLICES)

With just five ingredients, you can create this tender loaf with a colorful swirl of olives. This is a great bread to serve when you are having a large group at home or to take to a potluck.

Ann Major ★ Oskaloosa, Kansas

- 1 package (1/4 ounce) active dry yeast
- 1 cup warm water (110° to 115°)
- 1/4 cup canola oil
- 1-1/2 teaspoons sugar
- 1/2 teaspoon salt
- 2-1/2 to 3 cups all-purpose flour
- 3/4 cup sliced pitted green olives

In a large bowl, dissolve yeast in warm water. Add the oil, sugar, salt and 2 cups flour. Beat until smooth. Stir in enough remaining flour to form a firm dough.

Turn onto a floured surface; knead until smooth and elastic, about 6-8 minutes. Place in a greased bowl, turning once to grease top. Cover and let rise in a warm place until doubled, about 1 hour.

Punch dough down. Roll into a 16-in. x 12-in. rectangle. Sprinkle olives to within 1/2 in. of edges. Roll up jelly-roll style, starting with a long side; pinch seams to seal and tuck ends under. Place seam side down on a greased baking sheet. Cover and let rise until doubled, about 20 minutes.

Bake at 375° for 20-25 minutes or until golden brown. Cool on a wire rack.

Fruit & Nut Bread

PREP: 15 MIN. + RISING **BAKE:** 20 MIN. + COOLING
YIELD: 1 LOAF (12 WEDGES)

This recipe makes great use of convenient frozen bread dough. The tender bread makes a pretty loaf to bring to a holiday gathering or to give as a gift.

Priscilla Gilbert ★ Indian Harbour Beach, Florida

1	loaf (1 pound) frozen bread dough, thawed
1/3	cup chopped walnuts
1/4	cup golden raisins
1/4	cup raisins
1/4	cup dried cranberries
1/4	cup chopped dates
1	egg white
1	tablespoon honey

Turn bread dough onto a floured surface; roll out to 1-in. thickness. Sprinkle the walnuts, raisins, cranberries and dates over dough; fold over and knead well until the fruit and nuts are evenly mixed into dough. Shape into a round loaf and place in a greased 9-in. round baking pan.

Cover and let rise until doubled, about 30 minutes. Beat egg white and honey; brush over loaf. With a sharp knife, make 2 shallow crosses across top of loaf. Bake at 350° for 20-25 minutes or until golden brown. Transfer bread to a wire rack to cool.

TACO CHILI MIX

Gifts
FROM THE KITCHEN

Taco Chili Mix

(pictured on page 119)

PREP: 20 MIN. + SOAKING **COOK:** 1-3/4 HOURS
YIELD: 1 BATCH (9 SERVINGS AND 2-1/4 QUARTS)

Folks are thrilled to receive a jar of chili fixings for a slow-simmering dinner. The flavor is fantastic!

Suzette Jury ★ Keene, California

- 1/2 cup dried kidney beans
- 1/2 cup dried pinto beans
- 1/2 cup dried red beans
- 1 envelope taco seasoning mix
- 1 tablespoon dried minced onion
- 1/2 teaspoon chili powder
- 1/4 teaspoon ground cumin
- 1-1/2 cups tortilla chips

ADDITIONAL INGREDIENTS:
- 4 cups water
- 1 pound ground beef
- 1 can (14-1/2 ounces) diced tomatoes with mild green chilies
- 1 can (8 ounces) tomato sauce

Optional toppings: shredded cheddar cheese, shredded lettuce and sliced ripe olives

Layer the beans in a 1-qt. glass jar. Place seasonings in a small resealable plastic bag; place in jar. Top with chips. Cover and store in a cool dry place for up to 2 months.

TO PREPARE CHILI: Remove chips and seasoning packet from jar and set aside. Sort beans and rinse in cold water.

Place beans in a Dutch oven; add water to cover by 2 in. Bring to a boil; boil for 2 minutes. Remove from the heat; cover and let soak for 1 to 4 hours or until softened. Drain and rinse beans, discarding liquid.

Return beans to the pan. Add contents of seasoning packet and water. Bring to a boil. Reduce heat; cover and simmer for 1 hour or until beans are tender.

In a large skillet, cook beef over medium heat until no longer pink; drain. Add to the bean mixture; stir in tomatoes and tomato sauce. Bring to a boil. Reduce heat; cover and simmer for 30 minutes, stirring occasionally.

Crush tortilla chips. Stir into chili; cook for 5-10 minutes or until chili is thickened. Serve with cheese, lettuce and olives if desired.

Cranberry Walnut Biscotti

PREP: 25 MIN. **BAKE:** 40 MIN. + COOLING
YIELD: ABOUT 1-1/2 DOZEN

A chocolate glaze lends a little sweetness to biscotti loaded with walnuts and dried cranberries. Before your family has a chance to eat them all, wrap some up to give as gifts!

Joan Duckworth ★ Lee's Summit, Missouri

- 2 cups all-purpose flour
- 3/4 cup sugar
- 1 teaspoon baking powder
- 1/8 teaspoon salt
- 3 eggs
- 1-1/2 teaspoons vanilla extract
- 1 cup chopped walnuts, toasted
- 1 cup dried cranberries, chopped
- 1/2 cup milk chocolate chips
- 1 teaspoon shortening

In a large bowl, combine the flour, sugar, baking powder and salt. In a small bowl, whisk eggs and vanilla; add to dry ingredients just until moistened. Fold in walnuts and cranberries (dough will be sticky).

Divide dough in half. On a greased baking sheet, with lightly floured hands, shape each half into a 10-in. x 2-1/2-in. rectangle. Bake at 350° for 20-25 minutes or until golden brown.

Carefully remove to wire racks; cool for 10 minutes. Transfer to a cutting board; cut diagonally with a serrated knife into 1-in. slices. Place cut side down on ungreased baking sheets. Bake for 8-10 minutes on each side or until lightly browned. Remove to wire racks to cool completely.

In a microwave, melt chocolate chips and shortening; stir until smooth. Drizzle over biscotti. Let stand until set. Store in an airtight container.

Christmas Stollen

PREP: 1 HOUR + RISING   **BAKE:** 25 MIN.
YIELD: 4 LOAVES (12 SLICES EACH)

Colorful bits of candied fruit peek out from every sweet slice of this traditional recipe that's been in my family for generations. Mom would enlist me and my sister to drizzle the loaves with icing.

Ellen Teter ★ Arapahoe, Nebraska

- 2 packages (1/4 ounce *each*) active dry yeast
- 1/2 cup warm water (110° to 115°)
- 1-2/3 cups 2% milk (110° to 115°)
- 1 cup sugar
- 2/3 cup butter, melted
- 2 eggs
- 1 teaspoon grated lemon peel
- 3/4 teaspoon ground cardamom
- 1/2 teaspoon salt
- 1/2 teaspoon ground mace
- 5 to 5-1/2 cups all-purpose flour
- 1 cup coarsely chopped red candied cherries
- 1 cup coarsely chopped green candied cherries
- 1 cup sliced almonds
- 1 cup raisins
- 3/4 cup chopped candied pineapple
- 3/4 cup chopped candied citron

ICING:
- 1 cup confectioners' sugar
- 4 teaspoons 2% milk
- 1 teaspoon butter, melted
- 1/4 teaspoon vanilla extract

Dash salt

In a large bowl, dissolve yeast in warm water. Add the milk, sugar, butter, eggs, lemon peel, cardamom, salt, mace and 3 cups flour. Beat until smooth. Stir in enough remaining flour to form a soft dough (dough will be sticky). Stir in the cherries, almonds, raisins, pineapple and citron.

Turn onto a floured surface; knead until smooth and elastic, about 6-8 minutes. Place in a greased bowl, turning once to grease the top. Cover and let rise in a warm place until doubled, about 1 hour.

Punch dough down. Turn onto a floured surface. Divide into four portions. Shape each portion into a 12-in. x 7-in. oval. Fold long side over to within 1/2-in. of opposite side; press edges lightly to seal. Place 5 in. apart on lightly greased baking sheets. Cover and let rise until doubled, about 30 minutes.

Bake at 350° for 22-28 minutes or until golden brown. Remove to wire racks to cool.

For icing, in a small bowl, combine the confectioners' sugar, milk, butter, vanilla and salt. Drizzle over stollens.

TO MAKE AHEAD: Baked unfrosted loaves can be placed in airtight containers or resealable plastic bags and frozen for up to 3 months. Thaw overnight at room temperature; drizzle with icing as directed.

Christmas Jam

PREP: 40 MIN. **PROCESS:** 5 MIN./BATCH
YIELD: 12 HALF-PINTS

A few years ago, I hit upon the idea of presenting neighbors and relatives with baskets of homemade jam as gifts. With cherries, cinnamon and cloves, this smells and tastes like Christmas!

Marilyn Reineman ★ Stocton, California

- 3 packages (12 ounces *each*) frozen pitted dark sweet cherries, thawed and coarsely chopped
- 2 cans (8 ounces *each*) unsweetened crushed pineapple, drained
- 1 package (12 ounces) frozen unsweetened raspberries, thawed
- 9 cups sugar
- 1/4 cup lemon juice
- 1/4 cup orange juice
- 1/4 teaspoon ground cinnamon
- 1/4 teaspoon ground cloves
- 1/4 teaspoon butter
- 2 pouches (3 ounces *each*) liquid fruit pectin

In a Dutch oven, combine the fruit. Stir in the sugar, juices, cinnamon, cloves and butter. Bring to a full rolling boil over high heat, stirring constantly. Stir in pectin. Boil for 1 minute, stirring constantly.

Remove from the heat; skim off foam. Carefully ladle hot mixture into hot sterilized half-pint jars, leaving 1/4-in. headspace. Remove air bubbles; wipe rims and adjust lids. Process for 5 minutes in a boiling-water canner.

Editor's Note: The processing time listed is for altitudes of 1,000 feet or less. Add 1 minute to the processing time for each 1,000 feet of additional altitude.

Citrus Spiced Olives

PREP: 20 MIN. + CHILLING **YIELD:** 4 CUPS

Lemon, lime and orange bring a burst of sunny citrus flavor to marinated olives that are great for nibbling on at Yuletide buffets. You can even blend the olives and spread the mixture onto baguette slices.

Ann Sheehy ★ Lawrence, Massachusetts

- 4 cups pitted mixed olives
- 1/2 cup white wine
- 1/4 cup canola oil
- 3 tablespoons salt-free seasoning blend
- 3 tablespoons *each* orange, lemon and lime juices
- 4 garlic cloves, minced
- 2 teaspoons *each* grated orange, lemon and lime peels
- 1/2 teaspoon crushed red pepper flakes

In a large bowl, combine all ingredients. Cover and refrigerate for at least 4 hours before serving.

Dressed-Up Olives

Citrus Spiced Olives are a special hostess gift. To make them even more memorable, present them in a wide-mouth patterned glass jar with a lid. Or, package them in a canning jar and add some embellishments. Cover the lid with felt, tulle or organza and tie the fabric to the lid with a ribbon or small beaded chain.

Minty Cocoa Mix

PREP/TOTAL TIME: 15 MIN.
YIELD: 16 SERVINGS (3 CUPS MIX)

Instead of stirring hot chocolate with a candy cane, our home economists add crushed candies right to the mix. It's a mouthwatering, minty delight!

- 2-1/2 cups nonfat dry milk powder
- 1 cup confectioners' sugar
- 1/2 cup baking cocoa
- 1/2 teaspoon salt
- 1 cup miniature semisweet chocolate chips
- 1/2 cup crushed peppermint candies

ADDITIONAL INGREDIENT:
- 1 cup hot 2% milk

Place the milk powder, confectioners' sugar, cocoa and salt in a food processor; cover and process until a fine powder is formed. Transfer to a small bowl; stir in chocolate chips and candies. Store in a cool dry place for up to 2 months.

TO PREPARE HOT COCOA: Place 3 tablespoons cocoa mix in a mug; pour milk over mix and stir until blended.

Peanut Butter Cup Cookies

PREP: 25 MIN.   **BAKE:** 15 MIN./BATCH
YIELD: 1 BATCH (4 CUPS MIX AND 4 DOZEN COOKIES)

A cookie mix allows family and friends to easily bake a batch of homemade treats when they have time. No can resist the combination of chocolate and peanut butter!

Judy Crawford ★ Auxvasse, Missouri

- 1-3/4 cups all-purpose flour
- 1 teaspoon baking powder
- 1/2 teaspoon baking soda
- 3/4 cup sugar
- 1/2 cup packed brown sugar
- 18 miniature peanut butter cups, quartered

ADDITIONAL INGREDIENTS:
- 2/3 cup butter, softened
- 1 egg

In a small bowl, combine the flour, baking powder and baking soda. In a 1-qt. glass jar, layer the sugar, brown sugar and flour mixture; top with peanut butter cups. Cover and store in a cool dry place for up to 1 month.

TO PREPARE COOKIES: In a large bowl, beat butter and egg until well blended. Add contents of jar and stir until combined.

Shape dough into 1-in. balls. Place 2 in. apart on greased baking sheets (do not flatten). Bake at 375° for 12-14 minutes or until lightly browned. Remove to wire racks. Store in an airtight container.

Caramel Crispy Pops

PREP: 20 MIN. + COOLING   **YIELD:** 12 POPS

Ordinary rice cereal treats are fine for everyday, but the holiday calls for something a little more special. I dress them up with caramels and peanuts, then insert a stick to create a pleasing pop!

Linda Boufton ★ Dalton, Ohio

- 1 package (14 ounces) caramels
- 1/4 cup milk
- 4 cups crisp rice cereal
- 1 cup salted peanuts
- 12 Popsicle sticks

Unwrap caramels; place in a large heavy saucepan. Add milk; cook and stir over medium-low heat until melted. Remove from the heat. Stir in cereal and peanuts.

Press into a greased 8-in. square baking dish. Cool. Cut into 12 bars; gently insert a Popsicle stick into each bar. Store in an airtight container.

Rum Balls

PREP: 40 MIN.   **YIELD:** 3-1/2 DOZEN

Rum flavor comes through nicely in these traditional Christmas favorites. Roll half in powdered sugar and the other half in crushed vanilla wafers for visual appeal.

Audrey Larson ★ Bloomington, Minnesota

2-1/2 cups crushed vanilla wafers (about 75 wafers)
   1 cup ground pecans
   1 cup confectioners' sugar
   2 tablespoons plus 2 teaspoons baking cocoa
1/4 cup rum
   3 tablespoons honey
   2 tablespoons water
Additional confectioners' sugar *and/or* crushed vanilla wafers

In a large bowl, combine the wafer crumbs, pecans, confectioners' sugar and cocoa. Combine the rum, honey and water; stir into crumb mixture.

Shape into 1-in. balls. Roll in additional confectioners' sugar and/or wafer crumbs. Store in an airtight container.

Peach-Filled Muffins

PREP: 25 MIN.   **BAKE:** 20 MIN.   **YIELD:** 1 DOZEN

I altered an existing recipe to suit my family's taste and added an almond topping for a bit of crunch. For a change of taste with equally great results, use cherry preserves.

Lisa Varner ★ Charleston, South Carolina

   1 package (8 ounces) cream cheese, softened
1/4 cup butter, softened
   1 cup sugar
   2 eggs
1/4 cup 2% milk
1/2 teaspoon almond extract
1-3/4 cups all-purpose flour
1-1/2 teaspoons baking powder
1/4 teaspoon salt
1/2 cup peach preserves
1/4 cup sliced almonds
Confectioners' sugar

In a large bowl, beat the cream cheese, butter and sugar until light and fluffy. Add eggs, one at a time, beating well after each addition. Beat in milk and extract. Combine the flour, baking powder and salt; beat into creamed mixture just until moistened.

Fill paper-lined muffin cups half full. Drop 2 teaspoons preserves into center of each muffin; cover preserves with remaining batter. Sprinkle with almonds.

Bake at 350° for 18-22 minutes or until a toothpick inserted in muffin comes out clean. Cool for 5 minutes before removing from pan to a wire rack. Dust with confectioners' sugar.

Christmas Cookie Poppers

Christmas poppers (also called crackers) are a fun, festive way to bestow friends and family with little trinkets and treats at holiday parties. And the colorful ones shown here are no exception because they're filled with several homemade Rum Balls!

To make your own poppers, cut a piece of parchment paper that is large enough to cover the cookies or candies you want to give. Cut a piece of wrapping, tissue or foil paper about 5 inches wider than the parchment paper. Center the parchment paper over the wrapping paper. Place the cookies or candy down the center of the parchment paper. Wrap both papers around the cookies or candies. Twist ends and tie with ribbon to secure.

Outrageous Peanut Butter Sauce

PREP/TOTAL TIME: 10 MIN.   **YIELD:** 2 CUPS

I developed this thick and creamy sauce in an attempt to re-create a peanut butter topping we had at a restaurant. Served over any kind of ice cream, it's to die for!

Mary Long ★ Amherst, Virginia

- 1 cup creamy peanut butter
- 2/3 cup confectioners' sugar
- 1/2 cup corn syrup
- 1/4 cup water
- 1 teaspoon vanilla extract
- 1/4 teaspoon salt
- 1 Nutrageous candy bar (3.4 ounces), finely chopped

In a large bowl, combine the first six ingredients; fold in candy. Transfer to jars. Cover and store in a cool dark place for up to 4 weeks.

To serve, cook and stir in a small saucepan over medium-low heat until heated through. Serve with ice cream.

Spicy Praline Cashews

PREP/TOTAL TIME: 25 MIN.   **YIELD:** ABOUT 2-2/3 CUPS

This sweet-and-spicy snack makes an appearance at all of my holiday gatherings. As guests mingle and nibble on the cashews, I follow behind refilling the bowls!

Lillian Julow ★ Gainesville, Florida

- 1/2 cup sugar
- 1 tablespoon sherry vinegar
- 2 teaspoons salt
- 2 teaspoons ground cumin
- 1 teaspoon cayenne pepper
- 2-1/2 cups unsalted cashews, toasted

In a large heavy saucepan over medium heat, combine sugar and vinegar. Cook, without stirring, until mixture turns a golden amber color, about 8 minutes. Remove from the heat; stir in the salt, cumin and cayenne. Add cashews; stir until blended. Cool on waxed paper. Store the cashews in an airtight container.

Chocolate-Caramel Candy Bars

PREP: 50 MIN. **COOK:** 35 MIN. + CHILLING
YIELD: 3 DOZEN

Store-bought candy can't compare to irresistible, chewy nougat topped with a thick layer of caramel and covered in chocolate. For smaller bars, cut them in half before dipping.

- 2 teaspoons plus 1/2 cup butter, *divided*
- 2 cups sugar
- 1/2 cup evaporated milk
- 1-1/4 cups milk chocolate chips
- 1 jar (7 ounces) marshmallow creme
- 2 teaspoons vanilla extract

CARAMEL:

- 2 cups packed brown sugar
- 1-1/4 cups corn syrup
- 1 cup butter, cubed
- 1/4 teaspoon salt
- 1 can (14 ounces) sweetened condensed milk
- 1-1/2 teaspoons vanilla extract
- 3 pounds milk chocolate candy coating, coarsely chopped

Line a 13-in. x 9-in. pan with foil and grease the foil with 2 teaspoons butter; set aside.

In a large heavy saucepan over medium-high heat, melt remaining butter. Stir in sugar and evaporated milk. Bring to a boil; cook and stir 5 minutes longer. Remove from the heat; cool for 5 minutes. Stir in chocolate chips until melted. Stir in marshmallow creme and vanilla until smooth. Spread into prepared pan; set aside.

In another large heavy saucepan, combine the brown sugar, corn syrup, butter and salt; bring to a boil over medium heat, stirring constantly. Cook 4 minutes longer without stirring.

Remove from the heat; gradually stir in condensed milk. Return to the heat. Reduce heat to medium-low; cook and stir until a candy thermometer reads 244° (firm-ball stage). Remove from the heat; stir in vanilla. Pour over chocolate mixture (do not scrape saucepan). Refrigerate until caramel is set, at least 2 hours.

Using foil, lift candy out of pan. Gently peel off foil; cut into 3-1/4-in. x 1-in. bars. In a microwave, melt candy coating; stir until smooth. Dip bars in coating; allow excess to drip off. Place on a waxed paper-lined baking sheet; refrigerate until set. Store in an airtight container.

Editor's Note: For variety, stir 2 cups peanuts into the marshmallow creme mixture. We recommend that you test your candy thermometer before each use by bringing water to a boil; the thermometer should read 212°. Adjust your recipe temperature up or down based on your test.

Cranberry Orange Vinegar

PREP: 10 MIN. + STANDING   **YIELD:** 6 CUPS

I enjoy making an assortment of vinegars but this is a favorite. The longer the cranberries and oranges sit in the vinegar, the more intensely flavored it becomes.

Kathy Rairigh ★ Milford, Indiana

- 6 cups white wine vinegar
- 1 package (12 ounces) fresh *or* frozen cranberries, chopped
- 3 medium oranges, sectioned and chopped

In a large saucepan, heat vinegar to just below the boiling point. In a large bowl, lightly mash the cranberries and oranges; add heated vinegar. Cover and let stand in a cool dark place for 10 days.

Strain mixture through a cheesecloth and discard pulp. Pour into sterilized jars or decorative bottles. Seal tightly. Store in a cool dark place.

Cranberry Orange Vinaigrette

PREP/TOTAL TIME: 10 MIN.   **YIELD:** 1-1/4 CUPS

When I give jars of my Cranberry Orange Vinegar, I'm certain to include copies of this vinaigrette recipe. It pairs especially well with a green salad featuring dried cranberries, mandarin oranges and toasted walnuts. Or, use it as a marinade for chicken and salmon.

Kathy Rairigh ★ Milford, Indiana

- 1/2 cup Cranberry Orange Vinegar (recipe above) *or* raspberry vinegar
- 1/4 cup maple syrup
- 1/2 teaspoon salt
- 1/2 teaspoon grated orange peel
- 1/2 teaspoon ground mustard
- 1/8 teaspoon coarsely ground pepper
- 1/2 cup canola oil
- 1/2 teaspoon poppy seeds

In a blender, combine the first six ingredients. Cover and process for 1 minute. While processing, gradually add the oil in a steady stream. Stir in the poppy seeds. Store in the refrigerator.

Butterscotch Peanut Butter Fudge

PREP: 15 MIN + CHILLING   **YIELD:** ABOUT 2 POUNDS

You don't have to be experienced at making candy to try your hand at this no-fail fudge. The simply delicious confection makes a great gift everyone appreciates.

Marina Castle ★ North Hollywood, California

- 1 teaspoon plus 1/2 cup butter, *divided*
- 1 package (11 ounces) butterscotch chips
- 1 cup creamy peanut butter
- 2 cups miniature marshmallows
- 1/2 cup chopped unsalted peanuts

Line an 11-in. x 7-in. pan with foil and grease the foil with 1 teaspoon butter; set aside.

In a large saucepan, combine the butterscotch chips, peanut butter and remaining butter. Cook and stir over medium heat until melted. Remove from the heat; stir in marshmallows until smooth. Spread into prepared pan; sprinkle with peanuts. Chill until firm.

Using foil, lift fudge out of pan. Discard foil; cut fudge into 1-in. squares. Store in an airtight container.

TO MAKE AHEAD: Stored in an airtight container in a cool dry place, fudge will keep for about 2 to 3 weeks. For longer storage, wrap tightly and freeze for up to 1 year.

Amaretto-Peach Preserves

PREP: 1-1/4 HOURS **PROCESS:** 10 MIN.
YIELD: 5 HALF-PINTS

Chock-full of peaches, raisins and pecans, this lovely conserve enhances ordinary slices of toast.

Redawna Kalynchuk ★ Sexsmith, Alberta

    1   cup golden raisins
  3/4   cup boiling water
    2   pounds peaches, peeled and chopped
    4   teaspoons grated orange peel
  1/3   cup orange juice
    2   tablespoons lemon juice
    3   cups sugar
  1/2   cup chopped pecans
    3   tablespoons Amaretto

Place raisins in a small bowl. Cover with boiling water; let stand for 5 minutes. Place raisins with liquid in a large saucepan. Add peaches and orange peel. Bring to a boil. Reduce heat; cover and simmer for 10-15 minutes or until peaches are tender.

Stir in orange and lemon juices; return to a boil. Add sugar. Cook, uncovered, over medium heat for 25-30 minutes or until thickened, stirring occasionally. Add pecans; cook 5 minutes longer. Remove from the heat; stir in the Amaretto.

Carefully ladle hot mixture into hot sterilized half-pint jars, leaving 1/4-in. headspace. Remove air bubbles; wipe rims and adjust lids. Process in a boiling-water canner for 5 minutes.

Editor's Note: The processing time listed is for altitudes of 1,000 feet or less. Add 1 minute to the processing time for each 1,000 feet of additional altitude.

Tiramisu Snack Mix

(pictured below)

PREP: 15 MIN. + CHILLING   **YIELD:** 8 CUPS

This was inspired by one of my favorite desserts. It has the same great flavor combination of tiramisu but in a fun-to-eat snack mix.

Priscilla Yee ★ Concord, California

- 6 cups Chocolate Chex
- 1 can (6 ounces) salted roasted almonds
- 6 ounces white baking chocolate, chopped
- 2 teaspoons shortening, *divided*
- 2 teaspoons instant espresso powder
- 1/3 cup semisweet chocolate chips

Place cereal and almonds in a large bowl; set aside. In a microwave, melt white chocolate and 1 teaspoon shortening; stir in espresso powder until smooth. Pour over cereal mixture and toss to coat.

In a microwave, melt chocolate chips and remaining shortening; stir until smooth. Drizzle over cereal mixture and toss to coat. Spread onto waxed paper-lined baking sheets. Refrigerate until set. Store in an airtight container.

Spiced Caramel Corn

PREP: 35 MIN.   **BAKE:** 1 HOUR   **YIELD:** 3 QUARTS

For many years, we prepared this spiced popcorn during the holidays for gift-giving. We always had to make a triple batch because no one could stop eating it!

Lee Bremson ★ Kansas City, Missouri

- 3 quarts air-popped popcorn
- 2/3 cup packed brown sugar
- 1/2 cup butter, cubed
- 2 tablespoons maple syrup
- 1 teaspoon ground cinnamon
- 1/4 teaspoon ground nutmeg
- 1/4 teaspoon ground cloves
- 1/8 teaspoon salt
- 1/2 teaspoon vanilla extract
- 1/4 teaspoon baking soda

Place popcorn in a large bowl; set aside. In a large heavy saucepan, combine the brown sugar, butter, syrup, cinnamon, nutmeg, cloves and salt. Bring to a boil over medium heat, stirring constantly. Boil for 5 minutes without stirring.

Remove from the heat; stir in vanilla and baking soda (mixture will foam). Quickly pour over the popcorn and mix well.

Transfer to two lightly greased 15-in. x 10-in. x 1-in. baking pans. Bake at 250° for 1 hour, stirring every 15 minutes. Remove from pans and place on waxed paper to cool. Store in an airtight container.

Apple Brandy

(pictured at left)

PREP: 35 MIN. + STANDING   **YIELD:** 2 QUARTS

I spend a lot of time developing recipes for the many fruits and vegetables we grow on our farm. In this creation, brandy is enhanced with apples and spices for a pleasant drink.

Deanna Seippel ★ Lancaster, Wisconsin

- 4 cups sugar
- 2 cups water
- 4 pounds apples, sliced
- 1 liter brandy
- 3 whole cloves
- 1 cinnamon stick (3 inches)
- Additional whole cloves and cinnamon sticks

Combine sugar and water in a large saucepan. Bring to a boil; cook and stir until sugar is dissolved. Remove from the heat.

Place apples in a large glass or plastic container; add the sugar mixture, brandy, cloves and cinnamon stick. Cover and let stand at room temperature for at least two weeks, stirring once a week.

Strain brandy mixture; discard apples and spices. Pour into glass bottles. Place an additional three cloves and one cinnamon stick in each bottle.

Cinnamon Stir Sticks

(pictured at right)

PREP: 15 MIN.   **COOK:** 35 MIN. + COOLING
YIELD: 2-1/2 DOZEN

Our home economists use cinnamon sticks as holders for cute little lollipops that can be stirred into hot cider and tea.

- 1-1/2 cups sugar
- 3/4 cup water
- 2/3 cup corn syrup
- 1/2 teaspoon cream of tartar
- 1/2 teaspoon cinnamon oil
- 30 cinnamon sticks (5 inches)

Using a pencil, draw ten 2-in. ovals on three sheets of parchment paper. Place paper, pencil mark side down, on baking sheets; chill until ready to use.

In a large heavy saucepan, cook and stir the first four ingredients over medium heat until sugar is dissolved. Bring to a boil. Cook, without stirring, until a candy thermometer reads 325° or mixture is a golden amber color.

Remove from the heat; stir in oil (keep face away from mixture as oil is very strong). Immediately ladle mixture over ovals; press a cinnamon stick into each. Cool completely. Store in an airtight container for up to 1 month.

Editor's Note: We recommend that you test your candy thermometer before each use by bringing water to a boil; the thermometer should read 212°. Adjust your recipe temperature up or down based on your test.

Spiced Cider Bundles

PREP/TOTAL TIME: 30 MIN.
YIELD: 4 BUNDLES (8 SERVINGS EACH)

I like to enhance the naturally good taste of hot apple cider with these spice bundles. Make a Christmas gift basket of apple cider, spiced cider bundles and Cinnamon Stir Sticks for your friends. They'll be delighted.

Alissa Stehr ★ Gau-Odernheim, Germany

- Cheesecloth
- 24 whole cloves
- 24 whole allspice
- 4 teaspoons dried orange peel
- 4 cinnamon sticks (3 inches)
- ADDITIONAL INGREDIENTS FOR SPICED CIDER:
- 8 cups apple cider or juice

Cut eight 6-in. squares of cheesecloth; stack two squares on top of each other to make four stacks. Place 6 cloves, 6 allspice, 1 teaspoon orange peel and 1 cinnamon stick on each stack; bring up corners of cloth and tie with string to form a bag. Store in an airtight container for up to 1 month.

TO PREPARE CIDER: Place cider in a Dutch oven; add one spice bag. Bring to a boil over medium heat. Reduce heat; simmer, uncovered, for 15-20 minutes. Discard spice bag; ladle cider into mugs.

Editor's Note: To make dried orange peel, finely grate the peel from two oranges; spread in a greased 15-in. x 10-in. x 1-in. baking pan. Bake at 200° for 16-20 minutes or until dry.

In a small saucepan, bring cherries and water to a boil. Reduce heat; simmer, uncovered, for 20 minutes.

Add sugar and butter; cook and stir until sugar is dissolved. Remove from the heat; stir in extract and cinnamon. Cool; transfer to airtight containers. Store in the refrigerator for up to 2 weeks.

Waffle Mix

PREP/TOTAL TIME: 20 MIN.
YIELD: 6 BATCHES (1-1/3 CUPS MIX AND 6 WAFFLES EACH)

Thanks to apple pie spice and cinnamon, finicky eaters won't mind the heart-healthy use of whole wheat flour in these wonderful waffles. Give away half of the mix...and keep the other half for yourself!

- 4-1/2   cups all-purpose flour
- 3   cups whole wheat flour
- 2/3   cup sugar
- 1/4   cup baking powder
- 1   tablespoon apple pie spice
- 1   teaspoon salt
- 1   teaspoon ground cinnamon

ADDITIONAL INGREDIENTS:
- 1   cup 2% milk
- 1   egg
- 2   tablespoons canola oil

In a large bowl, combine the first seven ingredients. Store in an airtight container for up to 2 months.

TO PREPARE WAFFLES: Place 1-1/3 cups waffle mix in a large bowl. In another bowl, whisk the milk, egg and oil. Stir into dry ingredients just until moistened.

Bake in a preheated waffle iron according to the manufacturer's directions until golden brown.

Cherry Syrup

PREP: 5 MIN.   **COOK:** 25 MIN.   **YIELD:** 3 CUPS

My mom and grandma have been making this fruity syrup to serve with fluffy waffles and pancakes ever since I was a little girl. Now I make it for my sons, who love it as much as I do!

Sandra Harrington ★ Nipomo, California

- 1   package (12 ounces) frozen pitted dark sweet cherries, thawed
- 1   cup water
- 2-1/2   cups sugar
- 2   tablespoons butter
- 1/2   teaspoon almond extract

Dash ground cinnamon

Fabric Gift Bag

After taking the time to prepare a gift from your kitchen, it's important that you put some thought into the presentation. Dull-looking dry mixes become eye-catching offerings when tucked inside easy-to-make fabric gift bags.

Fold a 7-1/2-inch x 26-inch piece of fabric in half crosswise with the right sides facing. Sew or fuse the long edges together with a narrow seam. Turn right side out. If desired, trim the top edges with pinking shears.

Place the dry mix in a resealable plastic bag; seal. Place inside the fabric bag. Tie ribbon around the top; thread a gift tag on the ribbon and tie the ends.

Cookie EXCHANGE

Scrumptious Sugar Cookies

PREP: 15 MIN. + CHILLING **BAKE:** 10 MIN./BATCH
YIELD: ABOUT 2-1/2 DOZEN

My husband developed this crisp sugar cookie when he was a baker in Alaska. It's traveled with us to many states, along with requests for the recipe!

Nancy Gribble ★ Fort Wayne, Indiana

1	cup butter, softened
1/2	cup butter-flavored shortening
1	cup sugar
2	eggs
1	teaspoon almond extract
1/2	teaspoon vanilla extract
4	cups cake flour

1/2	teaspoon baking powder
1/2	teaspoon salt

ICING:

2-2/3	cups confectioners' sugar
6	tablespoons butter, softened
1	teaspoon vanilla extract
2	to 3 tablespoons 2% milk

Red paste food coloring, optional
Miniature semisweet chocolate chips and red-hot candies

In a large bowl, cream the butter, shortening and sugar until light and fluffy. Beat in eggs and extracts. Combine the flour, baking powder and salt; gradually add to creamed mixture and mix well.

Divide dough into thirds; flatten each portion into a circle. Wrap each in plastic wrap; refrigerate for 2 hours or until easy to handle.

On a lightly floured surface, roll out one portion of dough to 1/8-in. thickness. Cut with a floured 4-1/2-in. gingerbread boy cookie cutter; place 1 in. apart on ungreased baking sheets. Repeat with remaining dough; chill and reroll scraps.

Bake at 375° for 8-10 minutes or until edges begin to brown. Remove to wire racks to cool completely.

In a small bowl, beat the confectioners' sugar, butter, vanilla and enough milk to achieve desired consistency. Tint a portion red if desired. Decorate cookies as desired with icing, chocolate chips and red-hots.

TO MAKE AHEAD: Dough can be made 2 days in advance. Let stand at room temperature for 30 minutes before rolling out. Cookies can be baked 1 week ahead of time and stored in an airtight container at room temperature. Unfrosted cookies may be frozen for up to 1 month.

Gingerbread Boy Invitations

Try this quick and easy way to create invitations for your next cookie exchange or holiday party using a gingerbread cookie cutter as a template.

Begin by washing the cookie cutter in hot, soapy water and drying it thoroughly with a clean kitchen towel. Cut several pieces of brown fun foam into rectangles slightly larger than your cookie cutter. Firmly press the cookie cutter into the center of each rectangle so it leaves an imprint in the foam. Cut around each imprint.

Using a black marker with a fine point, handwrite the date, time and location in the center of each gingerbread boy invite. Using a standard hole punch, punch holes from red or green card stock for eyes and nose. Glue them to the foam using craft glue. Add any additional holiday stickers or decorations of your choice. If you like, you can also decorate using Foam Paint™ by DecoArt, which is specifically designed for foam surfaces. Just be sure to allow the paint to dry thoroughly before sending the invitations in the mail.

Raspberry Sandwich Cookies

PREP: 1-1/2 HOURS + CHILLING
BAKE: 15 MIN./BATCH + COOLING
YIELD: ABOUT 2 DOZEN

Pretty raspberry jam peeks out from buttery shortbread cookies for a festive treat from our Test Kitchen. Make them throughout the year with different cookie cutter shapes.

3	cups all-purpose flour
3/4	cup sugar
1/4	teaspoon salt
1-1/2	cups cold butter
2	tablespoons cold water
1/2	teaspoon almond extract
1/2	teaspoon vanilla extract
3/4	cup seedless raspberry jam

Confectioners' sugar

In a large bowl, combine the flour, sugar and salt; cut in butter until mixture resembles coarse crumbs. Stir in water and extracts until mixture forms a ball.

On a lightly floured surface, roll out dough to 1/8-in. thickness. Cut with floured 2-1/2-in. cookie cutters. From the center of half the cookies, cut out a 1-1/2 in. shape. Place 1 in. apart on parchment paper-lined baking sheets.

Bake at 325° for 12-15 minutes or until edges are lightly browned. Cool for 2 minutes before removing to wire racks to cool completely.

Spread 1/2 teaspoon jam over the bottoms of the solid cookies. Sprinkle cutout cookies with confectioners' sugar; place over cookies with jam.

Unwrap and cut into 1/4-in. slices. Place 1 in. apart on ungreased baking sheets. Bake at 375° for 8-10 minutes or until set. Remove to wire racks to cool.

For icing, in a large bowl, beat butter until fluffy. Add confectioners' sugar and eggnog; beat until smooth. Frost cookies. Store in an airtight container.

Editor's Note: This recipe was tested with commercially prepared eggnog.

TO MAKE AHEAD: Dough can be made 2 days in advance. Iced cookies can be stored for 1 week in an airtight container at room temperature.

White Chocolate Raspberry Cookies

PREP: 25 MIN. **BAKE:** 10 MIN./BATCH
YIELD: ABOUT 3-1/2 DOZEN

Featuring my family's favorite combination of white chocolate and raspberry, this cookie wins the hearts of those who sample it.

Mary Cooney ✶ Kettering, Ohio

1	cup butter, softened
2/3	cup sugar
4	ounces white baking chocolate, melted
1	egg
2	teaspoons vanilla extract
2-1/4	cups all-purpose flour
1	teaspoon baking powder
1/4	teaspoon salt

TOPPING:

1	jar (12 ounces) seedless raspberry jam
4	ounces white baking chocolate, melted

In a large bowl, cream butter and sugar until light and fluffy. Beat in the chocolate, egg and vanilla. Combine the flour, baking powder and salt; gradually add to creamed mixture and mix well.

Shape into 1-in. balls. Place 1 in. apart on ungreased baking sheets. Using a wooden spoon handle, make an indentation in the center of each cookie. Bake at 375° for 9-11 minutes or until set.

Remove to wire racks to cool completely. Spoon jam into cookies; drizzle with chocolate. Let stand until set. Store in an airtight container.

Eggnog Cookies

PREP: 30 MIN. + CHILLING **BAKE:** 10 MIN./BATCH + COOLING
YIELD: ABOUT 13-1/2 DOZEN

Prepared eggnog stars in both the cookie and frosting in this newfound recipe, imparting a subtle holiday flavor.

Amanda Taylor ✶ Glen Ewen, Saskatchewan

1	cup butter, softened
2	cups sugar
1	cup eggnog
5-1/2	cups all-purpose flour
1	teaspoon baking soda
3/4	teaspoon ground nutmeg

ICING:

1/4	cup butter, softened
3	cups confectioners' sugar
1/3	cup eggnog

In a large bowl, cream butter and sugar until light and fluffy. Beat in eggnog. Combine the flour, baking soda and nutmeg; gradually add to creamed mixture and mix well. Shape into four 10-in. rolls; wrap each in plastic wrap. Refrigerate overnight.

Almond Pillow Cookies

PREP: 40 MIN. + CHILLING **BAKE:** 10 MIN./BATCH
YIELD: ABOUT 4 DOZEN

I find people can't resist these buttery cookies with a soft almond center. The confectioners' sugar on top looks like a dusting of snow.

Laura McDowell ★ Lake Villa, Illinois

- 2 cups butter, softened
- 2 packages (3 ounces *each*) cream cheese, softened
- 2 cups sugar
- 2 egg yolks
- 1 teaspoon almond extract
- 1/2 teaspoon vanilla extract
- 4-1/2 cups all-purpose flour
- 1 teaspoon salt
- 1/2 teaspoon baking soda

FILLING:
- 1 can (8 ounces) almond paste
- 1/4 cup sugar
- 1 egg white
- 1/2 teaspoon vanilla extract
- Confectioners' sugar

In a large bowl, cream the butter, cream cheese and sugar until light and fluffy. Beat in egg yolks and extracts. Combine the flour, salt and baking soda; gradually add to creamed mixture and mix well.

Divide dough into fourths; cover and refrigerate for 2 hours or until easy to handle. In a small bowl, combine almond paste, sugar, egg white and vanilla until blended.

Roll one portion of dough to 3/8-in. thickness. Working quickly, place scant teaspoonfuls of filling 2-1/2 in. apart over half of dough. Fold dough over; press down around filling to seal. Cut out cookies using a scalloped round 2-1/4-in. cutter. Reroll scraps if desired; repeat with remaining dough and filling.

Bake at 350° for 10-14 minutes or until edges are lightly browned. Cool for 1 minute before removing from pans to wire racks. Sprinkle with confectioners' sugar.

Pumpkin Cookies with Cream Cheese Frosting

PREP: 30 MIN. **BAKE:** 10 MIN./BATCH + COOLING
YIELD: 4 DOZEN

A classic cream cheese frosting adds a finishing touch to these pleasantly spiced pumpkin cookies. Everyone enjoys the soft, cake-like texture.

Lisa Chernetsky ★ Luzerne, Pennsylvania

- 1 cup butter, softened
- 2/3 cup packed brown sugar
- 1/3 cup sugar
- 1 egg
- 1 teaspoon vanilla extract
- 1 cup canned pumpkin
- 2 cups all-purpose flour
- 1-1/2 teaspoons ground cinnamon
- 1 teaspoon baking soda
- 1/2 teaspoon salt
- 1/4 teaspoon baking powder
- 1 cup chopped walnuts

FROSTING:
- 1/4 cup butter, softened
- 4 ounces cream cheese, softened
- 2 cups confectioners' sugar
- 1-1/2 teaspoons vanilla extract

In a large bowl, cream butter and sugars until light and fluffy. Beat in egg and vanilla. Add pumpkin; mix well. Combine the flour, cinnamon, baking soda, salt and baking powder; gradually add to creamed mixture and mix well. Stir in walnuts.

Drop by rounded tablespoonfuls 2 in. apart onto greased baking sheets. Bake at 350° for 8-10 minutes or until edges are lightly browned. Remove cookies to wire racks to cool completely.

In a small bowl, beat the frosting ingredients until light and fluffy. Frost cookies. Store in an airtight container in the refrigerator.

Chocolate Reindeer

PREP: 40 MIN. + CHILLING **BAKE:** 10 MIN./BATCH
YIELD: 4 DOZEN

*You can enlist little hands to help position the antlers, eyes
and noses on these adorable crisp cookies.*

Pat Habiger ★ Spearville, Kansas

1	cup butter, softened
1-1/2	cups sugar
3	eggs
1	teaspoon vanilla extract
3-1/4	cups all-purpose flour
1/3	cup baking cocoa
2	teaspoons cream of tartar
1	teaspoon baking soda
1/2	teaspoon salt
96	miniature pretzels
96	M&M's miniature baking bits
48	small red gumdrops

In a large bowl, cream butter and sugar until light and
fluffy. Beat in eggs and vanilla. Combine the flour, cocoa,
cream of tartar, baking soda and salt; gradually add to
creamed mixture and mix well.

Divide dough into eight portions; cover and refrigerate
for at least 2 hours.

On a lightly floured surface, roll each portion into
a 6-in. circle; cut into six wedges. Place 2 in. apart on
ungreased baking sheets. Press in pretzels for antlers,
baking bits for eyes and a gumdrop for the nose.

Bake at 375° for 7-9 minutes or until set. Cool for 1
minute before removing from pans to wire racks. Store in
an airtight container.

Sour Cream Date Drops

PREP: 20 MIN.　**BAKE:** 10 MIN./BATCH　**YIELD:** 6 DOZEN

Sour cream lends a moist texture to these old-fashioned cookies. The recipe has earned me first prize at many fairs!

Carol Steiner ★ Arrowwood, Alberta

- 1/2　cup butter, softened
- 1　cup packed brown sugar
- 1/2　cup sugar
- 2　eggs
- 1　cup sour cream
- 1　teaspoon vanilla extract
- 2-1/2　cups all-purpose flour
- 1　teaspoon salt
- 1　teaspoon ground cinnamon
- 1/2　teaspoon baking soda
- 1/4　teaspoon ground cloves
- 1　cup finely chopped dates
- 1　cup chopped walnuts
- 1　cup candied cherries, chopped

In a large bowl, cream the butter and sugars until light and fluffy. Beat in the eggs, sour cream and vanilla. Combine the flour, salt, cinnamon, baking soda and cloves; gradually add to creamed mixture and mix well. Stir in the dates, nuts and cherries.

Drop by tablespoons 2 in. apart onto greased baking sheets. Bake at 325° for 10-12 minutes or until lightly browned. Remove to wire racks. Store in an airtight container with waxed paper between layers.

Coconut Pecan Joys

PREP: 15 MIN.　**BAKE:** 10 MIN./BATCH　**YIELD:** 4 DOZEN

My kids are always good judges as to whether or not a recipe is worth repeating. They eagerly eat these chewy goodies.

Lisa Moravek ★ Corning, New York

- 4　egg whites
- 1　teaspoon vanilla extract
- 1/8　teaspoon lemon juice
- 3/4　cup sugar
- 1　package (7 ounces) flaked coconut
- 1/4　cup chopped pecans
- 1/4　cup semisweet chocolate chips

In a large bowl, beat the egg whites, vanilla and lemon juice until soft peaks form. Gradually add sugar, 1 tablespoon at a time, beating until stiff peaks form and sugar is dissolved. Fold in coconut, pecans and chocolate chips.

Drop by rounded tablespoonfuls 2 in. apart onto greased baking sheets. Bake at 350° for 10-12 minutes or until lightly browned. Remove to wire racks to cool. Store in an airtight container.

Hazelnut Chocolate Chip Pizzelle

PREP: 15 MIN.　**COOK:** 5 MIN./BATCH　**YIELD:** 3 DOZEN

I've experimented with different varieties of pizzelle recipes, but this is definitely a favorite. My dad likes to help make them so that we don't run out!

Aimee McCullen ★ Youngwood, Pennsylvania

- 4　eggs
- 1　cup sugar
- 3/4　cup butter, melted
- 2　cups all-purpose flour
- 1/2　cup finely chopped hazelnuts, toasted
- 1/2　cup miniature semisweet chocolate chips

In a large bowl, beat the eggs, sugar and butter until smooth. Gradually add flour and mix well. Fold in hazelnuts and chocolate chips.

Bake in a preheated pizzelle iron according to manufacturer's directions until golden brown. Remove to wire racks to cool. Store in an airtight container.

Tart Tampers Make It Easy

Use a tart tamper to easily press dough into mini muffin cups and always yield a professional-looking treat.

Place a ball of dough in each mini muffin cup. Using firm pressure, push the dough down and up the sides of the cup. If the dough has not moved up the sides of the cup as far as you want, try rocking the tamper back and forth.

Chocolate Hazelnut Tassies

PREP: 25 MIN.   **BAKE:** 20 MIN./BATCH + COOLING
YIELD: 3 DOZEN

Your taste buds will be delighted to find these delicious tassies are not filled with the standard pecans but with dark chocolate and hazelnuts.

Joan Ranzini ★ Waynesboro, Virginia

- 1   cup butter, softened
- 2   packages (3 ounces *each*) cream cheese, softened
- 1   tablespoon sugar
- 2   teaspoons grated lemon peel
- 2   cups all-purpose flour

FILLING:
- 1/4   cup chocolate hazelnut spread
- 1/2   cup packed brown sugar
- 1   egg
- 1   tablespoon butter, melted
- 1   teaspoon vanilla extract
- 1/2   cup finely chopped hazelnuts
- 1/4   cup miniature semisweet chocolate chips

In a large bowl, cream the butter, cream cheese, sugar and lemon peel. Beat in flour. Shape into 36 balls. With floured fingers or a tart tamper, press dough onto the bottom and up the sides of ungreased miniature muffin cups.

For filling, in a small bowl, beat the hazelnut spread, brown sugar, egg, butter and vanilla until blended. Stir in hazelnuts and chocolate chips. Fill prepared cups three-fourths full.

Bake at 375° for 16-18 minutes or until set. Cool on wire racks for 10 minutes. Carefully remove from pans to wire racks. Store in an airtight container.

Editor's Note: Look for chocolate hazelnut spread in the peanut butter section of your grocery store.

Chocolate-Dipped Orange Cookies

PREP: 30 MIN.　**BAKE:** 10 MIN./BATCH + COOLING
YIELD: 3 DOZEN

With orange peel and extract, these tender cookies are bursting with fresh citrus flavor. Dipping them in chocolate adds a special touch.

Joanne Burkert ★ Beecher, Illinois

　1　cup butter, softened
1/2　cup confectioners' sugar
　1　teaspoon grated orange peel
　1　teaspoon orange extract
　2　cups all-purpose flour
1/4　teaspoon salt
　6　ounces dark chocolate candy coating
1/2　cup chopped almonds, toasted

In a large bowl, cream butter and confectioners' sugar until light and fluffy. Beat in orange peel and extract. Combine the flour and salt; gradually add to creamed mixture and mix well.

Divide dough into 36 pieces; shape each into a 2-1/2-in. rope. Place 2 in. apart on ungreased baking sheets. Bake at 350° for 10-12 minutes or until set. Cool for 2 minutes before removing from pans to wire racks to cool completely.

In a microwave, melt candy coating; stir until smooth. Dip ends of cookies in coating; allow excess to drip off. Sprinkle with almonds. Place on waxed paper; let stand until set. Store in an airtight container.

Vanilla Crescent Cookies

(pictured at left)

PREP: 25 MIN.   **BAKE:** 10 MIN./BATCH   **YIELD:** 4 DOZEN

This recipe originated in Croatia and has been in my husband's family for generations. I was thrilled when my mother-in-law shared it with me.

Beverly Williams ★ Rhinelander, Wisconsin

- 1 cup butter, softened
- 1 cup confectioners' sugar, *divided*
- 1 teaspoon vanilla extract
- 1/2 teaspoon grated lemon peel
- 2-1/2 cups all-purpose flour
- 1/4 teaspoon salt
- 1/2 cup finely chopped walnuts
- 2 tablespoons sugar
- 1 vanilla bean

In a large bowl, cream butter and 1/2 cup confectioners' sugar until light and fluffy. Beat in vanilla and lemon peel. Combine flour and salt; gradually add to creamed mixture and mix well. Stir in walnuts.

Shape tablespoonfuls of dough into crescent shapes. Place 2 in. apart on ungreased baking sheets. Bake at 375° for 10-12 minutes or until edges are lightly browned.

Place sugar in a food processor. Split vanilla bean and scrape seeds into food processor. Discard vanilla bean. Pulse mixture until combined. Transfer to a small bowl, stir in remaining confectioners' sugar. Coat warm cookies with sugar mixture. Cool completely on wire racks. Store in an airtight container.

Cream Cheese Slice-and-Bake Cookies

PREP: 25 MIN. + CHILLING   **BAKE:** 15 MIN./BATCH
YIELD: ABOUT 5-1/2 DOZEN

Chopped almonds add a bit of crunch to crisp refrigerator cookies fabulously flavored with rum extract and nutmeg.

- 1 cup butter, softened
- 1 package (3 ounces) cream cheese, softened
- 1 cup sugar
- 1 egg
- 1/2 teaspoon rum extract
- 1/4 teaspoon vanilla extract
- 3 cups all-purpose flour
- 1/2 teaspoon salt
- 1/2 teaspoon baking powder
- 1/4 teaspoon baking soda
- 1/2 teaspoon ground nutmeg
- 1 cup finely chopped almonds

In a large bowl, cream the butter, cream cheese and sugar until light and fluffy. Beat in the egg and extracts. Combine the flour, salt, baking powder, baking soda and nutmeg; gradually add to creamed mixture and mix well.

Shape into two 9-in. rolls. Roll each in almonds; wrap in plastic wrap. Refrigerate for 2 hours or until firm.

Cut into 1/4-in. slices. Place 2 in. apart on parchment paper-lined baking sheets. Bake at 375° for 11-13 minutes or until bottoms are lightly browned. Cool for 1 minute before removing from pans to wire racks.

TO MAKE AHEAD: Dough can be made 2 days in advance. Cookies can be baked 1 week ahead of time and stored in an airtight container at room temperature or frozen for up to 1 month.

Scraping a Vanilla Bean

Fresh vanilla beans add a wonderful rich flavor to baked goods. Here's how to remove those fantastic little seeds from the bean.

Split a vanilla bean lengthwise in half. Run the pointed end of a sharp knife or a small spoon down the center of the split bean to scrape out the seeds. Use seeds as directed in recipe.

Pistachio Buttons

PREP: 30 MIN. + CHILLING   **BAKE:** 10 MIN./BATCH
YIELD: 10 DOZEN

This recipe makes a big batch, which comes in handy during the holidays. The green center adds a festive touch.

Nella Parker ★ Hershey, Michigan

1/2	cup butter, softened
3/4	cup sugar
1	egg
1	teaspoon almond extract
1/4	teaspoon vanilla extract
2	cups all-purpose flour
1	teaspoon baking powder
1/2	teaspoon salt
1	ounce unsweetened chocolate, melted
1/3	cup finely chopped pistachios
10	drops green food coloring, optional

In a large bowl, cream butter and sugar until light and fluffy. Beat in egg and extracts. Combine the flour, baking powder and salt; gradually add to the creamed mixture and mix well.

Divide dough in half. Mix melted chocolate into half of dough; add pistachios and food coloring if desired to the remaining half. Divide each dough into four portions.

Roll out one chocolate portion into an 8-in. x 3-in. rectangle. Roll one green portion into an 8-in. log; place on chocolate dough 1 in. from a long side. Roll dough around filling and seal edges. Repeat with remaining dough. Wrap each in plastic wrap; refrigerate for 1 hour or until firm.

Unwrap and cut into 1/4-in. slices. Place 2 in. apart on lightly greased baking sheets. Bake at 350° for 8-10 minutes or until set. Remove to wire racks to cool.

Peppermint Meringue Clouds

PREP: 45 MIN. **BAKE:** 20 MIN./BATCH **YIELD:** 4 DOZEN

I love to bake so my kitchen gets a real workout every Yuletide. This unique recipe combines both sugar and meringue cookies. The mint candies add a seasonal flair.

June Rolf ★ Norwood, Minnesota

2/3	cup shortening
3/4	cup sugar
2	egg yolks
1/4	cup milk
1	teaspoon vanilla extract
2-1/2	cups all-purpose flour
1	teaspoon salt
1/2	teaspoon baking powder

MERINGUE:

2	egg whites
1/4	teaspoon salt
1/2	teaspoon white vinegar
1/2	teaspoon vanilla extract
1/2	cup sugar
1	cup (6 ounces) miniature semisweet chocolate chips
1/2	cup crushed peppermint candies
1/2	cup crushed spearmint candies

In a large bowl, cream shortening and sugar until light and fluffy. Beat in the egg yolks, milk and vanilla. Combine the flour, salt and baking powder; gradually add to creamed mixture and mix well. Cover and refrigerate for 30 minutes.

Meanwhile, in a small bowl, beat the egg whites, salt, vinegar and vanilla until soft peaks form. Gradually add sugar; beat until stiff peaks form. Fold in chocolate chips. Transfer half of the meringue to another bowl. Fold peppermint candies into one portion and spearmint candies into the remaining portion.

Shape cookie dough into 1-in. balls. Place 2 in. apart on ungreased baking sheets. Flatten with a glass dipped in sugar. Drop meringue by teaspoonfuls into the center of each cookie. Bake at 325° for 18-20 minutes or until lightly browned.

Any extra meringue can be dropped by tablespoons onto baking sheets and baked as directed.

Orange-Cranberry Bars

PREP: 30 MIN. **BAKE:** 35 MIN. + COOLING **YIELD:** 4 DOZEN

With the incredible combination of orange and cranberry, these bars are fast sellers at my church's Christmas bazaar.

Agnes Ward ★ Stratford, Ontario

2	cups all-purpose flour
1	cup packed brown sugar
1	teaspoon baking soda
1	teaspoon ground ginger
1	cup cold butter, cubed
1-1/2	cups quick-cooking oats
1	cup flaked coconut
2	teaspoons grated orange peel
1	cup chopped pecans, toasted
1	can (14 ounces) whole-berry cranberry sauce
1	cup orange marmalade

In a large bowl, combine the flour, brown sugar, baking soda and ginger; cut in butter until mixture resembles coarse crumbs. Stir in the oats, coconut and orange peel.

Place 3 cups of mixture in another bowl; stir in pecans. Set aside for topping. Press remaining oat mixture into a greased 15-in. x 10-in. baking pan. Bake at 350° for 10-12 minutes or until golden brown.

Combine cranberry sauce and orange marmalade; spread over crust. Top with reserved oat mixture. Bake for 25-30 minutes or until golden brown. Cool on a wire rack. Cut into bars.

In a large bowl, cream butter and sugar until light and fluffy. Beat in egg yolk and vanilla. Combine the flour, cinnamon and salt; gradually add to creamed mixture and mix well.

Using a cookie press fitted with the disk of your choice, press dough 2 in. apart onto ungreased baking sheets. Press chocolate chips into cookies as desired. Bake at 375° for 8-10 minutes or until set. Remove to wire racks. Store in an airtight container.

Editor's Note: A pastry bag fitted with a coupler and #32 star tip can be substituted for a cookie press. Pipe dough into concentric circles or shapes of your choice.

Piping Creates New Spritz Designs

Now you can make these buttery spritz even if you don't have a cookie press. By piping the dough with a star pastry tip these spritz (pictured left) have a festive new look.

Cut a small hole in the corner of pastry or plastic bag; insert # 32 star pastry tip. Fill the bag with dough. Pipe dough into concentric circles or other shapes 2 inches apart on ungreased baking sheets. Bake as directed.

Cinnamon Spritz

PREP: 15 MIN. **BAKE:** 10 MIN./BATCH
YIELD: 4-1/2 DOZEN

With lots of cinnamon flavor, these rich buttery cookies are similar to a classic Snickerdoodle. The spritz dough is so easy to work with.

Diane Cook ★ Phoenix, Arizona

    1   cup butter, softened
  3/4   cup sugar
    1   egg yolk
    1   teaspoon vanilla extract
    2   cups all-purpose flour
1-1/2   teaspoons ground cinnamon
  1/4   teaspoon salt
Semisweet chocolate chips

Red Velvet Cookies

PREP: 30 MIN. **BAKE:** 15 MIN./BATCH + COOLING
YIELD: 7-1/2 DOZEN

*These unique cookies have been a part of our holiday tradition
for as long as I can remember. My mother made them when I
was little, and now I often bake a batch for my own family.*

Mindy Young ★ Hanover, Pennsylvania

- 1 cup shortening
- 1 cup sugar
- 3/4 cup packed brown sugar
- 3 eggs, *separated*
- 2 teaspoons red food coloring
- 4 cups all-purpose flour
- 3 tablespoons baking cocoa
- 3 teaspoons baking powder
- 1 teaspoon salt
- 1 cup buttermilk
- 2 cups (12 ounces) semisweet chocolate chips

FROSTING:
- 1-1/2 cups butter, softened
- 3-3/4 cups confectioners' sugar
- 1/8 teaspoon salt
- 3 to 4 tablespoons 2% milk

In a large bowl, cream the shortening and sugars until light
and fluffy. Beat in egg yolks and food coloring. Combine
the flour, cocoa, baking powder and salt. Add to the
creamed mixture alternately with buttermilk, beating well
after each addition.

In another bowl with clean beaters, beat egg whites until
stiff peaks form; fold into batter. Fold in chocolate chips.
Drop by tablespoonfuls 2 in. apart onto greased baking
sheets. Bake at 350° for 12-14 minutes or until set. Remove
to wire racks to cool completely.

In a large bowl, beat the butter, confectioners' sugar
and salt until blended. Add enough milk to achieve desired
consistency. Crumble eight cookies and set aside. Frost
remaining cookies; sprinkle with cookie crumbs. Store in an
airtight container.

Glittered Snowflake Cookies

(pictured at left)

PREP: 25 MIN. + CHILLING   **BAKE:** 10 MIN./BATCH + COOLING
YIELD: ABOUT 3 DOZEN

The dough for these sugar cookies won't spread while baking, making it great for cookie cutters with intricate designs. Theses treats can also be drizzled with semisweet chocolate.

Kimberly DeWalt ★ Horseshoe Bend, Idaho

- 1 cup butter, softened
- 1 cup sugar
- 1 egg
- 1 teaspoon vanilla extract
- 3 cups all-purpose flour
- 1-1/2 teaspoons baking powder
- 1/2 teaspoon salt
- 4 ounces white baking chocolate, coarsely chopped

Edible glitter

In a large bowl, cream butter and sugar until light and fluffy. Beat in egg and vanilla. Combine the flour, baking powder and salt; gradually add to creamed mixture and mix well. Cover and refrigerate for 1-2 hours or until firm.

On a lightly floured surface, roll dough to 1/4-in. thickness. Cut with a floured 3-in. snowflake cookie cutter. Place 1 in. apart on greased baking sheets. Bake at 350° for 9-11 minutes or until edges are golden brown. Cool for 1 minute before removing to wire racks to cool completely.

In a microwave, melt chocolate; stir until smooth. Drizzle over cookies; sprinkle with edible glitter. Let stand until set. Store in an airtight container.

To Make Small Snowflakes: Cut dough with a floured 1-1/2-in. snowflake cookie cutter. Bake for 6-8 minutes or until edges are golden brown.

Editor's Note: Edible glitter is available from Wilton Industries. Call 1-800/794-5866 or visit *www.wilton.com.*

German Almond Cookies

PREP: 30 MIN.   **BAKE:** 15 MIN./BATCH
YIELD: 8-1/2 DOZEN

A dear German lady, who owned several restaurants, was well-known for these soft cookies. I feel honored to have received a copy of her cherished recipe.

Mrs. Edgar Stem Jr. ★ Old Forge, New York

- 2 cups butter, softened
- 2 cups sugar
- 1 can (9 ounces) almond paste
- 4 eggs
- 4-1/2 cups all-purpose flour

Chopped almonds and red and green sprinkles, optional

In a large bowl, cream the butter, sugar and almond paste. Add eggs, one at a time, beating well after each addition. Gradually add flour and mix well.

Roll into 1-in. balls and place 2 in. on ungreased baking sheets; flatten with a fork. Sprinkle with almonds and sprinkles if desired. Bake at 350° for 13-15 minutes or until lightly browned. Remove to wire racks to cool. Store in an airtight container.

Nutty Shortbread Cookies

PREP: 25 MIN.   **BAKE:** 30 MIN./BATCH + COOLING
YIELD: 2-1/2 DOZEN

My husband and I like the buttery flavor of shortbread cookies and have tweaked recipes through the years to come up with this mouthwatering version.

Angela Garcia ★ Oshkosh, Wisconsin

- 1-1/2 cups all-purpose flour
- 1/2 cup confectioners' sugar
- 1/2 cup ground almonds
- 1/2 teaspoon salt
- 1 cup cold butter
- 1/2 teaspoon almond extract *or* 1 teaspoon hazelnut liqueur
- 30 red *and/or* green candied cherries

In a large bowl, combine the flour, confectioners' sugar, almonds and salt; cut in butter until mixture resembles coarse crumbs. Stir in extract. Knead dough until smooth, about 6-10 times. Shape into 1-in. balls. Place 1 in. apart on ungreased baking sheets. Using the end of a wooden spoon handle, carefully make an indentation in the center of each. Fill each with a candied cherry.

Bake at 300° for 30-35 minutes or until set. Cool for 1 minute before removing from pans to wire racks to cool completely. Store in an airtight container.

Grinding Nuts

A food processor can make short work of grinding nuts, but if you're not careful you can end up with nut butter instead of ground nuts. To avoid this, toss the nuts with 1 or 2 tablespoons of flour from the recipe. This will absorb some of the nut oil and help keep the nuts moving freely in the processor. Also, pulse the processor on and off to help prevent overprocessing.

Chocolate Macaroon Bars

PREP: 20 MIN. **BAKE:** 20 MIN. + CHILLING
YIELD: 4 DOZEN

Here's a nice Christmas treat that takes very little effort. The classic combination of chocolate and coconut is timeless.

Loraine Meyer ★ Bend, Oregon

2	cups chocolate wafer crumbs
6	tablespoons confectioners' sugar
1/2	cup butter, melted
1	can (14 ounces) sweetened condensed milk
3-3/4	cups flaked coconut
1	cup sliced almonds, toasted
1-1/2	cups semisweet chocolate chips
1/3	cup heavy whipping cream

In a small bowl, combine the wafer crumbs, confectioners' sugar and butter; press into a greased 13-in. x 9-in. baking pan. In a large bowl, combine the milk, coconut and almonds. Drop by spoonfuls over crust; spread evenly.

Bake at 350° for 20-25 minutes or until edges begin to brown. Cool completely on a wire rack. In a microwave-safe bowl, melt chips and cream; stir until smooth. Drizzle over top. Refrigerate until firm. Cut into bars.

Holiday
SWEETS

Sprinkle with remaining confectioners' sugar. Garnish with additional whipped cream and chocolate stars if desired. Refrigerate for at least 1 hour before serving.

Editor's Note: This recipe was tested with Alessi crisp ladyfinger cookies. Look for chocolate hazelnut spread in the peanut butter section of your grocery store.

Chocolate-Caramel Dream Pie

PREP: 25 MIN. + CHILLING   **YIELD:** 8 SERVINGS

Chocolate, caramel and cream cheese come together to produce a pleasing pie that's packed with lots of rich flavor. Everyone will surely save room for dessert!

Anna Robb ★ Harrison, Arkansas

1-1/2	cups crushed crisp ladyfinger cookies
1/3	cup butter, melted
1/2	cup chocolate hazelnut spread
2/3	cup caramel ice cream topping
2	tablespoons plus 2 cups heavy whipping cream, *divided*
1-1/2	cups slivered almonds
1	package (8 ounces) cream cheese, softened
1/3	cup plus 1 tablespoon confectioners' sugar, *divided*
1-1/2	cups semisweet chocolate chips, melted
2	teaspoons vanilla extract

Additional heavy whipping cream, whipped
Chocolate Stars for garnish if desired, optional

Combine crushed cookies and butter; press onto the bottom and up the sides of a greased 9-in. pie plate. Refrigerate for 30 minutes.

Spread hazelnut spread over crust. In a large bowl, combine caramel topping and 2 tablespoons cream; stir in almonds. Spoon over hazelnut spread layer.

In a small bowl, beat cream cheese and 1/3 cup confectioners' sugar; stir in melted chocolate and vanilla until smooth. In a large bowl, beat remaining cream until stiff peaks form; fold into cream cheese mixture. Spread over caramel-almond layer.

Chocolate Stars

After taking the time to create a stunning holiday dessert, why not enhance it with some edible Chocolate Stars?

1. Trace a star design several times on a piece of paper. Place paper on a baking sheet and cover with waxed paper. Microwave 1 bag (12 ounces) semisweet chocolate chips and 1 teaspoon shortening on high for 1 minute; stir. Microwave at additional 10- to 20-second intervals, stirring until smooth. Cut a small hole in the corner of a pastry or plastic bag. Attach a small round pastry tip with a coupler. Fill bag with melted chocolate. Following traced designs, pipe chocolate onto waxed paper. Chill until the chocolate is firm, about 15 minutes.

2. Carefully remove the stars with a metal spatula. Store in a cool, dry place in a covered container.

Ruby Grapefruit and Shortcakes

PREP: 35 MIN. **BAKE:** 15 MIN. + COOLING
YIELD: 10 SERVINGS

Tender biscuits are filled with sweetened cream and grapefruit sections for a wonderful, wintry spin on strawberry shortcake.

Karla Johnson ★ East Helena, Montana

- 2 cups all-purpose flour
- 2 cups cake flour
- 1/2 cup plus 1 tablespoon sugar, *divided*
- 2-1/2 teaspoons baking powder
- 1-1/2 teaspoons baking soda
- 1/2 teaspoon salt
- 3/4 cup cold butter
- 1-1/3 cups buttermilk
- 1/2 cup crystallized ginger, finely chopped
- 2 tablespoons heavy whipping cream

FILLING:

- 1 cup ruby red grapefruit juice
- 3 tablespoons sugar
- 2 cans (15 ounces *each*) grapefruit sections, drained

GINGER WHIPPED CREAM:

- 1-1/2 cups heavy whipping cream
- 2 tablespoons confectioners' sugar
- 2 tablespoons finely chopped crystallized ginger

In a large bowl, combine the flours, 1/2 cup sugar, baking powder, baking soda and salt. Cut in butter until mixture resembles coarse crumbs. Stir in buttermilk and ginger just until moistened.

Turn onto a lightly floured surface; knead 8-10 times. Pat or roll out to 1-in. thickness; cut with a floured 3-in. biscuit cutter. Place 2 in. apart on an ungreased baking sheet. Brush tops with cream; sprinkle with remaining sugar. Bake at 400° for 12-15 minutes or until golden brown.

Meanwhile, place grapefruit juice and sugar in a small saucepan. Bring to a boil; cook until the liquid is reduced by half. Remove from the heat. Add the grapefruit; toss gently to coat.

In a large bowl, beat cream until it begins to thicken. Add confectioners' sugar; beat until stiff peaks form. Fold in the ginger.

Split warm shortcakes in half horizontally. Spoon filling over bottoms; replace tops and garnish with whipped cream.

TO MAKE AHEAD: Grapefruit mixture can be made the day before serving. For best results, make biscuits the same day they are served.

Apricot-Raspberry Angel Torte

PREP: 20 MIN. **BAKE:** 35 MIN. + COOLING
YIELD: 12 SERVINGS

Guests will never guess you used a prepared angel food cake and canned pie filling to create this gorgeous torte. The addition of fresh raspberries lends a from-scratch touch.

Sally Sibthorpe ★ Shelby Township, Michigan

- 1 package (16 ounces) angel food cake mix
- 2 packages (one 8 ounces, one 3 ounces) cream cheese, softened
- 1/3 cup sugar
- 1-1/4 teaspoons almond extract
- 1 carton (8 ounces) frozen whipped topping, thawed
- 1 can (21 ounces) apricot *or* peach pie filling
- 1-1/2 cups fresh raspberries
- 1 cup sliced almonds

Fresh mint leaves

Prepare and bake cake according to package directions, using a greased 10-in. baking pan. Cool.

In a large bowl, beat the cream cheese, sugar and extract until light and fluffy; fold in whipped topping.

Split cake into three horizontal layers. Place bottom layer on a serving plate; spread with a third of the cream cheese mixture. Top with a third of the pie filling, raspberries and almonds. Repeat layers twice. Garnish with mint. Refrigerate leftovers.

About Crystallized Ginger

Crystallized ginger, also known as candied ginger, is the root of the ginger plant that has been cooked in a sugar syrup. Larger grocery stores will carry candied ginger in the spice section. Store it in an airtight container in a cool, dark place for up to 3 months.

Lemon Poppy Seed Cake

(pictured at left)

PREP: 40 MIN.   **BAKE:** 25 MIN. + COOLING
YIELD: 12 SERVINGS

This lovely layered cake may not be made from scratch, but lemon curd filling and creamy frosting give it a gourmet taste. It's a tasty change from chocolate desserts.

Suzanne Earl ★ Spring, Texas

- 3 eggs, *separated*
- 1 package (18-1/4 ounces) lemon cake mix
- 1 cup 2% milk
- 1/3 cup buttermilk
- 1/3 cup canola oil
- 1/4 cup unsweetened applesauce
- 1/4 cup lemon juice
- 1 tablespoon grated lemon peel
- 4 teaspoons poppy seeds
- 2 cups heavy whipping cream
- 1/4 cup sugar
- 2 teaspoons vanilla extract
- 1 jar (10 ounces) lemon curd

Place egg whites in a large bowl; let stand at room temperature for 30 minutes.

In another large bowl, combine the cake mix, milk, buttermilk, oil, applesauce, lemon juice, egg yolks, lemon peel and poppy seeds; beat on low speed for 30 seconds. Beat on medium for 2 minutes. In another bowl, beat egg whites until stiff peaks form; fold into batter.

Transfer to two greased and floured 9-in. round baking pans. Bake at 350° for 22-28 minutes or until a toothpick inserted near the center comes out clean. Cool for 10 minutes before removing cakes from pans to wire racks to cool completely.

In a large bowl, beat cream until it begins to thicken. Add sugar and vanilla; beat until stiff peaks form.

Cut each cake horizontally into two layers. Place bottom layer on a serving plate; top with 1/3 cup lemon curd. Repeat layers twice. Top with remaining cake layer. Spread remaining lemon curd over top of cake within 1 in. of edges. Frost sides and top edge of cake with 3 cups whipped cream mixture. Pipe remaining mixture around edges.

Frozen Strawberry Dessert

PREP:: 25 MIN. + FREEZING   **YIELD:** 15 SERVINGS

When planning Christmas menus, I appreciate dessert recipes like this that can be made ahead and frozen. A light and creamy slice is welcome after a heavy meal.

Cassie Alexander ★ Muncie, Indiana

- 1-1/4 cups crushed pretzels
- 1/4 cup sugar
- 1/2 cup butter, melted

FILLING:

- 1 can (14 ounces) sweetened condensed milk
- 1/2 cup thawed nonalcoholic strawberry daiquiri mix
- 1 package (8 ounces) cream cheese, softened
- 1 container (16 ounces) frozen sweetened sliced strawberries, thawed
- 1 carton (8 ounces) frozen whipped topping, thawed

In a small bowl, combine the pretzels, sugar and butter. Press onto the bottom of a greased 11-in. x 7-in. dish. Refrigerate for 30 minutes.

For filling, in a large bowl, combine milk and daiquiri mix. Beat in cream cheese until smooth. Stir in strawberries; fold in whipped topping. Pour over crust (dish will be full). Freeze for 4 hours before serving.

TO MAKE AHEAD: This dessert can be made two weeks before serving. To serve with a strawberry sauce, puree 2 packages (10 ounces each) frozen sweetened sliced strawberries, thawed and undrained in a food processor or blender. Strain through a fine sieve. Makes 2 cups of sauce.

Cranberry-White Chocolate Trifle

(pictured at left)

PREP: 45 MIN. **COOK:** 15 MIN. + CHILLING
YIELD: 14 SERVINGS (3/4 CUP EACH)

Trifles are a great dessert to make when entertaining because they feed a crowd and often can be prepared in advance. Plus, they look so eye-catching on the table.

Janet Varble ★ Harrisville, Utah

    6 tablespoons sugar
    3 tablespoons cornstarch
  1/8 teaspoon salt
2-2/3 cups milk
    3 egg yolks, beaten
    5 ounces white baking chocolate, chopped
1-1/2 teaspoons vanilla extract
    1 can (14 ounces) jellied cranberry sauce
  1/3 cup raspberry liqueur
    1 loaf (10-3/4 ounces) frozen pound cake, thawed and cut
       into 1/2-in. cubes

TOPPING:
1-1/2 cups heavy whipping cream
  1/4 cup confectioners' sugar
    1 teaspoon vanilla extract

In a large saucepan, combine the sugar, cornstarch and salt. Stir in milk until smooth. Cook and stir over medium-high heat until thickened and bubbly. Reduce heat; cook and stir 2 minutes longer.

Remove from the heat. Stir a small amount of hot mixture into egg yolks; return all to the pan, stirring constantly. Bring to a gentle boil; cook and stir 2 minutes longer. Remove from the heat; stir in white chocolate and vanilla. Cool to room temperature without stirring.

In a small bowl, whisk cranberry sauce and raspberry liqueur until smooth.

Place half of the cake cubes in a 3-qt. trifle bowl or glass bowl. Spread with half of the cranberry mixture; top with half of the custard. Repeat layers. Cover and chill for at least 2 hours.

In a large bowl, beat cream until it begins to thicken. Add confectioners' sugar and vanilla; beat until stiff peaks form. Pipe over top.

Mini Pumpkin Custards

PREP: 25 MIN. **BAKE:** 20 MIN. + CHILLING
YIELD: 8 SERVINGS

Guests don't need to feel guilty about indulging in sweets when they're offered small cups of creamy custard. Each spoonful is like pumpkin pie without the calorie-laden crust.

Leslie Tripp ★ Potomac, Maryland

  1/2 cup half-and-half cream
  1/2 cup heavy whipping cream
    3 egg yolks
    2 tablespoons plus 2 teaspoons sugar
  1/8 teaspoon ground cinnamon
Dash *each* salt, ground cloves and nutmeg
  1/3 cup canned pumpkin
  1/4 cup maple syrup
  1/2 teaspoon vanilla extract
Whipped cream and additional ground nutmeg

In a small saucepan, heat half-and-half and heavy cream until bubbles form around sides of pan. In a small bowl, whisk egg yolks, sugar, cinnamon, salt, cloves and nutmeg.

Remove cream from the heat; stir a small amount of hot cream into egg mixture. Return all to the pan, stirring constantly. Stir in the pumpkin, syrup and vanilla.

Transfer to eight stoneware demitasse cups or 2-oz. ramekins. Place cups in a baking pan; add 1 in. of boiling water to pan.

Bake, uncovered, at 325° for 25-30 minutes for demitasse cups and 20-25 minutes for ramekins or until centers are just set (mixture will jiggle). Remove cups from water bath; cool for 10 minutes. Cover and refrigerate for at least four hours. Garnish with whipped cream and additional nutmeg.

TO MAKE AHEAD: These custards can be made the day before serving.

Lime Tartlets

(pictured at left)

PREP: 40 MIN.   **BAKE:** 10 MIN. + CHILLING   **YIELD:** 4 TARTS

Cool and refreshing, lime tarts are a much-requested recipe of family and friends throughout the year. I've even filled the buttery crusts with chocolate pudding.

Jennifer Lester ★ Billings, Montana

2/3	cup all-purpose flour
2	tablespoons sugar
1/4	cup cold butter
1	egg yolk
1-1/2	teaspoons cold water

FILLING:

1	cup sugar
1	tablespoon cornstarch
1	cup heavy whipping cream
1/3	cup lime juice
1	tablespoon grated lime peel
3/4	cup sour cream
3	tablespoons butter

Whipped cream

In a small bowl, combine flour and sugar; cut in butter until mixture resembles coarse crumbs. Add egg yolk. Gradually add water, tossing with a fork until a ball forms. Divide into four portions.

Press dough onto the bottoms and up the sides of four ungreased 4-in. fluted tart pans with removable bottoms. Place on a baking sheet. Bake at 400° for 8-10 minutes or until golden brown. Cool on wire racks.

In a small saucepan, combine sugar and cornstarch. Add the cream, lime juice and peel; stir until blended. Cook and stir over medium heat until mixture comes to a boil. Cook and stir 1-2 minutes longer or until thickened. Remove from the heat; stir in sour cream and butter. Cool to room temperature, stirring occasionally. Spoon into tart shells.

Refrigerate for 1 hour before serving. Garnish with whipped cream.

Chocolate Almond Pie

PREP: 30 MIN.   **BAKE:** 45 MIN. + COOLING
YIELD: 8 SERVINGS

Almonds replace pecans for a sweet and satisfying pie. The chocolate chips make it hard to eat just a single slice!

Rosemarie Weleski ★ Natrona Heights, Pennsylvania

Pastry for single-crust pie (9 inches)

1	cup unblanched almonds, coarsely chopped and toasted
1/2	cup semisweet chocolate chips
3	eggs, beaten
1	cup packed brown sugar
1	cup corn syrup
2	tablespoons butter, melted
3/4	teaspoon ground cinnamon
1/2	teaspoon almond extract
1/2	teaspoon vanilla extract
1/8	teaspoon salt

Whipped cream and grated chocolate, optional

Line a 9-in. pie plate with pastry; trim and flute edges. Fill with almonds and chocolate chips. In a large bowl, whisk the eggs, brown sugar, corn syrup, butter, cinnamon, extracts and salt. Pour into pastry.

Bake at 350° for 45-55 minutes or until set. Cool on a wire rack. Garnish with whipped cream and grated chocolate if desired. Refrigerate leftovers.

Citrus Loop Garnish

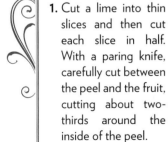

1. Cut a lime into thin slices and then cut each slice in half. With a paring knife, carefully cut between the peel and the fruit, cutting about two-thirds around the inside of the peel.

2. Fold the cut peel under so that the fruit on half of the slice is exposed. Place in a covered container and store in the refrigerator until needed.

Chocolate Cran-Raspberry Cheesecake Bars

PREP: 25 MIN. **BAKE:** 45 MIN. + CHILLING
YIELD: 2 DOZEN

Cranberries, raspberries and baking cocoa take ordinary cheesecake bars to a new level. The recipe makes a big batch so it's terrific for large gatherings.

Sharon Delaney-Chronis ★ South Milwaukee, Wisconsin

1-3/4   cups sugar, *divided*
   3   tablespoons cornstarch
   3   cups fresh *or* frozen cranberries, thawed
   1   cup fresh *or* frozen raspberries, thawed
1/2   cup cranberry juice
   2   cups crushed vanilla wafers (about 60 wafers)
   5   tablespoons butter, melted
   3   tablespoons baking cocoa
   3   packages (8 ounces *each*) cream cheese, softened
   1   cup (8 ounces) sour cream
3/4   cup egg substitute
3/4   cup semisweet chocolate chips, melted
1-1/2   teaspoons vanilla extract
Additional melted semisweet chocolate and fresh raspberries, optional

In a large saucepan, combine 3/4 cup sugar and cornstarch. Stir in berries and cranberry juice. Cook and stir over medium heat until mixture comes to a boil. Remove from the heat and cool slightly.

Meanwhile, in a large bowl, combine the wafer crumbs, butter and cocoa. Press onto the bottom of a greased 13-in. x 9-in. baking dish. Pour berry mixture over crust.

In another bowl, beat the cream cheese, sour cream and remaining sugar until smooth. Add egg substitute; beat on low speed just until combined. Stir in melted chocolate and vanilla. Pour over top.

Bake at 325° for 45-55 minutes or until center is almost set. Cool on a wire rack for 1 hour. Cover and refrigerate for 8 hours or overnight. Drizzle with additional melted chocolate and garnish with raspberries if desired.

Maple Pecan Cake

PREP: 35 MIN.   **BAKE:** 40 MIN. + COOLING
YIELD: 12 SERVINGS

While preparing to enter a baking contest many years ago, I kept fine-tuning this recipe until it was just right. My determination paid off...I was first runner-up! Chocolate frosting enhances the maple-nut flavor of the cake.

Darlene Brenden ★ Salem, Oregon

5	eggs, *separated*
1-1/2	cups all-purpose flour
3/4	cup sugar
1	teaspoon baking powder
3/4	teaspoon salt
3/4	cup maple syrup
1/2	cup water
1	teaspoon maple flavoring
3/4	cup chopped pecans
1-1/2	ounces semisweet chocolate, grated

FROSTING:

1/4	cup butter, cubed
3	ounces semisweet chocolate, chopped
4	cups confectioners' sugar
1/4	cup 2% milk
1/4	cup maple syrup
1-1/2	cups chopped pecans

Let eggs stand at room temperature for 30 minutes. In a large bowl, combine the flour, sugar, baking powder and salt. In another bowl, whisk the egg yolks, maple syrup, water and maple flavoring. Add to dry ingredients; beat until well blended. In another bowl, beat egg whites until stiff peaks form; fold into batter. Fold in pecans and chocolate.

Gently spoon into an ungreased 10-in. tube pan. Cut through batter with a knife to remove air pockets. Bake on the lowest oven rack at 350° for 40-45 minutes or until cake springs back when lightly touched. Immediately invert pan; cool completely, about 1 hour.

Run a knife around side and center tube of pan. Remove cake to a serving plate. For frosting, in a microwave, melt butter and chocolate; stir until smooth. Pour into a large bowl; beat in the confectioners' sugar, milk and maple syrup. Frost cake; press pecans onto the top and sides of cake.

TO MAKE AHEAD: The unfrosted cake can be made the day before serving. Store tightly wrapped at room temperature. Frost before serving.

Pumpkin Bread Pudding

PREP: 20 MIN. + STANDING   **BAKE:** 50 MIN.
YIELD: 6 SERVINGS

This old-fashioned treat is so warm and comforting on chilly evenings. Pumpkin gives it great seasonal appeal, and the white chocolate sauce makes it even more irresistible.

Shirley Glaab ★ Hattiesburg, Mississippi

2	eggs, lightly beaten
1-1/2	cups canned pumpkin
1	cup heavy whipping cream
1	cup half-and-half cream
2/3	cup packed brown sugar
1	teaspoon ground cinnamon
1/2	teaspoon vanilla extract
1/4	teaspoon salt
1/4	teaspoon ground nutmeg
5	cups cubed day-old French bread

WHITE CHOCOLATE SAUCE:

8	ounces white baking chocolate, chopped
1/2	cup heavy whipping cream

In a large bowl, combine the first nine ingredients. Add bread cubes; stir to coat. Let stand for 15 minutes. Transfer to a greased 2-qt. baking dish. Bake, uncovered, at 350° for 50-55 minutes or until a knife inserted near the center comes out clean.

Meanwhile, in a small saucepan, heat white chocolate and cream. Cook and stir over low heat until chocolate is melted. Cool until thickened, about 10 minutes. Serve warm sauce with warm pudding. Refrigerate leftovers.

Strawberry Chocolate Truffles

PREP: 45 MIN. + CHILLING   **YIELD:** 3-1/2 DOZEN

The ever-popular combination of strawberries and chocolate is showcased in these rich, decadent truffles. I often double the recipe and give the extras as gifts.

Pat Habiger ★ Spearville, Kansas

- 4 milk chocolate candy bars (7 ounces *each*), halved
- 1 cup heavy whipping cream
- 1/4 cup strawberry spreadable fruit
- 1-1/2 teaspoons vanilla extract
- 1-1/4 cups chopped almonds, toasted

Place chocolate in a food processor; cover and process until chopped. In a small saucepan, bring cream just to a boil. Pour over chocolate; cover and process until smooth. Stir in spreadable fruit and vanilla until combined. Transfer to a small bowl; cool to room temperature, stirring occasionally. Refrigerate until firm, about 3 hours. Shape into 1-in. balls. Roll in almonds.

TO MAKE AHEAD: These truffles can be made one week before serving. Store in an airtight container in the refrigerator.

Burnt-Sugar Chiffon Cake

PREP: 30 MIN. **BAKE:** 45 MIN. + COOLING
YIELD: 12 SERVINGS

This tall chiffon cake is a favorite when I take it to senior and church functions. The rich, creamy frosting complements every tender slice.

Mrs. LaVaughn Fisher ★ Kingfisher, Oklahoma

3/4	cup sugar
1	cup water

CAKE:

1	cup egg whites (about 7)
2-1/4	cups cake flour
1-1/4	cups sugar
3	teaspoons baking powder
1	teaspoon salt
5	egg yolks
1/2	cup canola oil
6	tablespoons water
1	teaspoon vanilla extract
1/2	teaspoon cream of tartar

FROSTING:

2	tablespoons plus 1/2 cup butter, *divided*
3	tablespoons cake flour
1/2	teaspoon salt
4	cups confectioners' sugar
1/4	cup 2% milk
1	teaspoon vanilla extract

In a small heavy skillet, heat sugar until golden brown. Gradually add water; cook and stir until sugar is dissolved. Set aside.

Let egg whites stand at room temperature for 30 minutes. In a large bowl, combine the flour, sugar, baking powder and salt. In another bowl, whisk the egg yolks, oil, water, vanilla and 6 tablespoons reserved syrup. Add to dry ingredients; beat until well blended. In another bowl, beat egg whites and cream of tartar until stiff peaks form; fold into batter.

Gently spoon into an ungreased 10-in. tube pan. Cut through batter with a knife to remove air pockets. Bake on the lowest oven rack at 325° for 45-50 minutes or until cake springs back when lightly touched. Immediately invert pan; cool completely, about 1 hour.

Run a knife around side and center tube of pan. Remove cake to a serving plate.

For frosting, in a small saucepan, melt 2 tablespoons butter. Stir in flour and salt until smooth; gradually add the remaining syrup mixture. Bring to a boil; cook and stir for 1 minute or until thickened. Transfer to a small bowl; beat in the confectioners' sugar, milk and vanilla. Cool to room temperature.

In a large bowl, beat remaining butter until fluffy, about 5 minutes. Gradually beat in confectioners' sugar mixture. Spread frosting over top and sides of cake.

TO MAKE AHEAD: Cake can be made the day before serving. Store the cake tightly wrapped at room temperature. The remaining caramelized sugar for the frosting can also be stored covered at room temperature overnight.

Mile-High Chiffon

To create tall, impressive chiffon cakes, remove the eggs from the refrigerator, then separate them while they are still cold. Let the whites and the yolks stand at room temperature for 30 minutes to warm up. Eggs are easier to separate when cold, but can obtain more volume when they are beaten at room temperature.

Pomegranate Creme Brulee

PREP: 25 MIN. **BAKE:** 30 MIN. + CHILLING
YIELD: 5 SERVINGS

Creme brulee is a decadent, elegant dessert that I reserve for the holidays and special occasions. This version features the tasty twist of pomegranate.

Ben Rogojan ★ Seattle, Washington

  1/2   cup pomegranate juice
  2/3   cup sugar, *divided*
  3/4   teaspoon lemon juice
    2   cups heavy whipping cream
1-1/2   teaspoons brown sugar
1-1/2   teaspoons water
    6   egg yolks, beaten
    1   teaspoon vanilla extract

TOPPING:

2-1/2   teaspoons sugar
  1/3   cup pomegranate seeds

In a small saucepan, combine the pomegranate juice, 1/3 cup sugar and lemon juice. Bring to a boil over medium heat; cook until liquid is reduced by half. Stir in the cream, brown sugar, water and remaining sugar. Cook until bubbles form around sides of pan.

Remove from the heat; stir a small amount of hot mixture into egg yolks. Return all to the pan, stirring constantly. Stir in vanilla. Transfer to five 4-oz. ramekins. Place cups in a baking pan; add 1 in. of boiling water to pan.

Bake, uncovered, at 325° for 30-35 minutes or until center is just set (mixture will jiggle). Remove ramekins from water bath; cool for 10 minutes. Cover and refrigerate for at least 4 hours.

If using a creme brulee torch, sprinkle custards with sugar. Heat sugar with the torch until caramelized. Sprinkle with pomegranate seeds and serve immediately.

If broiling the custards, place ramekins on a baking sheet; let stand at room temperature for 15 minutes. Sprinkle with sugar. Broil 8 in. from the heat for 4-7 minutes or until sugar is caramelized. Refrigerate for 1-2 hours or until firm. Sprinkle with pomegranate seeds before serving.

Holiday Spirits

PREP: 45 MIN. + STANDING   **YIELD:** 2-1/2 DOZEN

The green color of these chocolate-coated cookies is certain to put you in the Christmas mood. Sprinkling them with crushed candies enhances the minty taste.

Jeannette Buesing ★ Whitmore Lake, Michigan

  1   cup crushed vanilla wafers (about 30 wafers)
  1   cup confectioners' sugar
  1   cup finely chopped walnuts
1/4   cup green creme de menthe
  1   tablespoon light corn syrup
  8   ounces bittersweet chocolate, chopped
  1   teaspoon shortening
Crushed starlight mints, optional

In a large bowl, combine the wafer crumbs, confectioners' sugar, walnuts, creme de menthe and corn syrup. Roll into 3/4-in. balls; place on waxed paper.

In a microwave safe bowl, melt the chocolate and shortening; stir until smooth. Dip balls in chocolate; allow excess to drip off. Return to waxed paper; immediately sprinkle with crushed mints if desired. Let stand until set. Store in an airtight container.

TO MAKE AHEAD: These cookies can be made up to one week in advance. Store in an airtight container in a cool, dry place.

Peanut Butter Custard Blast

PREP: 30 MIN. **COOK TIME:** 25 MIN. + CHILLING
YIELD: 15 SERVINGS

"Ooey, gooey, great!" is how friends and family describe this scrumptious chocolate-peanut butter dessert. I appreciate the make-ahead convenience.

Marilee Evenson ★ Wisconsin Rapids, Wisconsin

2 cups cream-filled chocolate sandwich cookie crumbs
2 tablespoons sugar
1/3 cup butter, melted

FILLING:

1-1/2 cups sugar
1/3 cup cornstarch
2 tablespoons all-purpose flour
1/2 teaspoon salt
6 cups 2% milk
6 egg yolks, beaten
1 cup creamy peanut butter

TOPPING:

2 cups heavy whipping cream
1 tablespoon confectioners' sugar
6 peanut butter cups, chopped
1/2 cup chopped salted peanuts
2 tablespoons chocolate syrup

In a small bowl, combine cookie crumbs and sugar; stir in butter. Press onto the bottom of a greased 13-in. x 9-in. baking dish. Bake at 375° for 8 minutes or until set. Cool on a wire rack.

For filling, in a large saucepan, combine the sugar, cornstarch, flour and salt. Stir in milk until smooth. Cook and stir over medium-high heat until thickened and bubbly. Reduce heat; cook and stir 2 minutes longer.

Remove from the heat. Stir a small amount of hot mixture into egg yolks; return all to pan, stirring constantly. Bring to a gentle boil; cook and stir 2 minutes longer.

Remove from the heat. Stir 1 cup into peanut butter until smooth. Gently stir peanut butter mixture into the pan. Pour over crust. Cool to room temperature. Cover and refrigerate for at least 2 hours.

In a large bowl, beat cream until it begins to thicken. Add confectioners' sugar; beat until stiff peaks form. Spread over peanut butter mixture. Sprinkle with peanut butter cups and peanuts. Drizzle with chocolate syrup.

TO MAKE AHEAD: After peanut butter custard is poured over the crust, refrigerate overnight. Before serving, top with the sweetened whipped cream, peanuts, peanut butter candy and chocolate drizzle.

Cinnamon Pumpkin Truffles

(pictured at left)

PREP: 35 MIN. + CHILLING   **YIELD:** 2 DOZEN

Even novice candy makers can prepare these simple and satisfying confections. The blending of pumpkin and chocolate is wonderful!

Cherie Sechrist ★ Red Lion, Pennsylvania

- 2 cups white baking chips
- 1/4 cup heavy whipping cream
- 1/4 cup canned pumpkin
- 1 teaspoon ground cinnamon
- 1/4 teaspoon ground ginger
- 1/4 teaspoon ground cloves
- 14 ounces dark chocolate candy coating, coarsely chopped
- 2 tablespoons shortening
Chocolate and white sprinkles

In a microwave-safe bowl, microwave white chips with cream until chips are melted; stir until smooth. Add pumpkin and spices. Cover and refrigerate for 2 hours or until almost solid but still workable.

Shape into 1-in. balls. In a microwave, melt candy coating and shortening; stir until smooth. Dip truffles in chocolate mixture; allow excess to drip off. Roll in sprinkles; place on waxed paper-lined baking sheets. Refrigerate for 1-2 hours or until firm.

Store in an airtight container in the refrigerator.

TO MAKE AHEAD: These truffles can be made up to three days before serving.

Maple-Walnut Ice Cream

PREP: 20 MIN. + CHILLING
PROCESS: 20 MIN. + FREEZING   **YIELD:** 1 QUART

When my family has get-togethers, I frequently receive requests to make this scrumptious ice cream. The walnuts make a delicious complement to the maple flavor.

Sandra McKenzie ★ Braham, Minnesota

- 1 cup milk
- 2 eggs, lightly beaten
- 1/2 cup honey
- 2 cups heavy whipping cream, whipped
- 1-1/2 teaspoons maple flavoring
- 1/2 cup chopped walnuts, toasted

In a small saucepan, heat the milk to 175°. Combine eggs and honey. Whisk in a small amount of the hot mixture to the egg mixture. Return all to the pan, whisking constantly. Cook and stir over low heat until mixture reaches at least 160° and coats the back of a metal spoon. Remove from heat.

Cool quickly by placing pan in a bowl of ice water; stir for 2 minutes. Stir in cream and maple flavoring. Press plastic wrap onto surface of custard. Refrigerate for several hours or overnight.

Fill cylinder of ice cream freezer two-thirds full; freeze according to the manufacturer's directions. During the last 5 minutes of processing, add walnuts. When ice cream is frozen, transfer to a freezer container; freeze for 2-4 hours before serving.

Paper Candy Dish Party Favors

Create a festive party favor by filling a handmade paper bowl with cute Christmas candies like Cinnamon Pumpkin Truffles.

Template for the candy dish is on page 90. With a pencil, trace the pattern onto tracing paper. Cut out the pattern on a 6-in. square of heavy, double-sided scrapbook paper. Using an 1/8-in. hole punch, make holes where shown on the pattern. Fold the paper to the wrong side along the broken lines on the pattern; bring up sides to form a box. Starting and ending in the center of one side, thread a 20-in. length of 1/8-in.-wide grosgrain ribbon in and out through punched holes. Tie ribbon ends in a small bow on outside of box. Line the dish with tissue or parchment paper or a paper cupcake liner before filling to prevent oil stains.

Holiday Pumpkin Pie

PREP: 40 MIN. + CHILLING **BAKE:** 35 MIN. + COOLING
YIELD: 8 SERVINGS

With a flaky, from-scratch crust, creamy filling and crunchy sugar topping, this will likely be the best pumpkin pie you've ever tasted! One pie may not be enough to please your family.

Kim Adams Johnson ★ Lincoln, Nebraska

1-1/4 cups all-purpose flour
2-1/4 teaspoons sugar
1/4 teaspoon salt
1/3 cup cold unsalted butter
1 tablespoon plus 1-1/2 teaspoons shortening
2 to 4 tablespoons cold water

FILLING:
1-1/2 cups heavy whipping cream
1/2 cup whole milk
1-1/2 teaspoons ground cinnamon
1/2 teaspoon salt
1/4 teaspoon ground nutmeg
1/8 teaspoon ground ginger
1/8 teaspoon ground cloves
4 egg yolks
1/2 cup sugar
1 can (15 ounces) solid-pack pumpkin

1 teaspoon vanilla extract
3 tablespoons turbinado (washed raw) sugar *or* granulated sugar

In a large bowl, combine the flour, sugar and salt. Cut in butter and shortening until crumbly. Gradually add water, tossing with a fork until dough forms a ball. Wrap in plastic wrap. Refrigerate for 1 hour or until easy to handle.

Roll out pastry to fit a metal 9-in. pie pan. Transfer pastry to pie pan. Trim pastry to 1/2 in. beyond edge of plate; flute edges. Line pastry with a double thickness of heavy-duty foil. Bake at 450° for 8 minutes. Remove foil; bake 5 minutes longer. Cool on a wire rack.

In a large saucepan, heat the cream, milk, cinnamon, salt, nutmeg, ginger and cloves until bubbles form around sides of pan. In a small bowl, whisk egg yolks and sugar. Remove cream mixture from the heat; stir a small amount of hot mixture into egg yolk mixture. Return all to the pan, stirring constantly. Stir in pumpkin and vanilla. Pour into pie shell.

Bake at 350° for 35-45 minutes or until a knife inserted near the center comes out clean. Cool on a wire rack.

If using a creme brulee torch, sprinkle with turbinado sugar. Heat sugar with the torch until caramelized.

If broiling the pie, place pie on a baking sheet. Sprinkle with turbinado sugar. Broil 8 in. from the heat for 4-7 minutes or until sugar is caramelized. Refrigerate leftovers.

Double Chocolate Espresso Cheesecake

PREP: 35 MIN. **BAKE:** 1 HOUR + CHILLING
YIELD: 16 SERVINGS

Every slice of this creamy cheesecake is a standout. The classic pairing of chocolate and coffee is sure to please partygoers.

Cheryl Perry ★ Hertford, North Carolina

1-1/2 cups crushed vanilla wafers (about 45)
1/4 cup butter, melted
2 tablespoons sugar
1/4 teaspoon instant espresso powder

FILLING:

4 packages (8 ounces *each*) cream cheese, softened
1-1/2 cups sugar
1 cup sour cream
1 cup 60% cacao bittersweet chocolate baking chips, melted
1/2 cup baking cocoa
1/4 cup half-and-half cream
1 tablespoon all-purpose flour
5 eggs, lightly beaten
1-1/2 teaspoons instant espresso powder
1 teaspoon vanilla extract

TOPPING:

1 cup coffee liqueur
1 tablespoon half-and-half cream
1 cup heavy whipping cream

2 tablespoons confectioners' sugar
1/2 cup 60% cacao bittersweet chocolate baking chips, chopped
16 chocolate-covered coffee beans

Place a greased 9-in. springform pan on a double thickness of heavy-duty foil (about 18 in. square). Securely wrap foil around pan.

In a large bowl, combine the wafer crumbs, butter, sugar and espresso powder. Press onto the bottom and 1-in. up the sides of prepared pan.

In a large bowl, beat the cream cheese, sugar, sour cream, melted chocolate, cocoa, cream and flour until smooth. Add eggs; beat on low speed just until combined. Stir in the espresso powder and vanilla. Pour into crust. Place springform pan in a large baking pan; add 1 in. of hot water to larger pan.

Bake at 350° for 60-70 minutes or until center is just set and top appears dull. Remove springform pan from water bath. Cool on a wire rack for 10 minutes. Remove foil. Carefully run a knife around edge of pan to loosen; cool 1 hour longer. Refrigerate overnight. Remove sides of pan.

In a small saucepan, combine liqueur and half-and-half. Bring to a boil; cook until liquid is reduced by half. Meanwhile, in a large bowl, beat whipping cream until it begins to thicken. Add confectioners' sugar; beat until stiff peaks form.

Drizzle cheesecake with coffee syrup; garnish with whipped cream, chocolate and coffee beans.

Heavenly Praline Cake

(pictured at left)

PREP: 40 MIN. **BAKE:** 1 HOUR + COOLING
YIELD: 16 SERVINGS (5 CUPS CANDIED PECANS)

A moist cake and generous frosting are filled with the fabulous flavor of caramel. The candied pecans are almost a dessert by themselves!

Jennifer Rodriguez ★ Midland, Texas

```
 1    egg white
 4    cups pecan halves
1/3   cup sugar
1/3   cup packed dark brown sugar
```
CAKE:
```
 1    cup butter, softened
 1    package (8 ounces) cream cheese, softened
 2    cups packed dark brown sugar
 4    eggs
 2    teaspoons vanilla extract
2-1/2 cups all-purpose flour
 1    teaspoon baking powder
1/2   teaspoon baking soda
1/4   teaspoon salt
 1    cup (8 ounces) sour cream
 1    cup chopped pecans, toasted
```
ICING:
```
 1    cup packed dark brown sugar
1/2   cup butter, cubed
1/4   cup 2% milk
 1    cup confectioners' sugar
 1    teaspoon vanilla extract
```

In a large bowl, beat egg white until foamy. Add pecan halves; stir gently to coat. Combine sugar and brown sugar; add to pecan mixture and stir gently to coat.

Spread into two greased 15-in. x 10-in. x 1-in. baking pans. Bake at 325° for 18-22 minutes, stirring once. Cool. Store in an airtight container.

Meanwhile, in a large bowl, cream the butter, cream cheese and brown sugar until light and fluffy. Add eggs, one at a time, beating well after each addition. Beat in vanilla. Combine the flour, baking powder, baking soda and salt; add to the creamed mixture alternately with sour cream, beating well after each addition. Stir in chopped pecans.

Transfer to a greased and floured 10-in. fluted tube pan. Bake at 325° for 60-70 minutes or until a toothpick inserted near the center comes out clean. Cool for 10 minutes before removing from pan to a wire rack to cool completely.

In a small saucepan, combine brown sugar, butter and milk. Bring to a boil; cook and stir 1 minute longer. Remove from the heat; stir in confectioners' sugar and vanilla until smooth. Drizzle over cake. Serve with candied pecans.

TO MAKE AHEAD: The sugared nuts can be made a week in advance. Store tightly in an airtight container. The cake can be made a day in advance. Store, covered, at room temperature.

Caramel Apple Trifle Delight

PREP/TOTAL TIME: 25 MIN.
YIELD: 24 SERVINGS (2/3 CUP EACH)

Bring the popular taste of caramel apples to a terrific trifle brimming with pudding, pie filling and pound cake. English toffee bits add a delicious crunch.

Helen Fields ★ Springtown, Texas

```
 4    cups cold milk
 2    packages (3.4 ounces each) instant vanilla pudding mix
 2    cans (21 ounces each) apple pie filling
 1    cup English toffee bits
1/2   cup packed brown sugar
 1    teaspoon ground cinnamon
 1    loaf (16 ounces) frozen pound cake, thawed and cut
      into 1-inch cubes
1-1/4 cups caramel ice cream topping
1-1/2 cups heavy whipping cream, whipped
1/2   cup finely chopped walnuts, toasted
```
Additional caramel ice cream topping

In a large bowl, whisk milk and pudding mixes for 2 minutes. Let stand for 2 minutes or until soft-set. In another bowl, combine the pie filling, toffee bits, brown sugar and cinnamon.

In a 4-qt. trifle bowl or glass bowl, layer half of the cake cubes, pudding, apple mixture, ice cream topping, whipped cream and walnuts. Repeat layers; drizzle with additional ice cream topping. Chill until serving.

Banana-Hazelnut Cake

PREP: 40 MIN. **BAKE:** 25 MIN. + COOLING
YIELD: 12 SERVINGS

Special occasions call for outstanding desserts that take a little more time to prepare. I often bake and freeze the cake layers weeks in advance and thaw before assembling.

Trisha Kruse ★ Eagle, Idaho

3/4	cup butter, softened
2	cups sugar
3	eggs
2	teaspoons vanilla extract
1-1/2	cups mashed ripe bananas (3 to 4 medium)
1-1/2	cups buttermilk
1	tablespoon brandy *or* unsweetened apple juice
3	cups all-purpose flour
1	teaspoon baking soda
1/4	teaspoon salt

FILLING:

1-1/2	cups semisweet chocolate chips
3/4	cup heavy whipping cream
1/2	cup finely chopped hazelnuts, toasted

FROSTING:

2-1/4	cups heavy whipping cream
1/2	cup confectioners' sugar
1/2	cup finely chopped hazelnuts, toasted
12	hazelnuts

In a large bowl, cream butter and sugar until light and fluffy, about 5 minutes. Add eggs, one at a time, beating well after each addition. Beat in vanilla. In a small bowl, combine the bananas, buttermilk and brandy. Combine the flour, baking soda and salt; add to the creamed mixture alternately with banana mixture. Beat just until combined.

Transfer to three greased and floured 9-in. round baking pans. Bake at 350° for 25-30 minutes or until a toothpick inserted near the center comes out clean. Cool for 10 minutes before removing cakes from pans to wire racks to cool completely.

For filling, place chocolate chips in a small bowl. In a small saucepan, bring cream just to a boil. Pour over chocolate; whisk until smooth. Refrigerate until chilled. In a small bowl, beat chocolate mixture until soft peaks form, about 15 seconds. Fold in hazelnuts.

For frosting, in a large bowl, beat cream until it begins to thicken. Add confectioners' sugar; beat until soft peaks form. Fold in chopped hazelnuts.

Place one cake layer on a serving plate; spread with half of the chocolate mixture. Repeat layers. Top with remaining cake layer. Spread frosting over the top and sides of cake. Garnish with whole hazelnuts. Refrigerate until serving.

Deck THE HALLS

Glue gun and glue sticks

Standard sewing supplies

DIRECTIONS:

1. Enlarge mitten pattern below 200%. Trace onto tracing paper with pencil.

2. Cut out two mitten pieces from 7-in. x 4-1/2-in. piece of Polarfleece, reversing one.

3. With right sides facing and edges matching, sew around mitten with a 1/4-in. seam, leaving straight edge open where shown on pattern. Clip curves.

4. Turn mitten right side out and stuff firmly with stuffing.

5. For cuff, fold long edges of 2-in. x 5-in. piece of Polarfleece to wrong side with edges meeting in the center to make a 1-in. x 5-in. piece. Glue as needed to hold.

6. Fold cuff piece in half crosswise and mark fold. Pin cuff right side out to top of mitten with fold mark centered on front of mitten and short ends meeting at the back.

7. Glue cuff around top of mitten, overlapping the top edge of the mitten about 1/2 in. Let dry.

8. For hanging loop, stitch a length of metallic cord to opposite sides of cuff.

9. Glue leaves and berries to inside of mitten. Let dry.

10. Hand-sew charm to center front of cuff.

Merry Mitten Ornaments

CRAFT LEVEL: QUICK & EASY

FINISHED SIZE: Each mitten ornament measures about 3-1/2 inches across x 5 inches high without hanging loop.

Looking for a creative way to use up all those scraps of fleece and bits of Christmas greenery? Wrap up your tree with these pretty mitten ornaments. They're so quick and fun to make. Just add whatever you have on hand for a special sparkle.

Bette Veinot ★ Bridgewater, Nova Scotia

MATERIALS (FOR ONE):

Pattern at right

Tracing paper and pencil

7-inch x 4-1/2-inch piece of solid or print Polarfleece in color of choice for mitten

2-inch x 5-inch piece of contrasting solid or print Polarfleece for cuff

Thread to match fabrics

Polyester stuffing

Metallic cord for hanging loop

Coordinating small artificial berries and leaves for top of mitten

Cinnamon stick

2010 charm

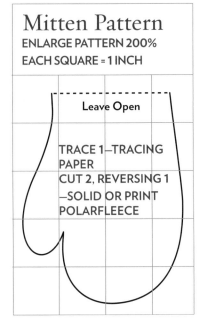

Mitten Pattern

ENLARGE PATTERN 200%
EACH SQUARE = 1 INCH

Leave Open

TRACE 1—TRACING PAPER

CUT 2, REVERSING 1 —SOLID OR PRINT POLARFLEECE

Retro Christmas Scene

Do you have an assortment of ornaments from decades ago (such as the Shiny Brites shown here) that you dare not hang on the tree in case they fall and break? Don't keep those beautiful baubles under wraps where no one can enjoy them.

Take holiday guests on a trip down memory lane by displaying those treasured ornaments in a retro-style tablescape.

Deck the dinner table in your finest linens, china and silverware. Then sprinkle artificial snow down the center to create a frosty scene. Place pretty ornaments inside assorted stemware.

Miniature bottle-brush trees easily complete the reminiscent, wintry wonderland.

Simple Snowflake Wreath

CRAFT LEVEL: QUICK & EASY

FINISHED SIZE: Wreath measures about 14 inches across.

Wrap a long feather boa from the craft store around a plain foam wreath, and you'll have the foundation for this winter-white delight. Silvery sequins on pins fill the wreath with shiny snow crystals, and a metallic wire-edged ribbon tops it all off.

Taste of Home Craft Editor

MATERIALS:

12-inch smooth white Styrofoam wreath form

White feather boa to cover wreath

Straight pins with silver ball heads

Silver snowflake sequins

Silver-lined bugle beads

3 yards of 1-1/2-inch-wide silver metallic wire-edged ribbon

Measuring tape

Scissors

DIRECTIONS:

1. Wrap the Styrofoam wreath form with the white feather boa, covering the wreath form completely. Pin the ends of the boa in place to hold it securely.

2. Place a silver snowflake sequin on a straight pin. Add one or two silver-lined bugle beads to the pin to prevent the sequin from falling into the boa. Insert the pin into the front of the wrapped Styrofoam wreath form where desired.

3. In the same way, add more sequins to the front of the wreath where desired.

4. For the ribbon hanger, cut a 24-in. length of silver metallic wire-edge ribbon. Loop the ribbon around the top of the wreath and tie the ribbon ends together. Use scissors to trim the ends.

5. Tie the remaining ribbon piece into a bow around the ribbon hanger on the wreath. Trim ends of bow as desired.

Clay roller

Craft knife

Stylus

Ruler

Sculpey Satin Glaze

Small flat paintbrush

Foam plate or palette

Candles—two tea light candles and one 3-inch pillar candle in color of choice

DIRECTIONS:

1. Trace patterns onto tracing paper with pencil.

2. Cut out each shape.

LARGE POINSETTIA CANDLEHOLDER:

Leaves:

1. Condition a large walnut-size piece of Clover clay.

2. Roll the clay to a 1/8-in. thickness.

3. Place the large leaf/bract pattern on the clay and use craft knife to cut out leaf shape. Repeat as needed to make three leaves.

4. Referring to Fig. 1 at right, place the leaves in a circle as shown with the wide points just touching.

5. Use stylus to draw veins on the leaves.

Bracts:

1. Condition a pea-size piece of Blush clay and a large walnut-size piece of Buttercream clay. Roll each color of clay into a long rope. Twist the ropes of clay together and roll them into a ball. Work the ball until the clay is mottled as shown in the photo at left.

2. Roll the clay to a 1/8-in. thickness.

3. Place the large leaf/bract pattern on the clay and use craft knife to cut out shape. Repeat, cutting out as many bracts as possible from the clay.

4. Repeat steps 1-3 until you have cut out 9 large bracts.

5. Use stylus to draw veins on the bracts.

6. Referring to Fig. 1 at right, place the bracts in a circle as shown.

Poinsettia Candleholders

CRAFT LEVEL: BEGINNER

FINISHED SIZE: Large candleholder measures about 9 inches across. Small candleholders measure about 5-1/2 inches across.

Transform ordinary oven-bake clay into pretty poinsettia petals that hold an assortment of candle sizes.

Taste of Home Craft Editor

MATERIALS (FOR ALL):

Patterns on page 179

Tracing paper and pencil

Scissors

Oven-bake clay—one 2.8-ounce package of Clover, one 2.8-ounce package of Blush and three 2.8-ounce packages of Buttercream (Studio by Sculpey clay shown)

Foil-lined baking tray

Clay oven

  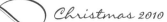

7. Press the center of the overlapped clay pieces together, in a 3-1/2-in. circle. Gently lift and shape the bracts as shown in the photo, leaving a 3-1/2-in. circle for the candle in the center.

8. Place assembled poinsettia on a foil-lined baking tray.

SMALL POINSETTIA CANDLEHOLDER (make 2):

Leaves:

1. Repeat steps 1-5 of instructions for large poinsettia candleholder, using small leaf/bract pattern at far lower right instead.

Bracts:

1. Repeat steps 1-5 of instructions for large poinsettia candleholder, using small leaf/bract pattern.

2. Press the overlapped clay together, leaving a 1-1/2-in. circle in the center. Gently lift and shape the bracts as shown in the photo, leaving a 1-1/2-in. circle for the tea light in the center.

3. Place assembled poinsettias on foil-lined baking trays.

Finishing:

1. Bake each candleholder at 275° for 30 minutes or as directed by clay manufacturer. Let cool.

2. Use small flat brush to apply satin glaze to each candleholder. Let dry.

3. Place candles in each candleholder.

Large Poinsettia
Large Leaf/Bract Pattern

TRACE 1—TRACING PAPER
CUT 3—CLOVER CLAY
CUT 9—MOTTLED BUTTERCREAM AND BLUSH CLAY

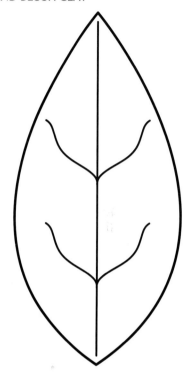

FIG. 1
Leaf Placement for Large and Small Candleholders

Small Poinsettia
Small Leaf/Bract Pattern

TRACE 1—TRACING PAPER
CUT 6—CLOVER CLAY
CUT 18—MOTTLED BUTTERCREAM AND BLUSH CLAY

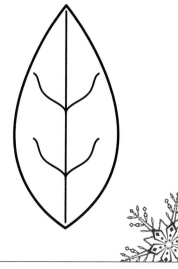

Countdown to Christmas

The month before Christmas is a hectic time of year that is filled with parties, school recitals, shopping, baking and so much more. Planning is the key to keeping the holidays stress-free. Here is a general checklist for the Yuletide season to help keep you organized. Feel free to adjust the checklist to suit your family's needs.

4 WEEKS BEFORE CHRISTMAS
Mark your calendar for all school activities and social events.
Write Christmas letter for cards.
Purchase cards and stamps.
Create Christmas card list and starting writing!
Decorate the outside of your home.
Write out a gift-shopping list.
Plan your holiday parties and send out invitations.

3 WEEKS BEFORE CHRISTMAS
Purchase any decorations.
Start your holiday baking with goodies that freeze well.
Purchase holiday wrapping supplies if needed.
Shop for gifts and wrap them.
Start decorating the house.

2 WEEKS BEFORE CHRISTMAS
Mail any gifts that need to be sent.
Plan the Christmas menu (breakfast and dinner).
Purchase a fresh tree, if using.
Buy stocking stuffers and candy.
Finish decorating the house.
Finishing writing and sending Christmas cards.

1 WEEK BEFORE CHRISTMAS
Write a grocery list for the holiday menus.
Finish the holiday baking.
Purchase nonperishable groceries.
Check battery and camera supplies.

CHRISTMAS WEEK
Finish last-minute shopping.
Purchase flowers and/or assemble a centerpiece.
Check, clean and iron table linens.
Do advance meal preparation for Christmas Day.

WEEK AFTER CHRISTMAS
Write thank-you notes.
Replace Christmas cards, gift bags, wrapping paper and ribbon as needed.
Purchase discounted seasonal serving dishes, towels, tablecloths or decorations to store for next year.

traditional heart for ears. Glue wiggle eyes to larger heart. Glue larger heart to front of yarn ball.

8. String gold bell onto ribbon and tie a bow. Trim ends to desired length. Glue bow to front of sheep.

9. For hanging loop, pull thread under a few strands of yarn at top of sheep and tie the ends in an overhand knot.

Crafter's Note: The directions call for a bulky-weight yarn to shape the sheep's body. If you'd like to use a lighter weight, you'll need additional yardage—as much as it takes for the ball to measure 2 in. across. Instead of choosing yarn that looks like mohair, try other textures such as boucle or chenille. You can replace the felt for the ears, face and tail with 1-in.-high x 1-in.-wide x 1/8-in.-thick wooden hearts (face) and 1-in.-high x 1/2-in.-wide x 1/8-in.-thick wooden primitive hearts (ears and tail).

Fluffy Sheep Ornament

CRAFT LEVEL: QUICK & EASY

FINISHED SIZE: Sheep ornament measures about 2-3/8 inches high x 2-1/2 inches long x 2 inches wide.

I created these sheep for Christmas trees as part of our family tradition. Every December I make an original ornament for each of our three children. When the kids are grown and leave home, I'll present them with a box of the trims I've crafted over the years.

Joyce Keklock ★ Archbald, Pennsylvania

MATERIALS:

Patterns on this page

Tracing paper and pencil

1-1/2-inch x 3-inch piece of stiffened black felt

Four 1/2-inch-high x 1/2-inch-wide wooden spools

Black acrylic paint

Small flat paintbrush

12 yards of white bulky-weight acrylic yarn (Lion Brand Jiffy yarn shown)

3/8-inch-high gold liberty bell

8-inch length of red 1/8-inch-wide satin ribbon

10-inch length of thread for hanger

Two 1/4-inch wiggle eyes

Glue gun and glue stick

Scissors

DIRECTIONS:

1. Trace patterns onto tracing paper with pencil.

2. Cut out three primitive hearts for ears and tail and one traditional heart for face from stiffened black felt.

3. Paint each wood spool black. Add coats as needed for complete coverage. Let dry.

4. Wind yarn into a 2-in. ball. Glue the end in place to secure. Let dry.

5. Referring to photo for position, use glue gun to attach the flat end of each spool to bottom of yarn ball for legs.

6. Turn one primitive heart upside down and glue it onto the back of the yarn ball for sheep's tail.

7. Referring to photo, turn each remaining heart upside down and glue the primitive hearts to the front of the

Sheep Patterns
TRACE 1 EACH PIECE—
TRACING PAPER

Traditional Heart
CUT 1—BLACK STIFFENED FELT

Primitive Heart
CUT 3—BLACK STIFFENED FELT

Checkerboard Tree Skirt

CRAFT LEVEL: INTERMEDIATE

FINISHED SIZE: Tree skirt measures about 32 inches square.

The checkerboard look of this tree skirt comes from napped fabric, which reflects the light differently when the squares are turned in opposite directions. Compared to round tree skirts, the rectangular shape makes it easier to lay flat around the base of the tree.

Taste of Home Craft Editor

MATERIALS:

1-1/8 yards of 44-inch-wide napped fabric (lightweight rayon upholstery fabric shown—see crafter's note)

1-1/4 yards of 44-inch-wide coordinating fabric for lining

Matching all-purpose thread

Rotary cutter and mat (optional)

Quilter's ruler

4 yards of coordinating bead trim

Standard sewing supplies

DIRECTIONS:

Cutting:

1. From napped fabric, cut sixty-four 5-in. squares.

2. From lining fabric, cut four 17-in. squares.

Piecing:

Do all piecing with right sides of fabrics facing and a 1/2-in. seam. Finger press seams to one side. Do not press napped fabric with an iron.

1. Place the napped fabric squares right side up on a flat surface in four rows with four squares in each row. Rotate every other square one-half turn to make a checkerboard pattern throughout as shown in layout diagram at right. Repeat with remaining fabric squares to make four sections.

2. Sew squares A-D in Rows 1-4 in each section together as planned.

3. Sew the rows in each section together, carefully matching all corners to form left front, right front, left back and right back sections.

4. Sew left and right front sections together along squares A and D to form a rectangle.

5. Sew the left back section to the top left edge of the front section.

6. Sew the right back section to the top right edge of the back section to form a square. Do not sew sections together along the center.

Lining:

1. With right sides facing and a 1/2-in. seam, sew two of the lining squares together to form a rectangle.

2. In the same way, sew one square to the top left side and the remaining square to the top right side to make a piece identical to the pieced tree skirt.

3. Pin the lining to the pieced tree skirt with right sides facing and edges matching.

4. Draw a circle in the center of the tree skirt to accommodate the trunk of your tree. Sew around the circle and then continue sewing around the outside edges of the tree skirt with a 1/2-in. seam, leaving an opening for turning along one short edge.

5. Cut circular opening for tree trunk, leaving a narrow seam. Clip into seam as needed to make a smooth circle.

6. Turn tree skirt right side out through opening. Turn raw edges of opening in and hand-sew opening closed.

Finishing:

1. Finger press edges as needed.

2. Hand-sew band of trim to wrong side of tree skirt, leaving beads extending beyond the edge.

Crafter's Note: The tree skirt could also be made from two different fabrics. Just cut thirty-two 5-in. squares each from the two fabrics and alternate the squares in a checkerboard pattern.

TREE SKIRT LAYOUT DIAGRAM

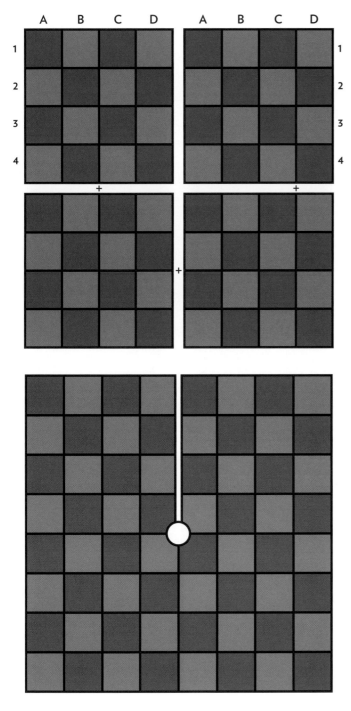

Chandelier Christmas Wreath

With an exquisite wreath and sparkling ornaments hanging in mid-air, your guests will focus on your beautifully set dining room table from the moment they walk in.

Buy an artificial pine wreath. Fluff out pine boughs to completely cover wreath form.

Decorate wreath with strands of inexpensive crystal beads or plastic beads that look like crystals. Secure the beads to wreath with florist's wire.

Hang the wreath from the chandelier securely with four or five strands of fishing line. Make sure the wreath is level, hanging 12 to 15 in. below the chandelier. Attach organdy ribbons from the wreath to the chandelier to cover the fishing line.

Hang an assortment of crystal ornaments (five to seven) from the wreath using organdy ribbon.

Standout Seasonal Seating

Most folks only focus on decorating their table for Christmas dinner, but you can also add an embellishment to the back of dining room chairs. Simply tie a wire-edge metallic-print ribbon into large multi-loop bows. (See "Making a Multi-Loop Bow" below.) What better way to draw guests to the table for an inviting holiday dinner?

Making a Multi-Loop Bow

1. Make loops of ribbon, alternating them up and down and twisting the ribbon as needed to keep the right side out.

2. Pinch the center of the ribbon together and wrap a small loop of ribbon (with the right side out) around your thumb for the center of the bow.

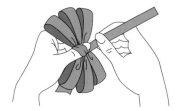

3. Make the same number of loops as before to complete the bow. Then thread a length of ribbon or craft wire through the small center loop and fasten it to secure the bow.

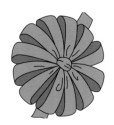

No-Sew Table Runner

CRAFT LEVEL: QUICK & EASY

FINISHED SIZE: Runner measures about 12 inches wide x 36 inches long.

Cute Christmas table runners at the store can be costly…and sometimes the color scheme just doesn't work for your home. You can create your own coordinating table runner by weaving together inexpensive ribbon!

Taste of Home Craft Editor

MATERIALS:

12-inch x 36-inch piece of one-sided fusible fleece or heavy fusible interfacing for base of runner

8-3/4 yards of 1-1/2-inch-wide white grosgrain ribbon cut into eight 38-inch lengths

9-1/2 yards of 1-1/2-inch-wide red-and-white polka dot ribbon cut into twenty-four 14-inch lengths

Two 12-inch lengths and two 36-inch lengths of 1/2-inch-wide no-sew paper-backed fusible web

14-inch x 38-inch piece of coordinating cotton fabric for backing

13-1/2-inch x 37-1/2-inch piece of paper-backed fusible web

Quilter's ruler

Rotary cutter and mat (optional)

Iron and ironing surface

Straight pins

DIRECTIONS:

Woven Front:

1. Place 12-in. x 36-in. piece of one-sided fusible fleece or heavy fusible interfacing for base of runner, non-fusible side up on no-stick ironing surface.

2. With long edges matching, fuse 1/2-in.-wide strips of paper-backed fusible web to matching edges of one-sided fusible fleece or heavy fusible interfacing. Remove paper from one short edge only.

3. With right side of ribbon up, align the ends of the eight 38-in. lengths of the white grosgrain ribbon along short edge of the base. Fuse ends in place.

4. Remove paper backing from one long edge and align the 14-in. lengths of red-and white polka dot ribbon along the long edge as before. Fuse the ends in place.

5. Carefully turn base over.

6. Fold ribbon ends over base to front of runner.

7. Weave ribbon pieces in an over-one, under-one pattern, keeping edges square and close together. Fuse ribbons in place.

8. Fold ends of ribbon to back, pinning as needed to hold. Remove paper backing from remaining short edge and

fuse ribbon ends in place. Repeat along remaining long edge.

Backing:

1. Center and fuse paper-backed fusible to web to wrong side of backing fabric. Let cool.

2. Trim fused backing fabric to a 11-3/4-in. x 35-3/4-in. piece. Remove paper.

3. Place fused backing fabric centered right side up on wrong side of woven runner. Fuse the backing to back of woven runner.

8.
Glue remaining flaps of top section to top flaps of center ring. Then glue remaining flaps of bottom section to bottom flaps of center ring.

9.
Glue ends of cord inside center top of ornament for hanging loop.

Ornament Patterns
Triangles
TRACE 1—TRACING PAPER
CUT 1—LIGHTWEIGHT CARDBOARD

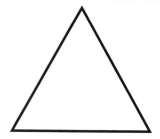

Circles
TRACE 1—TRACING PAPER
CUT 1—LIGHTWEIGHT CARDBOARD
CUT 20—SCRAPBOOK PAPER

Paper Globe Ornaments

CRAFT LEVEL: QUICK & EASY

FINISHED SIZE: Ornament measures about 3 inches across.

Ever wonder what to do with all of those scraps of pretty Christmas scrapbook papers? Here's a perfect way to recycle them—as delightful tree ornaments! It's so simple that even youngsters (with a little help from an adult) will have a ball making the tree trims.

Alma Barkman ★ Winnipeg, Manitoba

MATERIALS (FOR EACH):

Patterns at right

Tracing paper and pencil

Scrap of lightweight cardboard for templates

Scrapbook paper

1-1/2-inch circle punch (optional)

6-inch length of coordinating cord for hanging loop

Transparent tape

Zip Dry Paper Glue

Scissors

DIRECTIONS:

1. Trace triangle pattern at right onto tracing paper.

2. Tape pattern onto lightweight cardboard. Cut out shape on traced lines for template.

3. Punch out 20 circles from scrapbook paper or trace and cut 20 circles from pattern at right.

4. Center triangle template over right side of a circle. Fold the outside edges of circle upright around triangle template, creating a triangle shape with flaps. See Fig. 1 at right. Repeat with remaining circles.

5. Place five circles right side up on a flat surface with one point of each triangle pointing toward the center and wrong sides of flaps touching as shown in Fig. 2 at right.

6. Apply a small amount of glue to wrong side of flaps and glue flaps together with edges matching to make a dome shape for top of ornament. Repeat, using five circles for bottom dome of ornament.

7. Position 10 circles on a flat surface with points of triangles alternating up and down as shown in Fig. 3 at right. Glue flaps together that are touching to make a strip. Then glue end flaps together to make a ring for the center of ornament.

FIG. 1
Forming triangles

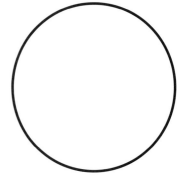

FIG. 2
Making top and bottom dome

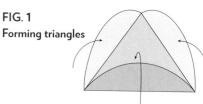

FIG. 3
Making center strip

Barbed Star

CRAFT LEVEL: QUICK & EASY

FINISHED SIZE: Star ornament measures about 7 inches wide x 7 inches high without hanging loop.

Made from rusted barbed wire, this star holds special meaning for me. My mother and I made them for a family reunion.

Robin Kile ★ Franklin, West Virginia

MATERIALS:

Five 7-inch-long pieces of rusty barbed wire (same size sticks could also be used)

Work gloves

3-ply jute string

Glue gun and glue stick

Gloss spray varnish

1/2-inch x 15-inch torn strip of cream-and-red plaid fabric

12-inch length of wired berry garland

Ruler

Scissors

DIRECTIONS:

Refer to Fig. 1 at lower right while making star as instructed. Wear gloves to protect your hands.

1. Stack two pieces of barbed wire with ends even. Wrap jute string several times around them about 1/2 in. from top. Knot securely and cut excess jute string.

2. With bottom ends even, place another piece of barbed wire on top of barbed wire piece on the right. Slip newly added barbed wire piece under piece on the left. Tie as before.

3. In the same way, place fourth barbed wire piece on the newly added piece, making sure it is under the barbed wire piece on the right. Tie as before.

4. Add fifth barbed wire piece to the right-hand end of the piece just added. All pieces should cross in the center in an over-under pattern. Tie as before.

5. Cut a 12-in. length of jute string and knot ends together for hanging loop. Place loop through top star point and thread knot through loop. Pull on knotted end to form hanging loop.

6. Add a bit of glue to each knot on back to secure. Let dry.

7. Following manufacturer's instructions, spray star with gloss varnish. Let dry.

8. Wrap berry garland around your finger to coil. Glue garland to front of star as shown.

9. Tie torn fabric strip into a bow and glue to star.

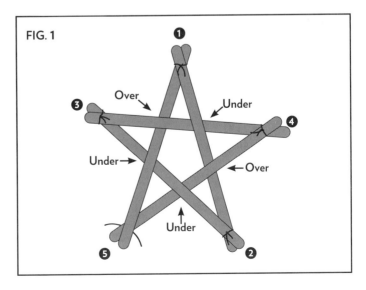

FIG. 1

Frosted Snowman

CRAFT LEVEL: QUICK & EASY

FINISHED SIZE: Snowman measures about 7 inches wide x 9 inches high.

This cute character will melt hearts during the holidays and keep your home brimming with cheer well into the New Year. The entire project can be completed in a few hours.

Taste of Home Craft Editor

MATERIALS:

Patterns on page 189

Tracing paper and pencil

9-inch x 12-inch piece of black felt for hat

Black all-purpose thread

Men's white over-the-calf tube sock

3-inch Styrofoam ball for snowman's head

Firm roll of toilet tissue for snowman's body

Clear plastic wrap to cover roll of toilet tissue

6-inch length of string or twist tie

Two black glass straight pins or small black beads for eyes

Three black buttons

1-1/4-inch-long piece of 1/4-inch wooden dowel for nose

Sandpaper

Small flat paintbrush

Orange acrylic paint

3/4-inch-wide x 20-inch-long torn strip of red print fabric for scarf

1/4-inch-wide x 7-1/2-inch-long strip of red fabric or ribbon for trim on hat

10-inch-length of 1/8-inch-wide green satin ribbon for bow on hat

Two 1/2-inch-long pinecones for trim on hat

Two small twigs for arms

Textured snow medium

Spray glitter or snow (optional)

Glue gun and glue sticks

Snowman accessories of your choice (artificial Christmas tree made from wired pine garland shown)

Standard sewing supplies

DIRECTIONS:

Hat:

1. Trace hat top and hat brim patterns onto tracing paper with pencil as directed on patterns.

2. Cut a hat top and hat brim piece from black felt. Also cut a 2-in.-wide x 7-1/4-in.-long piece from black felt for center band of hat.

3. Sew narrow ends of center band of hat together with a 1/4-in. seam to make a tube. Finger-press seam open.

4. With right sides facing and a 1/4-in. seam, sew one edge of band piece to hat top piece.

5. With right sides facing, sew opposite edge of band piece to inside edge of hat brim piece in the same way.

6. Turn hat right side out.

Snowman:

1. Sand one end of wooden dowel piece to make a cone shape for nose. Paint dowel piece orange for nose. Let dry.

2. Wrap roll of toilet tissue with clear plastic wrap.

3. Slip wrapped tissue roll into top of sock.

4. Insert Styrofoam ball into top of sock for head. Pull sock up to cover ball.

5. Push foot end of sock into opening on opposite end of tissue roll.

6. Adjust sock as needed so knit design of sock is straight and is the same over the roll of tissue and the snowman's head.

7. Tie top of sock together on top of head with string or twist tie. Glue as needed to hold. Trim excess sock if desired.

Assembly:

1. Glue felt hat to top of snowman's head.

2. Wrap narrow band of fabric or ribbon around hat near brim. Overlap ends in back and trim excess. Spot-glue as needed to hold trim in place.

3. Tie green ribbon into a small bow. Glue bow to hat where desired and pinecones to center of bow.

4. Glue black beads to snowman's head or insert black glass straight pins into head and glue in place for eyes.

5. Cut a tiny hole in the front of head below eyes for nose. Apply glue to the flat end of the snowman's nose and insert nose into hole.

6. Glue buttons down front of snowman.

7. Tie fabric for scarf around snowman's neck. Trim ends as desired. Spot-glue scarf to snowman as needed to hold.

8. Glue trims and accessories to snowman where desired.

9. Apply textured snow to hat, nose, buttons and accessories as desired. Let dry.

10. Spray snowman with glitter or snow if desired. Let dry.

Sock Snowman Patterns

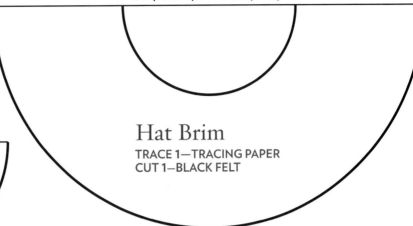

Trace, flop and repeat for complete pattern

Hat Brim
TRACE 1—TRACING PAPER
CUT 1—BLACK FELT

Trace, flop and repeat for complete pattern

Hat Top
TRACE 1—TRACING PAPER
CUT 1—BLACK FELT

"C" is for Christmas Wreath

CRAFT LEVEL: BEGINNER

FINISHED SIZE: Wreath measures about 9 inches across x 12 inches high.

You'll spell out fun when you assemble this delightfully different accent. A decoupaged papier-mache "C" forms the wreath, covered with purchased words that describe the holiday season.

Taste of Home Craft Editor

MATERIALS:

Papier-mache letter "C"

Green tissue paper

White craft glue

Water

Small container

1-inch foam brush

Scrapbook words of your choice

18-inch length of 2-inch-wide red satin ribbon

DIRECTIONS:

1. Make a mixture of half white glue and half water in small container.

2. Tear tissue paper into small squares.

3. Use foam brush to apply glue mixture to a small area of the letter.

4. Add a square of tissue and brush over it with more glue mixture.

5. Continue to add tissue paper in the same way, covering the front and sides of the letter. Let dry.

6. Glue scrapbook words to front of letter. Let dry.

7. Loop a length of ribbon around the top of the letter and tie the ends together to form a hanging loop.

"P" is for Personalizing

Instead of the letter "C," create this wreath with the first letter of your last name. By changing the background color and scrapbook words, you can make a door display for each season of the year.

4. Each square on the chart represents one set of fabric threads surrounded by four holes. Each stitch is worked over one set of threads with the needle passing through the holes.

5. The color and/or symbol inside each square on the chart, along with the color key, tells which color of six-strand embroidery floss to use to make the cross-stitch. Wide lines on the chart show where to work backstitches. See color key for French knot symbol. See Fig. 1 at right for stitch illustrations.

6. Use 18-in. lengths of six-strand embroidery floss. Longer strands tend to tangle and fray.

7. Separate the strands and thread the needle with one strand for the cross-stitched Christmas tree garland and two strands for all remaining cross-stitches. Use two strands for the French knots and one strand for all backstitches.

8. To begin stitching, leave a 1-in. tail of embroidery floss on back of work and hold tail in place while working the first few stitches over it.

9. To end stitching, run the needle under a few stitches in back before clipping the embroidery floss close to work.

Cross-Stitched Santa

CRAFT LEVEL: BEGINNER

FINISHED SIZE: Cross-stitched design area is 40 stitches wide x 44 stitches high. Excluding hanging loop, ornament measures 3-3/8 inches wide x 3-5/8 inches high.

Every Christmas, a friend of mine has a lovely hand-painted Santa Claus to give to my family. I'm only too happy to make one of my own designs to share with her. My latest creation shows Kris Kringle stuffing a stocking by a tree—and includes metallic threads for sparkle.

Penny Duff ★ Kennebunk, Maine

MATERIALS:

Chart on page 191

Two 6-inch squares of off-white 14-count Aida cloth

DMC six-strand embroidery floss in colors listed on color key

Size 24 tapestry needle

Polyester stuffing

Scissors

DIRECTIONS:

Cross-Stitching:

1. Zigzag or overcast the edges of both pieces of Aida cloth to prevent fraying.

2. Fold one piece of Aida cloth in half lengthwise, then fold it in half crosswise and mark where the folds intersect.

3. Draw lines across the chart connecting opposite arrows. Begin counting where the lines intersect to locate the first stitch of the top row, then locate the same spot on the Aida cloth and begin stitching there for a centered design.

Assembly:

1. When all stitching is complete, and only if necessary, gently wash the stitched piece in lukewarm water. Press right side down on a terry towel to dry.

2. Place the stitched piece right side up on top of the unstitched piece of Aida cloth with edges even.

3. With unseparated white floss, join the pieces with a running stitch, stitching through every other square one square outside the entire backstitched border and stuffing ornament as you stitch.

4. Trim the excess Aida cloth, cutting through both layers two squares out from the white running stitch.

5. Thread the needle with a 9-in. length of unseparated gold metallic floss. On back of the ornament, stitch in and out of one square at each top corner. Remove needle and knot ends together to form a hanging loop.

CROSS-STITCHED SANTA CHART

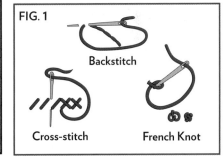

COLOR KEY	DMC
⊡ White	
◉ Light Shell Pink	224
▣ Medium Holiday Red	304
▣ Black	310
▣ Dark Pistachio Green	367
◉ Pearl Gray	415
▪ Very Light Brown	435
◻ Light Tan	437
✳ Light Old Gold	676
✖ Medium Garnet	815
● Medium Beige Brown	840
■ Dark Antique Blue	930
◙ Light Antique Blue	932
▧ Very Light Peach	948
▨ Gold Metallic (1 strand)	5282
BACKSTITCH	
▬ Black (1 strand)	310
▬ Red Metallic (1 strand)	5270
FRENCH KNOT	
⑤ Black (2 strands)	310

FIG. 1

Backstitch

Cross-stitch   French Knot

Christmas Countdown Chalkboard

CRAFTING LEVEL: QUICK & EASY

FINISHED SIZE: Frame shown measures 11 inches high x 13 inches wide with a 7-1/2-inch-high x 9-1/2-inch-wide opening.

Keep the kids' excited minds occupied by having them count down the days until Santa arrives on this clever chalkboard that starts with a basic picture frame.

Taste of Home Craft Editor

MATERIALS:

White flat picture frame with 7-1/2-inch x 9-1/2-inch opening and glass

Black chalkboard spray

Newspaper

Assorted stickers to decorate the frame

White chalk

White paint-writer or white paint and small round paintbrush

6-inch length of 16-gauge gold wire

Glue gun and glue stick

Sawtooth picture hanger

DIRECTIONS:

1. Remove glass from picture frame and place glass on newspaper covered work surface. Following manufacturer's instructions, spray glass with black chalkboard spray. Let dry.

2. Using white paint writer or white paint and paintbrush, write "_ _ _ _ days until Christmas!" on chalkboard-sprayed side of glass. Let dry.

3. Attach sawtooth picture hanger to center of back of picture frame.

4. Place glass back in frame.

5. Add stickers where desired to front of frame.

6. Coil wire piece to fit chalk. Glue coiled wire to top of picture frame.

7. Place chalk piece inside coiled wire to hold.

Dried Flower Angel

CRAFT LEVEL: QUICK & EASY

FINISHED SIZE: Angel measures about 20 inches high x 14 inches wide.

When it comes to crafting, I enjoy trying new techniques. I keep an idea file that I fill with all sorts of different projects that catch my eye. When I spotted a bunch of flowers hanging upside down, I thought they looked like an angel in the making.

Bobbie Glassberg ★ Desoto, Texas

MATERIALS:

Dried flowers with 15-inch-long stems for angel's skirt (green eucalyptus, sweet Annie, pink and lavender statice and baby's breath shown)

Six 10-inch-long stems of burgundy eucalyptus for wings

Large twist tie or rubber band

6-inch round white lace doily

3-inch Styrofoam ball for head

Serrated knife or craft knife

Skin-tone nylon stocking

Spanish moss for hair

Two 6mm black beads for eyes

Natural raffia for bow

Powdered cosmetic blush and cotton swab

Glue gun and glue sticks

Craft wire

Ruler

Craft scissors

DIRECTIONS:

Refer to photo above as a guide while assembling the angel as directed in the instructions that follow.

Skirt:

1. Arrange the dried flowers and green eucalyptus so that the different flower varieties and colors alternate and fan out, creating the appearance of fabric layers. When flowers are in the desired position, cut the stem ends even, leaving the longest stems about 14 in. long.

2. Wrap stem ends securely with twist tie or rubber band to hold the flowers in place.

Bodice:

1. In the center of the lace doily, cut a slit large enough to fit over the stems of the flower skirt.

2. Slip doily right side out over the stems.

3. Fold doily in half and spot-glue doily to stems to hold. Let dry.

Head:

1. Use serrated knife or craft knife to cut Styrofoam ball in half for head. Discard one half or save for another project.

2. Place one ball half inside nylon stocking. Smooth stocking over curved side of ball and tie or glue stocking on flat side of ball to secure stocking in place. Cut away excess stocking.

3. Glue flat side of covered half-ball to the stem end of the flowers for the angel's head. Let dry.

4. For hair, glue Spanish moss to the sides, top and back of head. Let dry.

5. Glue the black beads to head for eyes. Let dry.

6. Using cotton swab and a circular motion, apply cosmetic blush to cheeks.

7. Hold lengths of raffia together in a bundle and tie in a small bow. Center and glue the bow just below the head. Trim raffia as desired. Let dry.

8. For halo, glue lavender statice to the top of angel's head.

Wings:

1. Hold the lengths of burgundy eucalyptus together in a bunch, fanning the tips. Wrap wire around the center of the eucalyptus to hold and form wings.

2. Glue wings to the back of angel just below the head. Let dry.

Finishing:

1. Form a wire piece into a loop and attach it to the center back of the wings for hanger.

2. Glue single dried flowers where desired for trim. Let dry.

Tabletop Tree Boughs

CRAFT LEVEL: QUICK & EASY

FINISHED SIZE: Ornament tree shown measures about 24 inches across x 55 inches high. Size will vary depending on size of branches used.

Go out on a limb and put a spin on the traditional Christmas evergreen. Trim a few natural tree branches from your own backyard to hold ornaments and snowflakes. Be sure to select a sturdy container to prevent it from tipping over.

Taste of Home Craft Editor

MATERIALS:

Natural tree branches

Garden shears

Vase or other container

Sand to fill vase or container

White snowflake shapes in two different sizes

Ornaments in desired sizes and colors

Wire ornament hangers

Spanish moss

DIRECTIONS:

1. Fill container with sand.

2. Trim branches as needed and stand them upright in container.

3. Attach wire ornament hangers to snowflakes and ornaments. Wrap wire around branches to hold snowflakes and ornaments in place.

4. Place Spanish moss inside top of vase.

Hide a Picture

You don't have to go out and buy special holiday pictures and accents to decorate your home during the Christmas season. Add a touch of Yuletide merriment to any wall with inexpensive holiday wrapping paper. To have a well-put together display, select a motif for your artwork, such as Santas, snowmen or trees, or choose (as shown here) different patterns of papers that use the same color theme.

Look around your home for mirrors, pictures or even unused picture frames that may be tucked away in the basement or closets. Choose sizes and shapes that make an interesting arrangement. Wrap them up and hang on the wall. After the holidays, it is easy to remove the wrapping paper and return the items back to their original location.

Painting:

Keep container of water handy to thin paints and clean painting tools. Place dabs of each color as needed onto foam plate or palette. Apply additional coats as needed for complete coverage. Let paint dry after each application. Refer to photo at left as a guide while painting as directed in the instructions that follow.

1. Use flat brush and brown to paint pieces for stable roof, walls and floor. While paint is wet, wipe pieces with paper towel to reveal the grain.

2. Using flat brush, paint 1-3/4-in.-long craft stick piece white, 2-1/2-in.-long craft stick piece red and 3-in.-long craft stick piece green.

3. Paint all furniture plugs flesh for faces. Use round brush to add two small pink circles to each for cheeks.

4. Use flat brush to paint star gold.

5. With liner and black paint, add hair around faces, and add Baby's eyelashes.

6. Dip brush handle into black to add two tiny eyes to Mary and Joseph's faces, and two buttons to Joseph's body.

Assembly:

1. Glue stable wall pieces to back of stable floor. Glue roof pieces to top of walls, overlapping the cut edges a bit, and glue star to roof.

2. Glue Mary and Joseph to back of stable floor.

3. Cut small pieces of raffia and glue around the bottom edge of the Baby. Glue Baby to front of floor.

4. Glue faces to all figures.

5. Wrap green-and-tan fabric around Joseph and glue to hold. Wrap red print fabric around Mary and glue to hold. Glue on brown button.

6. Thread a piece of raffia through each green button and knot ends in front. Trim raffia close to knot. Glue buttons to stable floor as shown.

7. Glue paper clip to back top of stable for hanger. Thread with torn fabric strip, and tie ends in a knot for hanging loop.

Finishing:

1. Use black marker to add dashed lines around star and on Baby, and to write the verse and "Luke 2."

Craft Stick Nativity

CRAFT LEVEL: BEGINNER

FINISHED SIZE: Nativity measures about 7-1/4 inches across x 5-1/2 inches high without hanging loop.

This miniature Nativity is fashioned from jumbo craft sticks, which makes it simple enough for little ones to do with adult supervision.

Julee Chambers ★ Logansport, Indiana

MATERIALS:

Six jumbo craft sticks

Two 1-inch wooden domed furniture plugs

One 1/2-inch wooden domed furniture plug

1-1/4-inch-high wooden star

Sandpaper

Water container

Paper towels

Foam plate or palette

Acrylic craft paints—black, brown, flesh, gold, green, pink, red and white

Paintbrushes—small flat, small round and liner

Black fine-line permanent marker

Natural raffia

Two green 1/2-inch two-hole buttons

One 3/8-inch brown button

Fabric—1/2-inch x 10-inch torn strip of green-and-tan fabric for hanging loop, 3/8-inch x 4-1/2-inch strip of green-and-tan fabric for Joseph's cloak, and 3/8-inch x 4-1/4-inch strip of red print for Mary's cloak

Craft knife or craft scissors

Paper clip

Ruler

Craft glue

DIRECTIONS:

Cutting:

Refer to photo above when cutting and assembling craft sticks.

1. Cut two 5-in.-long craft stick pieces for stable roof, and cut one craft stick in half diagonally to make two 3-in. pieces for stable walls.

2. Cut one 3-in.-long craft stick piece for Joseph, and one 2-1/2-in.-long craft stick piece for Mary. Cut one 1-3/4-in.-long craft stick piece for Baby. Use sandpaper to round cut end as shown. (Leave remaining craft stick for stable floor.)

3. Sand as needed to smooth, and wipe with damp paper towel to remove sanding dust.

Christmas Tree Floor Mat

CRAFT LEVEL: BEGINNER

FINISHED SIZE: Floor mat measures 18 inches high x 27 inches wide.

With this home accent idea, I have a cheery yet practical project that I can display at our door all season long. The project started with a rectangle of ordinary vinyl flooring, which I painted dark blue. A simple sponge-painting technique produces the basic evergreen tree and matching border, while stamping creates the star and gift package shapes. All that's left to do is add the easy-to-paint details and finish the mat with sealer.

Sue Smith ★ Forest, Ontario

MATERIALS:

18-inch x 27-inch piece of vinyl flooring

Palette or foam plate

Water container

Paper towels

Small sponge roller or small household paintbrush

1-inch-wide painter's or masking tape

Ruler

Acrylic craft paints (Delta Ceramcoat and Ceramcoat Gleams paints shown)— Apple Green, Black Cherry, Black Green, Crocus Yellow, Custard, Forest Green, Golden Brown, Liberty Blue, Metallic Gold, Midnight Blue, Napthol Red Light, Purple and Tangerine

Paintbrushes—3/4-inch flat and small round

1-inch foam brush

Sea sponge

Pieces of new household sponge or compressed sponge (for stamping gift designs)—2-1/2-inch x 3-inch piece, 1-3/4-inch x 1-inch piece, 1-3/4-inch x 1-1/2-inch piece, 1-1/2-inch x 1-1/4-inch

piece, 1-3/4-inch x 2-1/4-inch piece and 1-1/2-inch x 1-1/2-inch piece

1-inch-high wooden star for stamping star

Acrylic semi gloss sealer

DIRECTIONS:

General Painting Instructions:

1. Keep paper towels and container of water handy to clean brushes and sponge pieces.

2. Place a quarter-size puddle of each paint color onto palette or foam plate as needed. Let paint dry after every application.

3. Painting is done on the back of the vinyl flooring piece. Make sure it is free of dirt and oil before applying paint.

4. Refer to the photo above and the painting diagram on page 196 as guides while painting as directed in the instructions that follow.

(continued on page 196)

Diagram measurements:

1/4" · 1" · 2" · 18" · 3-1/4" · 2-1/2" x 3" · 1-3/4" x 1-1/2" · 1-1/2" x 1-1/4" · 5" · 1-3/4" x 2-1/4" · 1-1/2" x 1-1/2" · 1-3/4" x 1" · 6-1/2" · 4-1/2" · 6-1/2" · 27"

Painting Background:

1. Using small sponge roller or household paintbrush, apply two coats of Midnight Blue to entire back side of vinyl flooring.

2. For border, apply 1-in.-wide tape around the edge of flooring piece to mask off a 1-in.-wide border around the outside edge of flooring piece. In the same way, apply more tape 2 in. in from the taped border, creating a 2-in.-wide space between the two sets of tape.

3. To create a guideline for stamping, apply another piece of tape so that the top edge of tape is about 4-1/2 in. from one long edge of the vinyl flooring. Do not extend the masking tape into the 2-in.-wide border.

Sponge-painting:

Border:

1. Wet sea sponge with clean water and squeeze out all excess water.

2. Dip sea sponge into Apple Green, Forest Green and Custard paints. Dab sponge onto paper towel to remove excess paint.

3. Using an up-and-down motion, lightly sponge-paint the 2-in.-wide masked-off border space area, allowing the blue background to show through a bit. Remove border tape.

Tree:

1. Wet sea sponge with clean water and squeeze out all excess water.

2. Dip sea sponge into Apple Green, Black Green and Forest Green, then dip one corner into Custard. Dab sponge onto paper towel to remove excess paint.

3. With the Custard corner at the bottom, lightly sponge-paint the bottom of the Christmas tree, starting in the center of the flooring piece at the taped stamping guideline. Continue sponge-painting in the same way to create a large triangle for the tree.

General Stamping Instructions:

1. Wet the household or compressed sponge pieces with clean water and squeeze out all excess water.

2. Using flat brush, apply paint to one side of sponge pieces as directed.

3. Press the painted side of the sponge piece onto flooring piece to transfer design onto flooring piece.

4. Let paint dry after stamping.

5. If needed, apply additional matching paint to make the stamped shapes opaque.

Gifts:

1. Apply Liberty Blue to a 2-1/2- x 3-in. side of a sponge piece. Stamp gift about 3-1/4 in. from inside edge of left border with the 2-1/2-in. edge of sponge piece just above the taped stamping guideline.

2. Apply Liberty Blue to a 1-3/4- x 2-1/4-in. side of a sponge piece. Stamp gift about 5 in. in from inside edge of right border with the 1-3/4-in. edge of sponge piece just above the stamping guideline.

3. Apply Purple to a 1-3/4- x 1-in. side of a sponge piece. Place the 1-3/4-in. edge just above the stamping guideline and stamp gift so it overlaps about 1 in. of the 2-1/2- x 3-in. Liberty Blue gift.

4. Apply Purple to a 1-1/2- x 1-1/4-in. side of a sponge piece. Place the 1-1/4-in. edge just above the stamping guideline and stamp gift on the left edge of the 2-1/4- x 1-3/4-in. Liberty Blue gift, overlapping the tree.

5. Apply Napthol Red Light to a 1-3/4- x 1-1/2-in. side of a sponge piece. Place the 1-1/2-in. edge just above the stamping guideline and stamp gift to the right of the 1-3/4- x 1-in. Purple gift, overlapping the tree.

6. Apply Napthol Red Light to a 1-1/2- x 1-1/2-in. side of a sponge piece. Place one corner just above the stamping guideline and stamp gift to the right of the 2-1/4- x 1-3/4-in. Liberty Blue gift.

7. Remove stamping guideline tape.

Star:

1. Using round brush, apply Crocus Yellow to one side of wooden star.

2. Press painted side of star down onto top of tree so star is about 1/4 in. below the inside edge of top border. Let dry.

Finishing:
Tree:

1. Dip handle end of round paintbrush into Crocus Yellow and randomly dab dots onto the tree for ornaments.

2. In the same way, add Napthol Red Light, Purple and Tangerine ornaments to the tree.

Gifts:

1. Using round brush and Tangerine, add small comma strokes to each Liberty Blue gift and several squiggles to the top of gifts for bows.

2. Using round brush, apply wide Black Cherry and narrow Metallic Gold diagonal stripes to each Napthol Red Light gift. Add a Metallic Gold bow to the top of same gifts.

3. Using round brush and Crocus Yellow, add ribbons and a bow to each Purple gift.

Sled Runner:

1. Using round brush and Golden Brown, paint sled runner freehand under the three gifts on the left side of the tree.

Snow:

1. Wet the flat brush with water. Touch brush on a paper towel until shine leaves bristles. Dip one corner of brush into Custard. Work brush back and forth on palette or foam plate to soften color and blend on one half of brush.

2. Pull the color-side of the brush along the bottom edge of the sled runner, tree and gifts for snow.

Sealing:

1. Using foam brush, apply three coats of sealer to front of floor mat following manufacturer's instructions. Let dry.

Cloth Silverware Holder

Add a bit of pizzazz to your buffet by displaying cutlery in a unique way. Place a large, starched cloth napkin wrong side up on a flat surface. (Our napkin measured 22 inches.) Fold up the bottom third of napkin, forming a rectangle. Carefully turn the napkin over. Fold bottom folded edge halfway up. On each short end, tuck about 1-1/2 inches of the napkin under to form a long pocket. Insert silverware into the pocket.

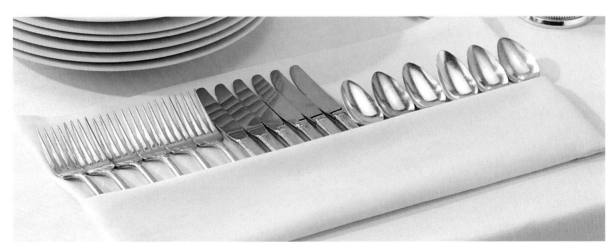

Festive Felt Stocking

CRAFT LEVEL: QUICK & EASY

FINISHED SIZE: Stocking measures about 4-1/2 inches wide x 7-5/8 inches long without hanging loop.

This felt stocking can hang from a mantel or fill it with candy or other treats and give to guests as a party favor.

Cindy Lund ★ Sandy, Vermont

MATERIALS:

Patterns on page 199

Tracing paper and pencil

Felt—one 9-inch x 12-inch piece of off-white for stocking and scraps of gold for star and dark red for heart

Scraps of two different dark green print fabrics for trees

Paper-backed fusible web

1/2-inch buttons—one gold, one red and two green

Dark green six-strand embroidery floss and embroidery needle

4-inch length of 3/8-inch-wide dark green grosgrain ribbon

Iron and ironing surface

DIRECTIONS:

1. Trace the stocking pattern onto tracing paper.

2. Fold off-white felt piece in half crosswise so the 9-in.-long sides are matching. Pin stocking pattern to folded felt.

3. Cut out stocking following pattern.

4. Trace heart, star and tree patterns onto paper side of fusible web, leaving 1/2 in. between shapes.

5. Cut apart shapes, leaving a margin of paper around each.

6. Fuse shapes to fabrics as directed on patterns and following manufacturer's instructions.

7. Cut out shapes, following patterns. Remove paper backing.

8. Referring to photo for position, fuse shapes to front of stocking.

9. With embroidery floss, sew the red and gold buttons to the front of stocking as shown.

10. Fold ribbon in half to form a loop. Sandwich the ends of the folded ribbon between the front and back stocking pieces at the upper back corner.

11. With embroidery floss and a long running stitch, hand-sew the front and back stocking pieces together, making sure to catch the ends of the hanging loop in the stitching. See Fig. 1 below for stitch illustration.

12. Sew the remaining green buttons to the upper back corner on the front and back of the stocking.

Stocking
TRACE 1—TRACING PAPER
CUT 2 AS DIRECTED—
OFF-WHITE FELT

Star
TRACE 1—PAPER-BACKED
FUSIBLE WEB
CUT 1-FUSED GOLD FELT

Large Tree
TRACE 1—PAPER-BACKED
FUSIBLE WEB
CUT 1-FUSED DARK GREEN PRINT

Small Tree
TRACE 1—PAPER-BACKED
FUSIBLE WEB
CUT 1-FUSED DARK GREEN PRINT

Heart
TRACE 1—PAPER-BACKED
FUSIBLE WEB
CUT 1-FUSED DARK RED FELT

Felt Stocking Patterns

FIG. 1

Running Stitch

KEY

—— Outline/cutting line
- - - - Overlapped portion
of pattern

Palette or foam plate

Acrylic craft paints—dark red, black, flesh, dark green, rose and white

Textured snow medium

Fine iridescent glitter

1-inch foam brush

Paintbrushes—small flat, small round and small stiff bristle brush

Toothpick

Craft glue

Ruler

Matte sealer

DIRECTIONS:

Painting:

Keep paper towels and container of water handy to clean brushes. Place small amounts of paint as needed onto foam plate or palette. Let paint dry after every application. Refer to patterns and photo at left as a guide while painting as directed in the instructions that follow.

1. With flat brush, paint front and edges of mustache white. Set aside.

2. With foam brush, paint the outside of cone dark red.

3. Use flat brush to paint a 1-1/2-in. flesh circle on cone for the face, starting about 2 in. from the top.

4. Glue furniture plug onto face for nose.

5. Paint the plug flesh.

6. Dip end of paintbrush handle into black and dab eyes above the nose, spacing them about 1/8 in. apart.

7. Use toothpick to dab a tiny white highlight in each eye.

8. Dip a stiff bristle brush into rose. Wipe brush on a paper towel to remove excess paint. With a nearly dry brush and a dabbing motion, apply a light coat of rose to the nose and each cheek.

9. Locate center the bottom edge of the face and lightly pencil-in a vertical line from bottom edge of face to bottom edge of cone as shown in Fig. 1 on page 201.

Santa Tree Topper

CRAFT LEVEL: QUICK & EASY

FINISHED SIZE: Santa measures about 6 inches high x 2-3/4 inches wide.

Instead of making his Christmas arrival up on a housetop, this Claus likes to pause on treetops! Since I painted my Santa pattern on a hollow cone, the design can fit right over the highest branch of my family's holiday evergreen.

Irene Wegener ★ Corning, New York

MATERIALS:

Patterns on page 201

Tracing paper and pencil

Scissors

6-inch-high cardboard cone

1/4-inch wooden domed furniture plug

1-inch wooden mustache or wooden angel wings for mustache

1-inch Styrofoam ball

Paper towels

Water container

10. Trace patterns onto tracing paper with pencil and cut out shapes.

11. Lay boot pattern on one side of vertical line so boot's straight edge matches bottom edge of cone. Trace outline of pattern with pencil. Repeat on opposite side of line.

12. Referring to Fig. 1, lay mitten pattern on cone about 3/4 in. from vertical line and trace around the pattern. Turn pattern over and trace around the pattern on the opposite side of vertical line.

13. Use flat brush to paint the mittens dark green and to paint the boots black.

14. Thin white paint with clean water to an ink-like consistency. Use round brush and white to highlight boots and mittens as shown on patterns, reversing the direction on second boot and mitten.

15. Thin black paint with clean water. Use round brush and black to add a 1-1/2-in.-long stroke above mittens to create shading for arms. Shade bottom of mittens in the same way.

16. Apply matte sealer following manufacturer's instructions. Let dry.

17. Glue mustache below the nose.

Textured Snow:

1. Use the stiff bristle brush to apply textured snow around cone at top of Santa's head to look like fur trim on the hat.

2. Cover mustache with textured snow and add a beard around the face, shaping it as desired. Add fur trim down the front of coat, around bottom of coat and to the cuff of each sleeve.

3. Add a textured snow eyebrow above each eye.

4. Sprinkle glitter onto textured snow while it is still moist. Let dry. Shake off excess glitter.

5. Apply glue to point of cone and push Styrofoam ball onto the point. When dry, apply textured snow and glitter to the ball as before.

6. Use a toothpick to dab on a small red dot for a mouth, centering it just below the mustache.

Crafter's Note: If you plan to put your Santa on a flat surface, you could paint even more cones green to look like trees and display them along with the Santa.

Twinkling Star Ornament

CRAFT LEVEL: QUICK & EASY

FINISHED SIZE: Each star ornament measures about 5 inches across.

Star light, star bright…these ornaments sparkle as brilliantly as the stars in the night! Enlist the kids to help make the easy adornments, then have them trim your tree or give some to the grandparents as gifts.

Taste of Home Craft Editor

MATERIALS:

Papier-mache star

White acrylic craft paint

Small flat paintbrush

Gem-Tac Embellishing Glue or tacky craft glue

Assorted small glass beads

DIRECTIONS:

1. Paint entire papier-mache star ornament white. Let dry.

2. Spread one side of the ornament with glue. Sprinkle beads over glue. When dry tap off excess beads and repeat on other side.

3. Spread side edges with glue and apply beads as before.

Boot Pattern
TRACE AND CUT 1—TRACING PAPER

Mitten Pattern
TRACE AND CUT 1—TRACING PAPER

FIG. 1
Positioning Patterns

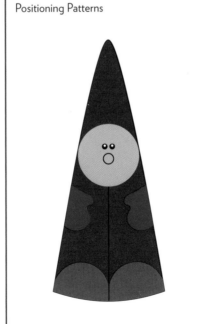

Let it Snow
Wall Hanging

CRAFT LEVEL: QUICK & EASY

FINISHED SIZE: Wall hanging measures 8 inches wide x 10 inches high, excluding the hanger.

My family's motto is "No winter wonderland is complete without a snowman." Of course, after the snowman is built, the wet mittens need to dry— which is why I fashioned some to hang from the bottom of my mini-quilt!

Donna Stefanik ★ Westfield, Massachusetts

MATERIALS:

Patterns on page 204

Tracing paper and pencil

44-inch-wide 100% cotton fabrics—3/8 yard of muslin, 1/4 yard of sky blue print, 1/8 yard each or scraps of green print and red print for mittens and heart appliques and a tiny scrap of orange solid for carrot nose

Off-white all-purpose thread

Six-strand embroidery floss—black, brown, light blue and red embroidery needle

8-1/2-inch x 10-1/2-inch piece of lightweight quilt batting

Paper-backed fusible web

Black acrylic craft paint

Small paintbrush

Black fine-line permanent marker

12-inch length of string for hanger

Small amount of polyester stuffing

Standard sewing supplies

DIRECTIONS:
Background:
Cutting:

1. From muslin, cut one 8-1/2- x 10-1/2-in. piece for backing, two 2- x 7-1/2-in. strips and two 2- x 8-1/2-in. strips for border.

2. From sky blue print, cut one 5-1/2- x 7-1/2-in. for background.

Piecing:

Do all stitching with right sides of fabrics together, edges even, and accurate 1/4-in. seam allowances.

1. Sew long edge of one 2- x 7-1/2-in. border strip to each 7-1/2-in. side of sky blue print piece. Open and press seams toward blue print piece.

2. Sew long edge of one 2- x 8-1/2-in. strip to each 8-1/2-in. edge. Open and press seams toward blue print piece.

Applique:

1. Trace all patterns on page 204 except mitten onto paper side of fusible web as directed on patterns, leaving 1/2 in. between shapes.

2. Cut apart shapes, leaving a margin of paper around each.

3. Following web manufacturer's instructions, fuse shapes to wrong side of fabrics as directed on patterns. Let cool.

4. Cut out all shapes following outlines of each.

5. Remove paper backing from shapes for wall hanging and place them right side up, on front of pieced top as shown in photo at left. Fuse shapes in place.

6. Separate black six-strand floss and use two strands to blanket-stitch around snowman and along inside design lines. See Fig. 2 on page 204 for stitch illustrations.

7. Use two strands of red to blanket-stitch around scarf, hat and along inside design lines. Straight-stitch the fringe on scarf and the pom-pom on hat.

8. Use two strands of blue to blanket-stitch around each corner heart.

9. Use three strands of brown to stem-stitch each twig arm and fingers.

10. Dip end of paintbrush handle into black and dab on dots for eyes, mouth and buttons.

11. Use black fine-line permanent marker to write "Let it Snow" on each border as shown in the photo.

Assembly:

1. Pin string to front of appliqued piece as shown in Fig. 1 at right.

2. Place appliqued piece right side up on a flat surface.

3. Center the 8-1/2- x 10-1/2-in. piece of muslin on top.

4. Center batting on top of muslin and pin to hold.

5. Sew around wall hanging with a 1/4-in. seam, catching the ends of string in the stitching and leaving an opening for turning. Clip corners diagonally.

6. Turn piece right side out.

7. Turn raw edges in and hand-sew opening closed with matching thread.

Mittens (make four):

1. Trace mitten pattern on page 204 onto tracing paper.

2. Cut out mittens as directed on patterns.

3. On two mittens of each color, fuse a contrasting color heart.

4. With edges even and wrong sides together, pair each set of matching mitten pieces and blanket-stitch around the edges with two strands of floss, matching the color of the floss to the appliqued heart and adding a small amount of stuffing before closing top edge.

Finishing:

1. For each pair of mittens, cut a 6-in. length of floss to match blanket stitching.

2. Thread floss on embroidery needle and knot one end.

3. Insert needle through the top of one mitten, through bottom of wall hanging about 2 in. from a corner and through second mitten. Knot floss to secure the mitten. Repeat for remaining pair of mittens.

Crafter's Note: The colors used on this wall hanging make it ideal to display throughout the winter season. But, it would also look cute made up in Christmas fabrics.

Let It Snow Blanket

Make multiple quilt blocks of this snowman design and sew them together to make a fun blanket.

FIG. 1 Hanger

1-1/4" 1-1/4"

Let it Snow

Let it Snow

Let it Snow

Let It Snow Wall Hanging Patterns

NOTE: Snowman patterns are given in reverse so they will face in the correct direction after being fused to the back of your fabric.

Mitten

TRACE 1—TRACING PAPER
CUT 4, REVERSING 2—RED PRINT
CUT 4, REVERSING 2—GREEN PRINT

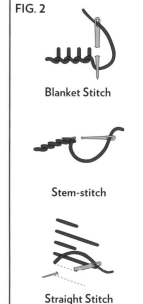

Hat

TRACE 1—PAPER-BACKED
FUSIBLE WEB
CUT 1—FUSED GREEN
PRINT

Carrot Nose

TRACE 1—NO-SEW
FUSIBLE WEB
CUT 1—FUSED ORANGE SOLID

Heart

TRACE 4—PAPER-BACKED
FUSIBLE WEB
CUT 4—FUSED RED PRINT
TRACE 4—NO-SEW FUSIBLE WEB
CUT 2—FUSED RED PRINT
CUT 2—FUSED SKY BLUE PIN-DOT

Scarf

TRACE 1—PAPER-BACKED
FUSIBLE WEB
CUT 1—FUSED GREEN PRINT

Grain

Grain

Grain

Snowman

TRACE 1—PAPER-BACKED
FUSIBLE WEB
CUT 1—FUSED MUSLIN

Grain

APPLIQUE KEY

—— Outline/cutting line
- - - Overlapped portion of piece
— Inside design lines

FIG. 2

Blanket Stitch

Stem-stitch

Straight Stitch

Gifts
TO GIVE

Pretty Painted Soap

CRAFT LEVEL: BEGINNER

FINISHED SIZE: Penguin soap shown measures about 2-1/2 inches across x 3-3/4 inches high. Snowflake soap measures about 2 inches across x 3 inches high. Patterns can be enlarged or reduced to fit other size bars of soap.

Don't forget the powder room when decorating your house for Christmas! I like to paint ordinary bars of soap with seasonal images and then give them as gifts to neighbors, teachers and friends.

Jena Weiler ★ Milwaukee, Wisconsin

MATERIALS (FOR BOTH):

Patterns on page 207

Tracing paper and pencil

Graphite paper

Two bars of white soap (see Crafter's Note)

Rubbing alcohol

Cotton ball

Spray or brush-on sealer or decoupage medium (see Crafter's Note)

Water container

Paper towels

Foam plate or palette

Acrylic craft paints—black, dark blue, light blue, orange, magenta, pink, purple, turquoise, white and yellow

Paintbrushes—small round and liner

Toothpick

DIRECTIONS:

1. Unwrap the bar of soap and let it dry for at least eight hours.

2. Using a cotton ball, wipe the side to be painted with rubbing alcohol. Do not touch the side to be painted after wiping with the alcohol.

3. Seal the side to be painted with spray or brush-on sealer. Let dry for at least 12 hours.

Painting:

Keep container of water handy to thin paints and clean painting tools. Place dabs of each paint color as needed onto foam plate or palette. Apply additional coats of paint as needed for complete coverage. Let paint dry between coats. Refer to patterns and photo above as a guide while painting as directed in the instructions that follow.

1. Trace patterns onto tracing paper.

2. Slip graphite paper between patterns and soap and trace over pattern lines.

Penguin Soap:

1. Use round brush and light blue to paint water.

2. Use round brush and yellow to paint penguin's feet. While paint is still wet, shade lower edge of each foot with orange.

3. Use round brush and purple to paint penguin's body, wings and head.

4. Use round brush and white to paint center circle on body and to paint face.

5. Dip handle end of paintbrush into black and dab on two small dots for eyes.

6. Dip round brush into pink and wipe on paper towel to remove excess paint. Add pink shading to cheeks. In the same way, add purple shading to penguin's stomach.

7. Dip toothpick into white and add a tiny dot to each eye.

8. Use liner and black to outline penguin and add details as shown.

9. Use liner and black to paint four Xs with a line through each for stars.

10. Dip toothpick into black and add random dots around penguin.

Snowflake Soap:

1. Use round brush and turquoise to paint large snowflake and liner to paint three small turquoise snowflakes.

2. Use liner to paint magenta and blue snowflakes.

3. Use liner and dark blue to paint detail in center of large snowflake.

4. Dip toothpick into dark blue to add tiny dots around large snowflake. In the same way, add turquoise and magenta dots where shown.

Finishing:

1. Add spray or brush-on sealer to painted area.

2. Let soap dry at least 24 hours before using or packaging.

Crafter's Note: Any brand or color of bar soap may be used. Walgreen's brand white bar soap has a logo on one side only. If your bar has a logo on both sides, use a straight-edge knife to shave off the logo. Then use a damp washcloth to smooth the surface for painting.

Spray sealer dries faster and harder. Brush-on sealer may leave brush strokes on surface.

Painted Soap Patterns

**TRACE 1–TRACING PAPER
PAINT AS DIRECTED**

Penguin Pattern

Snowflake Pattern

3-in-1 Greeting Cards

CRAFT LEVEL: QUICK & EASY

FINISHED SIZE: Each card measures 5-1/2 inches across x 4-1/4 inches high.

Making Christmas cards from scratch allows me to tap into my inner artist. I feel my holiday greetings are sent out with a little extra love!

Barb Czysz ★ Greendale, Wisconsin

MATERIALS:

5-1/2-inch x 4-1/4-inch purchased greeting cards—blue, green and red

Scrapbook stickers—two snowflakes, one snowman, nine green evergreen trees, two potted glitter trees, one ornament, "all is merry and bright" grosgrain ribbon, green, silver and red metallic glitter strips, red, green and silver metallic stars

Glue dots

Craft glue

Ruler

Scissors

DIRECTIONS:

Blue Snowman Card:

1. Place card on a flat surface with the fold at the top. Adhere snowflakes to card.

2. Place glue dots on the back of three evergreen trees and adhere the trees to the card.

3. Glue a star to the top of each tree.

4. Adhere snowman between the trees.

Red Tree Card:

1. Place card on a flat surface with the fold at the top. Adhere a green and a silver metallic glitter strip across the top and bottom of the card.

2. Cut away excess flush with sides of card.

3. Place glue dots on the back of three evergreen trees and adhere the trees to the card.

4. Glue ornament to upper right corner of card.

Green Tree Card:

1. Place card on a flat surface with the fold at the top. Adhere red metallic glitter strip across the bottom of the card. Cut away excess flush with sides of the card.

2. Place glue dots on the back of three evergreen trees and adhere the trees to the card.

3. Glue a glitter tree to the left and right evergreen trees.

4. Place glue dots on the back of the "all is merry and bright" grosgrain ribbon piece.

5. Adhere ribbon to card below center evergreen tree.

2. Slip a purple pearl on a length of 24-gauge wire or headpin with ends removed, and form a loop at opposite sides of purple pearl. Repeat with remaining purple pearl.

Strand One:

1. Connect a 1-in. length of the medium-linked chain to each loop of a flat black bead. This bead will be the center front of the necklace.

2. To each side of the black bead add the following: one light purple oval bead, 1-in. length of medium-link chain, one dark purple rectangular bead, 1-in. length of medium-link chain, one black faceted round bead, 1-in. length of medium-link chain, one pearl, 1-in. length of medium-link chain, one flat black bead, 1-in. length of medium-link chain, light purple oval bead, 1-in. length of medium-link chain, dark purple rectangular bead. Attach 2-in. length of chain to last bead on each end to make a 30-in.-long strand.

3. Attach a jump ring about 1 in. from each of the last beads on the first strand.

4. Attach the lobster claw clasp to ends of medium-linked chain.

Strand Two:

1. Attach the length of open-loop decorative chain to jump rings on first strand.

Purple Bead & Chain Necklace

CRAFT LEVEL: QUICK & EASY

FINISHED SIZE: Necklace measures about 30 inches long.

Purple is one of my favorite colors. Paired with black and the gunmetal chain, this makes a great necklace for fall and winter and looks great with sweaters.

Sarah Farley ★ Menomonee Falls, Wisconsin

MATERIALS:

Thirteen 1-1/2-inch-long gunmetal eye pins

Three 20mm black flat Czech glass beads

Four 10mm light purple oval glass beads

Four 10mm x 16mm dark purple rectangular glass beads

Two 10mm black faceted round plastic beads

24-gauge gunmetal wire or 2 gunmetal headpins with heads removed

Two 8mm purple pearls

20-inch length of oval and round medium-linked gunmetal chain

24-inch length of medium-link open-looped decorative gunmetal chain

One gunmetal lobster claw clasp

Two gunmetal jump rings

DIRECTIONS:

Preparation:

1. Attach a 1-1/2-in.-long eye pin to all the beads except the pearls and form a loop on opposite sides of each bead.

Beads & Chain Necklace

It's so easy to change the look of this necklace. Use silver- or gold-colored chain and white, brown, tan or even clear beads for the black beads. Experiment with the various shades and shapes of beads in your favorite color for the purple beads.

Skyline Purse

CRAFT LEVEL: INTERMEDIATE

FINISHED SIZE: Purse measures about 13 inches wide x 7 inches high without handles.

Making homemade purses is a fun hobby of mine. This stunning handbag with a sparkling city skyline is perfect for special occasions.

Lynn LeFever ★ Waterford, Minnesota

MATERIALS:

Pattern on page 210

Tracing paper and pencil

Light transfer paper and tracing wheel

44-inch-wide fabrics—1/3 yard of black wool crepe and 1/3 yard of coordinating fabric for lining

1/2 yard of fusible interfacing

All-purpose thread to match fabrics

Water container

Paper towels

Foam plate or palette

Piece of cardboard

Masking tape

Acrylic craft paints and fabric medium or fabric paints—black, gold, grey, pink, purple, red and silver

Paintbrushes—medium and small flat

Glitter glue

Approximately 30 clear seed beads

Magnetic purse closure

5-inch square black purse handles

Quilter's ruler

Standard sewing supplies

DIRECTIONS:

Cutting:

1. From black wool crepe, cut two 8-in. x 14-in. pieces for outside of purse and four 4-1/2-in. squares or size needed for attaching purse handles.

2. From coordinating fabric, cut two 8-in. x 14-in. pieces for lining of purse.

3. From fusible interfacing, cut two 8-in. x 14-in. pieces and four 4-1/2-in. squares or size needed for attaching purse handles.

Painting:

Keep container of water handy to thin paints and clean painting tools. Place dabs of each paint color as needed onto foam plate or palette. Apply paint sparingly for a translucent look. Refer to photo above as a guide while painting as directed in the instructions that follow.

1. Trace enlarged pattern on page 210 onto tracing paper with pencil.

2. Tape one piece of black fabric right side up to cardboard piece to hold.

3. With grain lines matching, center pattern over fabric and slip transfer paper between pattern and fabric. Pin or tape as needed to hold.

4. Using ruler and tracing wheel, go over lines of pattern to transfer pattern onto fabric.

5. Using medium flat brush, paint the buildings the colors as shown on the pattern.

6. Using small flat brush and glitter glue, add highlights to buildings.

7. Using small flat brush and black, add windows to buildings.

8. Using small flat brush and silver, outline and add rooflines to buildings.

Beading:

1. Hand-sew seed beads above buildings where shown on pattern.

Sewing:

Lining:

1. Following the manufacturer's instructions, fuse an interfacing piece to wrong side of each lining piece.

2. With right sides facing and edges matching, sew sides and bottom edges together with a 1/2-in. seam.

3. Press 1/2 in. along top edge of lining to wrong side.

4. Attach magnetic purse closure to center top edge of lining.

(continued on page 210)

Outside:

1. With right sides facing and edges matching, sew sides and bottom edges of purse together with a 1/2-in. seam.

2. Press 1/2 in. along top edge of purse to wrong side.

3. Turn purse right side out.

Attaching Handles:

1. Fuse an interfacing piece to the wrong side of each 4-1/2-in. black wool crepe square.

2. Place two pieces together with right sides facing and edges matching. Sew two opposite sides together with a 1/2-in. seam allowance. Turn piece right side out.

3. Slip through a purse handle and align raw edges. Pin as needed to hold. Center handle along top of lining with ends extending beyond top edge. Baste as needed to hold.

4. Repeat steps 2-3 for remaining handle.

Finishing:

1. Slip lining into the purse with wrong sides facing and side seams and top edges matching. Pin as needed to hold.

2. With matching thread, topstitch along top edge of purse catching edge of lining and handles in stitching.

Skyline Purse Pattern

EITHER USE PHOTOCOPIER TO ENLARGE PATTERNS 200% OR DRAW A 1-INCH GRID ON TRACING PAPER AND DRAW PATTERNS AS SHOWN ONTO TRACING PAPER WITH PENCIL.

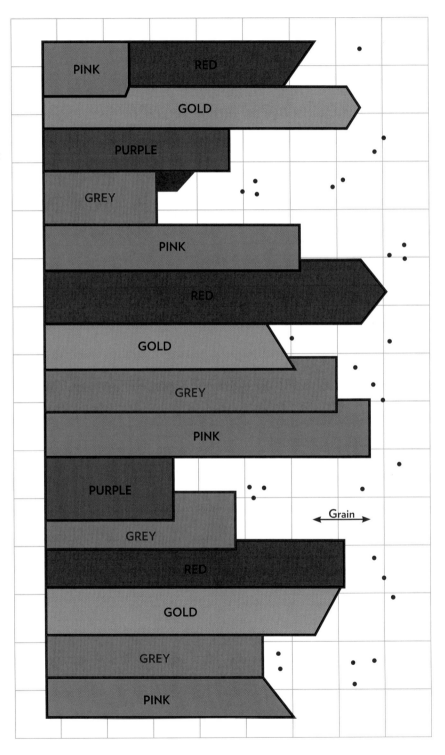

Off-white crochet cotton

1/4-inch black pom-pom for nose

Two 5mm brown beads for eyes

Two small forked twigs for antlers

4-inch length of leather shoelace for collar

Acrylic craft paints—brick red and gold

Small flat paintbrush

3/4-inch wooden bead for pull handle

5-inch-long x 3-1/2-inch-wide x 1/4-inch-thick piece of wood for base

Four 3/4-inch wooden wheels for base

Four small nails to fit through wheels

Hammer

Drill with 1/8-inch drill bit

Polyester stuffing

Hand-sewing needle with large eye

Glue gun and glue stick

Ruler

Scissors

DIRECTIONS:

Reindeer:

1. Trace patterns onto tracing paper with pencil.

2. Cut out shapes following outline of patterns.

3. Cut out pattern pieces from felt as directed on patterns, paying attention to direction of nap.

4. Separate six-strand embroidery floss and thread embroidery needle with two strands of floss for all stitching. See Fig. I on page 212 for stitch illustrations. With wrong sides together and edges even, sew body pieces together with light brown floss and a small blanket stitch, starting at stomach area and leaving an opening for stuffing. Stuff body firmly. Blanket-stitch wrong sides of opening together.

5. Blanket-stitch four sets of legs together in the same way, beginning and ending at the bottom of each leg. Stuff each leg firmly. Then blanket-stitch a sole to the bottom of each leg opening, matching the front of the sole to the front seam of the leg.

6. Blanket-stitch around curved edges of tail with light brown floss.

(continued on page 213)

Reindeer Pull-Toy

CRAFT LEVEL: INTERMEDIATE

FINISHED SIZE: Reindeer measures about 9 inches tall x 7 inches long x 4 inches wide.

Old-fashioned childhood treasures like dolls and other antiques are a source of inspiration for my crafts. I had already designed a series of pull toys—a horse, rabbit, giraffe and elephant. For the Christmas season, I added this adorable reindeer to the herd!

Karen Wittkop ★ Duluth, Minnesota

MATERIALS:

Patterns on page 212

Tracing paper and pencil

18- x 22-1/2-inch piece of light brown plush felt

3-inch square of dark red felt

Six-strand embroidery floss—dark green, gold and light brown

Embroidery needle

Four 1/2-inch two-hole brown buttons for legs

26-inch length of green 3-ply jute string

Reindeer Pull-Toy Patterns

TRACE AND CUT 1 EACH SHAPE—
TRACING PAPER

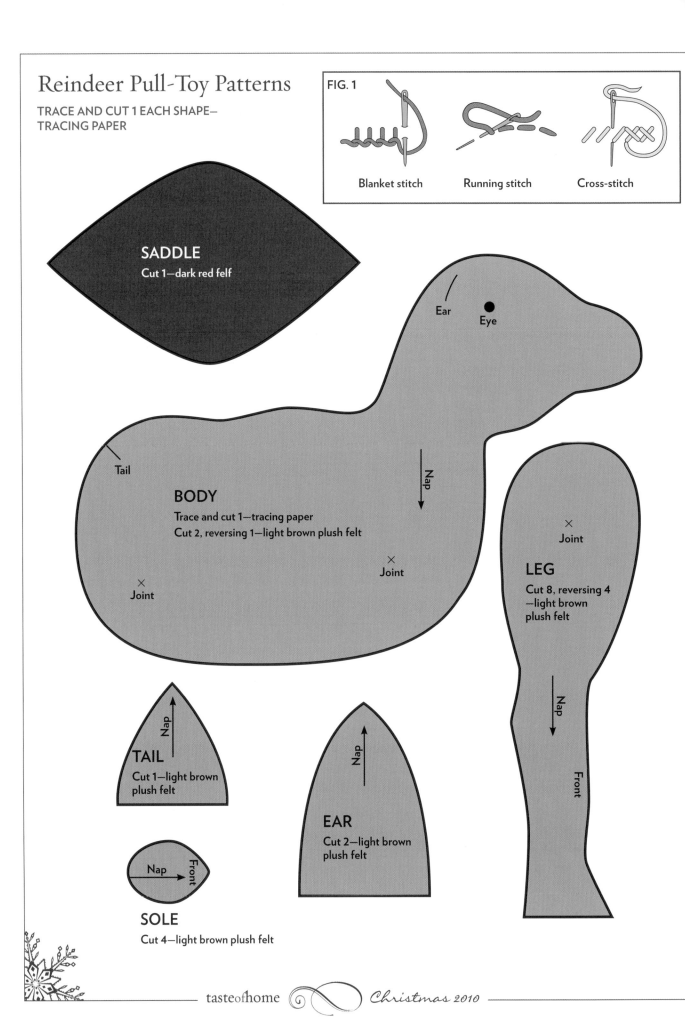

FIG. 1

Blanket stitch   Running stitch   Cross-stitch

SADDLE
Cut 1—dark red felf

Ear   Eye

Tail

Nap

BODY
Trace and cut 1—tracing paper
Cut 2, reversing 1—light brown plush felt

✕
Joint

✕
Joint

✕
Joint

LEG
Cut 8, reversing 4
—light brown
plush felt

Nap

Nap

Front

Nap

TAIL
Cut 1—light brown
plush felt

EAR
Cut 2—light brown
plush felt

Nap   Front

SOLE
Cut 4—light brown plush felt

7. Sew a running stitch along the straight edge of the tail with light brown floss. Pull the floss tight to gather edge and secure floss. Repeat along straight edge of each ear.

8. Cut two 8-in. lengths of crochet cotton. Thread both pieces onto large-eye hand-sewing needle.

9. Place a leg on each side of front of body where shown on pattern, making sure front of leg is facing forward. Insert threaded needle through joint marking at the top of one leg, through body joint marking and out joint at the top of the leg on the other side. Remove needle, leaving the ends of both pieces of crochet cotton extending from each side. On one side of reindeer, insert each strand of crochet cotton into separate holes of one brown button. Tie crochet cotton in a firm knot to secure button. Attach button on other side in same way, except pull crochet cotton tightly before tying knot. Trim ends of crochet cotton, leaving 1/2-in. tails. Repeat for back legs.

10. Glue bead eyes and pom-pom nose to head where shown on pattern. Let dry.

11. Glue straight edges of ears and tail to body where shown in photo. Let dry.

12. Use point of scissors to make two small holes in head between the ears for antlers. Apply a dab of glue to ends of twigs and insert ends into holes. Let dry.

13. Wrap leather shoelace around reindeer's neck for collar and glue ends together so they meet.

14. Cut a 14-in. length of jute string. Tie a loose slip knot in center of string and place loop over nose. Tighten knot and spot-glue in place, leaving ends free.

Saddle:

1. Blanket-stitch around edges of saddle with dark green embroidery floss. Then add a single row of cross-stitches with gold floss just inside the blanket-stitching.

2. Place saddle over reindeer's back with pointed ends on each side.

3. Cut a length of jute string to fit under reindeer from one point of saddle to opposite point.

4. Glue jute to wrong side of saddle at points and spot-glue edges of saddle to reindeer.

Base:

1. In the center of one short side, drill a hole through base about 1/2 in. from edge.

2. Paint wood base and bead brick red and wheels gold. Let dry.

3. Dip end of paintbrush handle into gold paint and dab small dots along each short edge of the wood base.

4. For pull cord, tie a knot in one end of an 8-in. length of jute string. Insert opposite end through hole in base from bottom to top. Thread bead onto other end of string and knot string.

5. Mark spots for wheels on each long side of wood base, positioning them 1 in. from each corner.

6. Attach wheels to sides of base with nails.

7. Stand reindeer on top of base as shown in photo.

8. Glue the bottom of each foot to base. Let dry.

It's a Wrap!

Think outside the box when wrapping Christmas gifts this holiday season with these clever ideas:

Go Beyond Gift Wrap. On some of our pretty packages, we used white butcher block paper, faux suede and tulle. Other ideas include felt, flannel, dish towels, newspaper, magazine pages and brown paper bags.

Get Rid of Ribbon. Secure a wrapped bottle of wine with a ponytail holder or wrap a necktie around a box (both ideas shown at right). You can also use twine, raffia, gold wire and upholstery trim. For a little girl's gift, tie on a new jump rope!

Easy Embellishments. Dress up a wrapped gift with inexpensive things like pom-poms or feathers. Other finishing touches include pine sprigs, pinecones, small jingle bells and cinnamon sticks.

You can even add a little extra gift on the outside of the package. Tie on a silver key ring (as we did), a cookie cutter or candy cane.

DIRECTIONS:

1. Wash and dry the inside of wax-coated paper cartons. Prepare commercial candles molds as directed by manufacturer. (Half-pint milk cartons, 64-ounce juice cartons and commercial molds shown.)

2. Place molds on foil-lined cookie sheet or tray.

3. In a double boiler over low heat, melt clear wax and add candle dye in the color of your choice. Or melt purchased candles, removing and discarding the wicks as the wax melts.

4. Pour a few drops of melted wax into bottom of a mold. Immediately place the end of a taper candle into the wax. Let the wax set.

5. Fill the mold with pieces of ice in different sizes and shapes, taking care to keep the taper candle upright.

6. Pour enough melted wax into the mold to cover the ice.

7. Let stand until the wax is hardened and the ice is melted.

8. Pour out the water and carefully tear the carton away or remove candle from commercial mold as directed.

9. Let the candle stand a few days to dry completely before using.

10. If the taper candle is taller than the ice candle, light and burn the taper candle until it is the same height as the ice candle.

11. When using, place the lighted candle on a holder to collect the wax as it melts.

Crafter's Note: Estimate how much wax you'll need to fill each carton about half full. Having too much wax is better than not having enough.

Ice Candles

CRAFT LEVEL: BEGINNER

FINISHED SIZE: Size will vary depending on size of candle molds used.

These lacy-looking candles are easy to make using wax and candle dye—or even old candles! They take a few days to dry so make them well in advance.

Taste of Home Craft Editor

MATERIALS:

Clear wax for candle making and candle dye in color of choice or purchased candles in color of choice (see Crafter's Note)

Double boiler

Matching taper candle for each candle

Commercial candle molds or wax-coated paper cartons

Crushed ice (enough to fill candle molds)

Foil-lined cookie sheet or tray

Scented Ice Candles

The ice candles can be scented with fragrance oils. Add the oil to the melted wax in step 3, following package directions. If you plan to use the candles on the dinner table, it is best to leave them unscented.

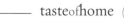

Classy Coupon Holder

CRAFT LEVEL: BEGINNER

FINISHED SIZE: Closed coupon holder measures about 4-1/4 inches high x 8 inches long.

Go to the grocery store in style by storing clipped coupons in this handcrafted holder. Feel free to use whatever color microsuede fabric you prefer.

Taste of Home Craft Editor

MATERIALS:

1/3 yard of red mircosuede fabric

1/3 yard of heavy-weight interfacing or buckrum

All-purpose thread to match fabric

Rotary cutter and mat (optional)

Quilter's ruler

Black square button

Magnetic purse closure

Standard sewing supplies

DIRECTIONS:

Cutting:

1. From red fabric, cut one 8-in. x 16-in. piece for outside of holder and pocket one; one 8-in. x 7-in. piece for pocket two; and one 8-in. x 8-in. piece for pocket three.

2. From interfacing or buckrum, cut one 7-7/8-in. x 8-in. piece for outside of holder and pocket one; one 3-1/2-in. x 7-7/8-in. piece for pocket two; and one 4-in. x 7-7/8-in. piece for pocket three.

Assembly:

1. Fold 8-in. x 16-in. piece of red fabric for outside of holder in half crosswise, right side out to make an 8-in. square. Slip 7-7/8-in. x 8-in. piece of interfacing or buckrum between folded layers.

2. Place fabric and interfacing on a flat surface with the fold at the top. Referring to Fig. 1 at right for placement, attach thinner side of magnetic closure to inside folded edge (top) of coupon holder. Refold fabric with right side out and raw edges matching.

3. With matching thread and a narrow satin stitch, stitch around raw edges only. Do not stitch along folded edge.

4. With a slightly wider stitch, satin-stitch along narrow edge again (top of pocket one) only.

Pockets:

1. Fold 8-in. x 7-in. red fabric piece in half crosswise with right side out to make a 3-1/2-in. x 8-in. piece. Slip 3-1/2-in. x 7-7/8-in. piece of interfacing or buckrum for pocket two inside folded red piece with long raw edges matching.

2. Fold 8-in. x 8-in. red fabric piece in half with right side out to make a 4-in. x 8-in. piece. Slip 4-in. x 7-7/8-in. piece of interfacing of buckrum for pocket three inside folded red piece with long raw edges matching.

3. Stitch over first stitching with a slightly wider satin stitch.

4. Referring to Fig. 1 below, fold satin-stitched edge of outside of holder up as shown to form pocket one. Attach thicker side of magnet closure to outside of first pocket.

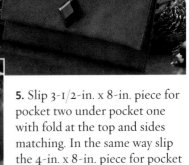

5. Slip 3-1/2-in. x 8-in. piece for pocket two under pocket one with fold at the top and sides matching. In the same way slip the 4-in. x 8-in. piece for pocket three under pocket two.

6. Holding all layers securely with edges matching, satin-stitch opposite sides with a slightly wider stitch. Fasten off all loose threads.

Finishing:

1. Attach button to front flap of coupon holder.

2. Fold top down to close.

FIG. 1

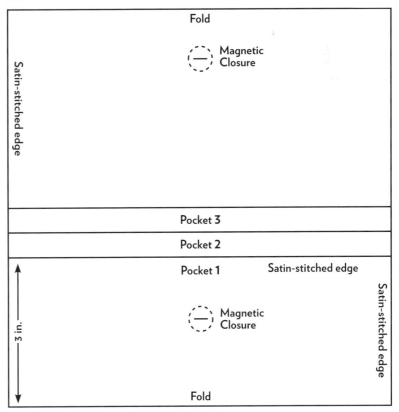

Festive Package Tags

CRAFT LEVEL: QUICK & EASY

FINISHED SIZE: Excluding ribbon loop, each gift tag measures about 3-3/8 inches high x 3 inches wide.

Give your gifts a special handcrafted touch with these fun tags. They're so quick and easy to make, you may never use store-bought ones again!

Loretta Mateik ★ Petaluma, California

MATERIALS (FOR TWO TAGS):

Patterns at right

Tracing paper and pencil

Card stock—3-inch x 6-inch piece of solid in color of choice for each ornament; 2-inch square of coordinating color for trees; scrap of contrasting color for ornament top and scrap of brown for tree trunk

1/8-inch circle hole punch

Glue-on rhinestones for trims

Two 6-inch lengths of 1/8-inch-wide coordinating satin ribbon

Black fine-line marker

Tacky (white) glue

Scissors

DIRECTIONS:

1. Trace patterns, separately onto tracing paper with pencil. Cut out each.

2. Fold each 3-in. x 6-in. piece of card stock in half crosswise to make a 3-in. square.

3. Place ornament pattern on top of a piece of folded card stock, positioning the fold of pattern on fold of card stock piece. Trace around pattern and cut out. Repeat with remaining pieces of folded card stock.

4. Fold scrap card stock in half. Place ornament top pattern on folded card stock, positioning the fold of pattern on fold of card stock. Trace around pattern. Trace one more ornament top in the same way. Cut out two tops.

5. Trace the tree pattern onto coordinating card stock pieces. Trace the trunk pattern twice onto brown card stock. Cut out two trunks and two trees.

6. Glue an ornament top to the top of each ornament, positioning the fold of the ornament top over fold of ornament.

7. Referring to the photo at left for position, glue a tree trunk and then a tree to each ornament.

8. Glue trims to trees.

9. Use punch to make a hole through each ornament top.

10. Thread a length of ribbon through the hole in each ornament top and tie the ends together to form a loop.

11. Use marker to write "To:" and "From:" on inside or front of each gift tag.

Gift Tag Patterns

TRACE 1 EACH—TRACING PAPER

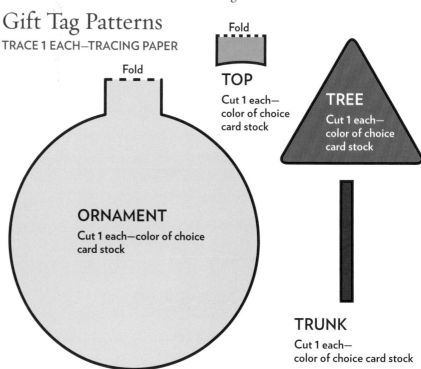

Fold

ORNAMENT
Cut 1 each—color of choice card stock

Fold

TOP
Cut 1 each—color of choice card stock

TREE
Cut 1 each—color of choice card stock

TRUNK
Cut 1 each—color of choice card stock

St. Nick Finger Towel

CRAFT LEVEL: QUICK AND EASY

FINISHED SIZE: Design area of towel is 32 stitches high x 177 stitches wide and measures about 2-1/4 inches high x 12-3/4 inches wide.

With a bundle of toys flung over his back, this right jolly old elf will keep Christmas memories and dreams close at hand. This cross-stitched festive fingertip towel makes a handy holiday keepsake or gift.

Penny Duff ★ Kennebunk, Maine

MATERIALS:

Chart at right

14-inch x 24-inch white fringed terry cloth towel with 3-inch-wide 14-count Aida cloth insert (Charles Craft Kitchen Mates towel shown)

DMC six-strand embroidery floss in colors listed on color key

Size 24 tapestry needle

Scissors

DIRECTIONS:

1. Fold Aida cloth insert of towel in half lengthwise and then in half crosswise to determine center and mark this point. To find center of towel chart, draw lines across chart, connecting opposite arrows. Begin stitching Santa at this point so design will be centered.

2. Stitch border section on each side of Santa where shown on chart.

3. Use 18-in. lengths of six-strand floss. Longer strands tend to separate and fray.

4. Separate strands and use three strands for cross-stitches and one strand for backstitches. See Fig. 1 below for stitch illustrations.

5. Each square on chart equals one stitch worked over a set of fabric threads. Use colors indicated on color key to complete cross-stitching.

6. Do not knot floss on back of work. Instead, leave a tail of floss on back of work and hold it in place while working the first few stitches over it. To end a strand, run needle under a few neighboring stitches in back before cutting floss close to work.

7. When stitching is complete, and only if necessary, gently wash stitched towel in lukewarm water. Press right side down on another terry towel to dry.

COLOR KEY	DMC
☐ White	000
▨ Light Shell Pink	224
▨ Medium Holiday Red	304
▨ Medium Navy Blue	311
▨ Dark Pistachio Green	367
▨ Pearl Gray	415
■ Medium Garnet	815
▨ Light Antique Blue	932
▨ Very Dark Peach Flesh	948
— Very Dark Coffee Brown	898

CROSS-STITCHED SANTA CHART

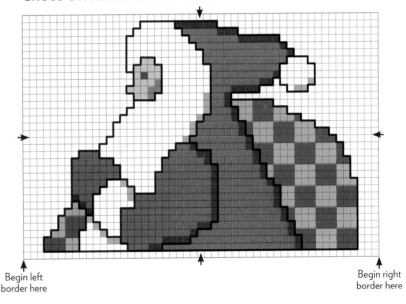

Begin left border here

Begin right border here

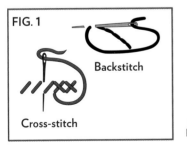

FIG. 1

Backstitch

Cross-stitch

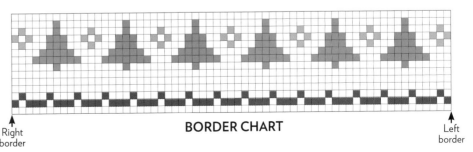

Right border

BORDER CHART

Left border

Polar Bear Money Holder

CRAFT LEVEL: **QUICK & EASY**

FINISHED SIZE: Polar bear money holder measures about 6-3/4 inches across x 5-3/4 inches high.

Give your loved ones a holiday hug by hanging "beary" cute money holders on your Christmas tree. They make the gift of giving currency and gift cards alike more memorable.

Taste of Home Craft Editor

MATERIALS:

Patterns below

Tracing paper and pencil

9-inch x 12-inch piece of white wool felt

1/2-inch black pom-pom for nose

Needle-felting equipment or tacky craft glue

Two 1/4-inch wiggle eyes

Clear monofilament thread for hanging loop

Hand-sewing needle

Scissors

DIRECTIONS:

1. Trace enlarged patterns onto tracing paper with pencil.

2. Cut out patterns following outline of patterns.

3. Cut three body pieces from felt.

4. Stack two body pieces with edges matching and either glue the pieces together or needle-felt them together.

5. Glue or needle-felt the tail piece to the back of the body piece.

6. Glue or needle felt the front legs to the back of the bottom edge of the body.

7. Glue or needle-felt the back legs to the front of the bottom edge of the body piece, leaving the upper curved edges free.

8. Glue or needle-felt the ears to the back of the head piece.

9. Glue or needle-felt the pom-pom nose to the center of the head piece.

10. Gluc or needle-felt the head to the body piece, leaving the upper and side edges free.

11. Place the remaining body piece on the back of the assembled bear with edges matching.

12. Glue or needle-felt the bottom and sides where shown on the pattern, leaving room to insert a gift card or money.

13. Thread hand-sewing needle with monofilament thread. Stitch through back piece of body. Tie ends in a knot to form a hanging loop.

Polar Bear Patterns

ENLARGE PATTERN 200%
EACH SQUARE = 1 INCH
TRACE 1 EACH PIECE—
TRACING PAPER

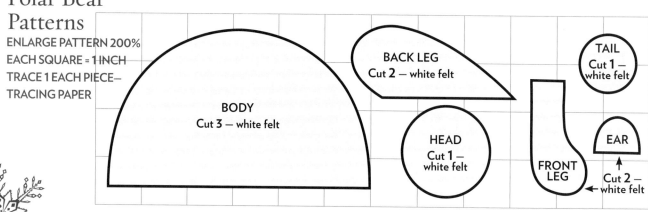

BACK LEG
Cut 2 — white felt

TAIL
Cut 1 —
white felt

BODY
Cut 3 — white felt

HEAD
Cut 1 —
white felt

FRONT LEG
Cut 2 —
white felt

EAR
Cut 2 —
white felt

Toothpick

Business-size envelope

Craft knife

Ruler

Rub-on glue stick

Scissors

DIRECTIONS:

1. From white card stock cut one 8- x 9-1/2-in. piece and one 3- x 8-1/2-in. piece.

2. Fold the larger piece of white card stock in half to form a 4- x 9-1/2-in. card.

3. Glue the blue card stock piece to the center front of the card.

4. Glue the smaller piece of white card stock to the center of the construction paper.

5. Trace the tree pattern at bottom, onto tracing paper and cut out tree.

6. Lay tree cutout on corrugated cardboard and trace around the shape with pencil. Cut out tree with craft knife.

7. Pour a small puddle of green paint onto foam plate or palette. Use paintbrush to apply paint to one side of cardboard tree.

8. Press the painted side of the tree onto the front of the card with the tree trunk centered about 1-1/4 in. from the bottom edge of the top piece of card stock. Carefully lift off the cardboard tree. Let dry.

9. Referring to photo at left for position, use gold metallic dimensional paint to draw a garland on tree. Add several random small gold dots around tree for snow.

10. Add a larger dot of gold metallic dimensional paint above top point of tree. Before paint dries, use toothpick to pull out the points of a star from the center of this dot. Let dry.

Stamped Christmas Tree Card

CRAFT LEVEL: QUICK & EASY

FINISHED SIZE: Card measures 4 inches wide x 9-3/8 inches high.

Pressed for time during the Christmas season? With my evergreen idea, you can still send out homemade greetings to everyone on your list. This design is surprisingly simple.

Emilda Harrington ★ Halifax, Nova Scotia

MATERIALS:

Pattern at right

Tracing paper and pencil

Cutting board or self-sealing mat

Two 8-1/2-inch x 11-inch sheets of white card stock

3-1/2-inch x 9-inch piece of blue card stock

6-inch square of corrugated cardboard

Green acrylic craft paint

Gold metallic dimensional paint

Foam plate or palette

1/2-inch flat paintbrush

Stamped Card Pattern

TRACE 1—TRACING PAPER
CUT 1—CORRUGATED CARDBOARD

A Forest of Trees

This tree design would be wonderful on note cards, gift tags or place cards. Just reduce the size of the tree pattern to fit the paper. The tree will also look great with silver metallic garland.

Flying Geese Crocheted Pillow

CRAFT LEVEL: INTERMEDIATE

FINISHED SIZE: Pillow measures
14 inches x 14 inches.

*The flying geese quilt pattern was
the inspiration for this design. These
comfortable black and tan pillows will
enhance any decor throughout the year.*

Jacqueline Jewett ★ Blauvelt, New York

MATERIALS (FOR ONE):

Red Heart Luster Sheen crochet thread—
one skein of black and two skeins of tan

Size 1 steel crochet hook or size needed to
obtain correct gauge

14-inch x 14-inch pillow form

Yarn or tapestry needle

Hand-sewing needle

Matching all-purpose thread

Three small snap sets

Scissors

GUAGE: Each complete square measures
about 3 inches square. Slight variation in gauge
will change finished size a bit.

DIRECTIONS:

Front:

Two-color square (make 16):

With tan, ch 5, join with a sl st in first
ch made to form a ring.

Round 1: Ch 3 for first dc, work 2 dcs in
ring, ch 3, work 3 dcs in ring, ch 3, drop
tan and pick up black, [work 3 dcs in
ring, ch 3] twice, join with a sl st in top
of beginning ch-3, turn: four 3 dc sets
and four ch-3s.

Round 2: Sl st in ch-3 sp, ch 3 for first
dc, dc in same ch-sp, work 1 dc in each
of the next 3 dcs of previous round,
(work 2 dcs, ch 3, 2 dcs) in next ch-3 sp,
work 1 dc in each of the next 3 dcs of
previous round, work 2 dcs in next ch-3
sp, ch 3, drop black, pick up tan, work 2
dcs in same ch-sp, work 1 dc in each of
the next 3 dcs of previous round, (work
2 dcs, ch 3, 2 dcs) in next ch-3 sp, work 1
dc in each of the next 3 dcs of previous
round, work 2 dcs in next ch-3 sp, ch 3,
join with a sl st in top of beginning ch-3,
turn: 28 dcs and four ch-3 corners.

Round 3: Sl st in ch-3 sp, ch 3 for first
dc, dc in same ch-sp work 1 dc in each
of the next 7 dcs of previous round,
(work 2 dcs, ch 3, 2 dcs) in next ch-3
sp, work 1 dc in each of the next 7 dcs
of previous round, work 2 dcs, in next
ch-3 sp, ch 3, drop tan, pick up black,
work 2 dcs in same ch-sp, work 1 dc
in each of the next 7 dcs of previous
round, (work 2 dcs, ch 3, 2 dcs) in next
ch-3 sp, work 1 dc in each of the next
7 dcs of previous round, work 2 dcs in
next ch-3 sp, ch 3, join with a sl st in top
of beginning ch-3, turn 44 dcs and four
ch-3 corners.

Round 4: Sl st in ch-3 sp, ch 3 for first dc,

dc in same ch-sp work 1 dc in each of the
next 11 dcs of previous round, (work 2
dcs, ch 3, 2 dcs) in next ch-3 sp, work 1
dc in each of the next 11 dcs of previous
round, work 2 dcs, in next ch-3 sp, ch 3,
drop black, pick up tan, work 2 dcs in
same ch-sp, work 1 dc in each of the next
11 dcs of previous round, (work 2 dcs, ch
3, 2 dcs) in next ch-3 sp, work 1 dc in each
of the next 11 dcs of previous round, work
2 dcs in next ch-3 sp, ch 3, join with a sl st
in top of beginning ch-3. Fasten off: 60
dcs and four ch-3 corners.

Joining Squares:

Referring to photo at left, lay out
completed squares right side up as
shown. Sew squares together, securing
corners with tan and then with black.

Front Border:

Round 1: Starting at the lower right front
edge and using black, * ch 3 for first
dc, work 1 dc same ch-sp, dc around,
working 2 dcs tog along center of each
square to next corner, (work 2 dcs,
ch 3, 2 dcs) in next corner, dc around,
working 2 dcs along center of each tan
square to next corner, work 2 dcs, ch
3 in next corner, change to tan; repeat
from * around, join with a sl st in top of
beginning ch-3 top.

Round 2: Working in matching colors, dc
in each dc and (work 2 dcs, ch 3, 2 dcs) in
each ch-3 of previous round. Fasten off.

Back:

Row 1: With tan, ch 65, dc in fourth
ch from hk and in each remaining ch
across: 63 dcs.

Rows 2-35: Turn, ch 3, dc in each dc
across: 63 dcs.

Sc one row along ends of rows,
decreasing 5 sts evenly along edge.
Repeat on other side.

Back Border:

Round 1: Starting at one corner with tan,
ch 3, for first dc, work 1 dc in same sp, *
work 1 dc in each st across, (work 2 dcs, ch
3, 2 dcs) in next corner, work 1 dc in each
st across, work 2 dcs in next corner, ch
3, change to black, work 2 dcs in corner,
repeat from * around, join with a sl st in
top of beginning ch-3.

Round 2: Working in matching colors, dc in each dc and (work 2 dcs, ch 3, 2 dcs) in each ch-3 of previous round. Fasten off.

Finishing:

Place front and back of pillow together with wrong sides facing and colored edges matching. With front of pillow facing you, join black to bottom right edge, sc through both front and back of pillow. Work along first side edge, work 4 scs in first corner, sc across top to next corner, work 2 scs in corner, with tan, work 2 scs in corner, sc along other side of pillow, work 4 scs in corner, then working along bottom front of pillow only, sc to next corner, work 2 scs in corner, join with a sl st in first st of round. Fasten off.

Sc along remaining edge of back of pillow. Fasten off.

Inside Flap:

Row 1: With tan, join yarn to open edge of pillow top, dc across.

Row 2-6: Turn, ch 3, dc in each st across.

Row 7: Turn ch 1, sc in each st across. Fasten off.

Weave in all loose ends.

Sew one side of snaps sets to inside flap and remaining sides to opposite side of inside back of pillow.

Insert pillow form and snap closed.

ABBREVIATIONS	
ch(s)	chain(s)
dc(s)	double crochet(s)
hk	hook
RS	right side
sc(s)	single crochet(s)
sl st	slip stitch
st(s)	stitch(es)
tog	together
( )	Instructions between parentheses are all worked in same stitch or space indicated.
* or [ ]	Instructions following astericks or within brackets are repeated as directed.

Three-Tiered Beaded Necklace

CRAFT LEVEL: BEGINNER

FINISHED SIZE: Necklace is about 27-3/4 inches long.

The sparkling strands of this beaded necklace make a gorgeous gift for Christmas—or any time at all. When I came across an assortment of frosted blue beads at a store, I knew right away I wanted to string them into this necklace. I use red and green varieties when I want a more Christmasy look. No matter what kind I choose, though, the simple design always works up quickly—in about an hour.

Jenna Osborne ★ Jackson, Ohio

MATERIALS:

One shallow, rimmed container for each bead variety and mixture

White beading thread

No. 11 beading needle

Measuring tape

Scissors

Two silver cup bead tips

Toggle clasp set

Needle-nose pliers

Jewelry glue

Beads for Inner Strand:

Mixture of at least 288 size 10 glass seed beads—dark blue transparent, light blue transparent, powder blue opaque and white opaque

Twenty-four 3mm denim blue seed beads

Four 9mm x 10mm frosted blue barrel beads

Four 12.5mm x 14mm frosted crystal barrel beads

Four 17mm x 19mm blue lapis barrel beads

Beads for Center Strand:

At least 500 size 10 powder blue opaque glass seed beads

Nineteen 6mm round blue transparent glass beads

Beads for Outer Strand:

Mixture of at least 336 size 10 glass seed beads—dark blue transparent, medium blue transparent and powder blue opaque

Five 6mm x 9mm opaque blue oat beads

About 22 coordinating dark blue, medium blue and white glass beads in assorted shapes and sizes ranging from 6mm to 1/2 inch

DIRECTIONS:

General Instructions:

1. Pour each size 10 glass seed bead mixture, the assorted glass beads for outer strand and each remaining bead variety into separate shallow, rimmed containers.

2. Keep the thread tension tight as you work.

3. Dab jewelry glue on all knots and let dry before continuing.

Beading:

Inner strand:

1. Cut a 36-in. length of thread. Add needle to one end.

2. Holding loose end of thread between your fingers so bead does not fall off, string one size 10 glass seed bead onto thread. Leaving a tail of thread, knot the loose end of the thread.

3. String one silver bead tip onto the thread, positioning the bead tip so the seed bead rests tightly inside the cup of the bead tip.

(continued on page 222)

4. String 22 randomly mixed seed beads, one 3mm denim blue bead, the barrel bead of your choice and another 3mm denim blue bead onto the thread. Repeat this pattern 11 times or until the inner strand measures about 19-1/2 in., alternating the different barrel beads as desired.

5. Add 22 more randomly mixed seed beads, the remaining silver bead tip and another seed bead, positioning it inside the cup of the bead tip as before.

6. Pull beads together and bring the thread back through the silver bead tip. Knot thread.

7. Bring the tail of thread back through the last 10 beads on the strand. Trim the excess thread.

Center strand:
1. Cut a 36-in. length of thread. Add needle to one end.

2. Tie loose end of thread to one silver bead tip on first strand.

3. String 25 powder blue seed beads and one 6mm round blue transparent glass bead onto thread. Repeat this pattern 18 times or until center strand measures about 23-1/2 in.

4. Add 25 powder blue seed beads.

5. Pull beads together and bring the thread through the second silver bead tip. Knot thread.

6. Bring the tail of thread back through the last 10 beads on the strand. Trim the excess thread.

Outer strand:
1. Cut a 36-in. length of thread. Add needle to one end.

2. Tie loose end of thread to one bead tip on first and second strands.

3. String 12 randomly mixed seed beads, then add one bead of your choice from the oat beads or assortment of glass beads. Repeat this pattern 26 times or until outer strand measures about 27 in.

4. Add 12 randomly mixed seed beads.

5. Pull the beads together and bring the thread through the second silver bead tip. Knot thread.

6. Bring the tail of thread back through the last 10 beads on the strand. Trim the excess thread.

Finishing:
1. Add one half of the toggle clasp to each silver bead tip.

2. Gently use the needle-nose pliers to close the hooks of the bead tips around the toggle clasp rings.

Crafter's Note: Three of the assorted glass beads shown have large holes. On each side of those beads, add a blue 3mm seed bead to prevent the assorted glass beads from sliding over the size 10 seed beads next to them.

Depending on the sizes of assorted glass beads you choose, you may need to string additional beads onto the outer strand so that it reaches the appropriate length (about 27 inches).

Lacy Christmas Balls
CRAFT LEVEL: INTERMEDIATE
FINISHED SIZE: Size will vary depending of size of ball ornaments. Gold ornament is about 2-3/4 inches in diameter. Purple ornament is about 3 inches in diameter. Silver ornament is about 2-1/2 inches in diameter. Teal ornament is about 1-3/4 inches in diameter.

For instant elegance, cover plain ball ornaments with these lacy crocheted pieces. With the four patterns included here, you'll love to dress up your Christmas tree.

Edith Calhoun ★ Elba, Alabama

MATERIALS (FOR ALL):
Twilley's Goldfingering metallic yarn— one ball each of Multi-Goldfingering Golddigger metallic yarn; Purple Goldfingering metallic yarn; Silver Goldfingering metallic yarn and Teal Goldfingering metallic yarn

Size 6 (1.75mm) steel crochet hook

Scissors

Assorted ball ornaments

DIRECTIONS:

Gold Ornament:

With gold yarn, ch 8, join with a sl st in first ch made to form a ring.

Round 1: Ch 4 for first tr, work 2 trs in ring keeping last lp of each on hk, yo and draw yarn through all lps on hk to make a tr cl, ch 5, [work 3 tr cl in ring, ch 5] five times, join with a sl st in top of first tr cl: 6 tr cls.

Round 2: In each ch-sp around, work (1 sc, 1 hdc, 2 dcs, 1 hdc, 1 sc), join with a sl st in first sc.

Round 3: Ch 8 [sc between the next 2 dcs, ch 5, dc between the next 2 scs, ch 5] around, join with a sl st in the third ch of the beginning ch-8.

Round 4: Sl st in next ch-sp, sc in ch-sp, ch 3, sc in same sp, [ch 5, (sc in next ch-sp, ch 3, sc) in same sp] around, ch 2, dc in first sc to bring yarn up to start next round.

Round 5: Sc in same ch-sp, [ch 6, sc in next ch-sp] around, ch 3, dc in first sc.

Rounds 6-10: Repeat Round 5. Leave an 8-in. length of yarn at the end of last round. Thread end through ch-sps of last round made.

Slip cover over ornament. Pull yarn end to tighten cover around top of ornament. Fasten yarn and clip end.

Purple Ornament:

With purple yarn, ch 6, join with a sl st in first ch made to form a ring.

Round 1: Ch 3 for first dc, work 17 dcs in ring, join with a sl st in top of beginning ch 3: 18 dcs.

Round 2: Ch 8, [sk 1 dc, sc in next dc] around, ch 4, tr in last dc to bring yarn up to start next round.

Round 3: Sc in top of lp, ch 3, sc in same sp, [ch 6, sc in next ch-sp, ch 3, sc in same ch-sp] around, ch 3, dc in first sc.

Rounds 4-7: Repeat Round 3. Leave an 8-in. length of yarn at the end of last round. Thread end through ch-sps of last round made.

Slip cover over ornament. Pull yarn end to tighten cover around top of ornament. Fasten yarn and clip end.

Silver Ornament:

With silver yarn, ch 6, join with a sl st in first ch made to form a ring.

Round 1: Ch 3 for first dc, dc in ring, [ch 2, work 2 dcs in ring] seven times, ch 2, join with a sl st in top of beginning ch-3.

Round 2: Sl st in next ch-2 sp, ch 3, work (1 dc, ch 2, 2 dcs) in same ch-sp, [in next ch-sp, work 1 dc, ch 2, 1 dc, in next ch-sp, work 2 dcs, ch 2, 2 dcs] around, join with a sl st in top of beginning ch-3.

Round 3: Sl st in next ch-2 sp, ch 5, dc in same ch-sp, ch 1, [in next ch-2 sp, work 2 dcs, ch 2, 2 dcs, ch 1, in next ch-2 sp, work 1 dc, ch 2, 1 dc, ch 1] around, join with a sl st in third ch of beginning ch-5.

Round 4: Sl st in next ch-2 sp, sc in same ch-sp, [ch 8, sc in next ch-2 sp] around to beginning ch-2 sp, ch 4, tr in first sc to bring yarn up to start next round.

Round 5: Sc in same sp, ch 3, sc in same sp, [ch 6, sc in next ch-sp, ch 3, sc in same sp] around, ch 3, dc in first sc.

Rounds 6-7: Sc in ch-sp [ch 6, sc in next ch-sp] around, ch 3, dc in first sc. Leave an 8-in. length of yarn at the end of last round. Thread end through ch-sps of last round made.

Slip cover over ornament. Pull yarn end to tighten cover around top of ornament. Fasten yarn and clip end.

Teal Ornament:

With teal yarn, ch 6, join with a sl st in first ch made to form a ring.

Round 1: [Ch 8, sc in ring] six times, ch 4, tr in ring to bring yarn up to start next round: 7 ch-sps.

Round 2: Sc in same sp, [ch 6, sc in next ch-8 sp] around, ch 3, dc in first sc.

Round 3: [Sc in ch-6 sp, ch 6] around, ch 3, dc in first sc.

Rounds 4-5: Repeat Round 3. Leave a 6-in. length of yarn at the end of last round. Thread end through ch-sps of last round made.

Slip cover over ornament. Pull yarn end to tighten cover around top of ornament. Fasten yarn and clip end.

ABBREVIATIONS

ch(s)	chain(s)
cl	cluster
dc(s)	double crochet(s)
hdc(s)	half double crochet(s)
hk	hook
lp(s)	loop(s)
sc(s)	single crochet(s)
sl	slip
sk	skip
sp(s)	space(s)
st(s)	stitch(es)
tr(s)	treble crochet(s)
yo	yarn over
[ ]	Instructions between brackets are repeated as directed.
( )	Instructions between parentheses are all worked in stitch or space indicated.

Add Your Own Touch

The balls, pictured at left, use a monochromatic color scheme. Mix-and-match the balls and yarn...try a light blue with the silver balls, brown or copper with a gold ball and pink or silver with a purple ball. For more variety, experiment with various metallic yarns.

pattern below and photo at left as a guide while painting.

1. Trace pattern below onto tracing paper with pencil.

2. Slip graphite paper between pattern and glass ornament and trace over pattern lines to transfer pattern onto ornament.

3. Use flat brush and flesh to paint face.

4. Use flat brush and gold to paint hair.

5. Use flat brush and turquoise to paint wings.

6. Use round brush and orange to paint halo around angel's head.

7. Use liner and white to add details to wings.

8. Use liner and gold metallic paint to outline halo and wings. Paint over left side of angel's hair with gold metallic paint.

9. Use fine-line marker to outline hair and to add details to angel's face.

10. Use round brush and pink to add cheeks.

Finishing:

1. Glue rhinestones to halo. Let dry.

2. Tie both lengths of narrow metallic ribbon to hanging loop of ornament. Tie one piece in a small bow. Coil all ribbon ends.

3. Thread blue-and-white ribbon through hanger of ornament.

4. Place feathers inside ornament.

Painted Angel Christmas Bulb

CRAFT LEVEL: BEGINNER

FINISHED SIZE: Painted angel ornament measures 4 inches across. Design area measures about 3-1/8 inches across x 2-1/2 inches high.

I turn ordinary clear glass ornaments into an extraordinary adornment by painting on an angel face. Hang them from your evergreens or from a single ornament stand.

Emma Acevedo ★ Milwaukee, Wisconsin

MATERIALS:

4-inch-diameter clear glass ornament

Rubbing alcohol and cotton ball

Pattern at right

Tracing paper and pencil

Graphite paper

Water container

Paper towels

Foam plate or palette

Acrylic craft paints—flesh, gold, gold metallic, orange, pink, turquoise and white

Paintbrushes—small flat, small round and liner

Black fine-line permanent marker

Five flat-back rhinestones

Craft glue

White craft feathers

Two 12-inch lengths of narrow gold metallic wire-edge ribbon

6-inch length of 5/8-inch-wide blue-and-white polka dot ribbon

DIRECTIONS:

Wipe outside of ornament with cotton ball and rubbing alcohol to remove fingerprints and oil. Avoid touching area to be painted.

Painting:

Keep paper towels and container of water handy to clean brushes. Place small amounts of paint as needed onto foam plate or palette. Let paint dry after every application. Refer to

Painted Angel Pattern

**TRACE 1—TRACING PAPER
PAINT AS DIRECTED**

Wine Bottle
Gift Sack

CRAFT LEVEL: QUICK & EASY

FINISHED SIZE: Wine bottle cover has a 4-inch diameter and is about 11 inches high. Size can be adjusted to fit other size bottles.

When taking a bottle of wine as a hostess gift, make it more of a present by tucking it inside a fabric gift bag. You'll be pleasantly surprised at how easy they are to make!

Taste of Home Craft Editor

MATERIALS (FOR ONE):

White chenille fabric—two 13-1/2 x 6-1/2-inch pieces and one 4-1/2-inch circle

White all-purpose thread

28-inch length of 2mm red bead string, two 24-inch lengths of purple satin rattail cord or two 34-inch lengths of turquoise cording

Small safety pin or bodkin

4-inch circle of lightweight cardboard

Standard sewing supplies

DIRECTIONS:

1. Place the two 13-1/2- x 6-1/2-in. pieces of white chenille together with right sides facing and edges matching. Sew the long edges together with a 1/4-in. seam, leaving a 1/4-in. opening 4 in. from one end on each side.

2. Fold 2-1/4 in. of the same edge to the wrong side. Pin as needed to hold. Sew around close to the raw edge. Sew 1/4 in. from previous stitching to form a channel for the ribbon or cording.

3. With right sides facing, pin the 4-1/2-in. circle of white chenille to the bottom opening. Sew circle piece to bottom edge with a 1/4-in. seam.

Drawstring:

1. Attach small safety pin or bodkin to one end of ribbon or cording. Insert safety pin or bodkin in opening on one side of bottle cover. Thread ribbon or cording through the entire channel and exit it through the same opening. Tie ends in a knot.

2. In the same way, insert the other length of ribbon or cording into the channel at the opening on the opposite side of the bottle cover.

Finishing:

1. Place circle of cardboard inside bottom of bottle cover.

2. Place bottle inside bottle cover. Pull knotted ends of ribbon or cording to close opening or wrap bead string around top. Tie ends in a bow on the front of the bottle cover.

Cozy Gift Sacks

Make the sacks in different sizes and with different soft materials, such as velveteen, flannel, polar fleece and micro-suede. Use them to package perfume, bubble bath or homemade jams and jellies.

Peppermint Twist Afghan

CRAFT LEVEL: INTERMEDIATE

FINISHED SIZE: Afghan measures about 67 inches long x 51 inches wide.

I've found that crochet patterns for double-ended hooks are scarce. When my sister asked me to design projects using double-ended hooks, I began experimenting and came up with this design on my own. The red and white color scheme is as pretty as peppermint candy.

Darla Fanton ★ Portland, Oregon

MATERIALS:

4-ply worsted-weight yarn (Red Heart Super Saver and Red Heart Classic yarn shown)—35 ounces of Cherry Red, 28 ounces of White and 12 ounces of Paddy Green

10-inch-long size P double-ended crochet hook (Cro-Hook) Size N/15 (10mm) crochet hook

Yarn or tapestry needle

Scissors

GAUGE: 12 sts and 16 rows = 4 inches. Check guage to save time.

DIRECTIONS:

This afghan is worked with two strands of yarn held together and worked as one throughout. As you work, remember that every lp has two strands. When picking up a lp in a horizontal st, always insert the hk under both strands of the top lp only.

Strip (make 5):

Row 1: With double-ended hk and two strands of Cherry Red held together as one, ch 23 (remembering that the lp on hk never counts as a ch); insert hk in top lp of second ch from hk, yo and draw yarn through so there are 2 lps on hk; * insert hk through top lp of next ch, yo and draw yarn through, adding another new lp; repeat from * across: count 23 lps on hk. Slide all stitches to opposite end of hook, then turn hk so these sts are at left end of hk. Leave Cherry Red uncut to be picked up and worked again later.

Votive Trim Kits

Some festive trims are all you need to fashion cute candleholders for the holidays. Trim the candleholders yourself and give them as gifts. Or if the recipient is crafty, assemble a kit for them to put together.

Taste of Home Craft Editor

CRAFT LEVEL: QUICK & EASY

FINISHED SIZE: Vases shown each measure 3 inches high x 3 inches square. Trim can be added to any size vase.

MATERIALS (FOR ONE):

3-inch-high x 3-inch-square clear glass vase

Double-sided transparent tape

12-inch length of trim of choice or enough to go around each vase the number of desired times

Scissors

Tea light or votive candle for each vase

DIRECTIONS:

1. Place a strip of double-sided transparent tape around vase where trim is desired.

2. Starting at one corner, add trim over tape. Trim excess.

3. Place tea light or votive candle inside vase.

4. Repeat with remaining vases.

5. Give trimmed vases as a gift and include additional trims for other occasions.

Row 2: With two strands of White held together as one, make a slip knot on left end of hk and draw this lp through first lp on hk; * working from left to right, yo and draw yarn through next 2 lps on hk (one of each color); repeat from * until 1 lp remains. Do not turn work.

Row 3: Working from right to left with White, ch 1, insert hk through top lp of second horizontal st, yo and draw through a new lp, insert hk under next vertical bar, yo and draw through a new lp; * sk next horizontal st and vertical bar, insert hk through top lp of next horizontal st, yo and draw through a new lp, insert hk under next vertical bar, yo and draw through a new lp; repeat from * across: count 23 lps on hk. Slide all sts to opposite end of hk and turn hk as before. Leave White uncut to be picked up and worked again later.

Row 4: Working from left to right with Cherry Red, yo and draw yarn through first lp on hk; * yo and draw yarn through 2 lps on hk (one of each color); repeat from * until 1 lp remains. Do not turn work.

Row 5: Repeat Row 3 with Cherry Red instead of White.

Row 6: Repeat Row 4 with White instead of Cherry Red.

Rows 7-144: Repeat Rows 3-6, ending with a Row 4.

Row 145: Working from right to left with Cherry Red, ch 1, sk first vertical bar; * insert hk in top lp of next horizontal st, yo and draw yarn through this st and the lp on hk; repeat from * across. Fasten off Cherry Red. Cut White.

Edging:
Round 1: With the predominantly red side of strip facing you and Row 145 at the top, use size N hk to join two strands of Cherry Red with a sl st in the upper right corner of strip, ch 3, work 2 dcs in same sp; working in sts at top and bottom edges of strip and in the end of each row on long edges of strip, * [ch 1, sk 1 st (or row), dc in next st] to corner, ending last repeat with 3 dcs in corner st; repeat from * around, ending with a sl st in top of beginning ch-3. Fasten off.
Round 2: Join two strands of Paddy Green with a sc in first dc of any corner

3-dcs. * Work 3 scs in each corner dc, [dc in skipped st (or row) below next ch-1 sp, sc in next dc] to next corner; repeat from * around, ending last repeat with a sl st in beginning sc. Fasten off.

Add edging to two more strips in the same way. Turn the remaining two strips over so the predominantly White side is facing, then add the two rounds of edging as before.

Assembly:
1. With the predominantly red side of one strip facing the predominantly white side of another strip and edges even, whipstitch one long edge of two strips together through back lps only with Paddy Green. See Fig. 1 at right for stitch illustration.

2. Continue to add strips in this manner so the colors alternate.

Afghan Edging:
Round 1: Join Paddy Green with a sl st in any st, ch 2, hdc in each st around, join with a sl st in top of beginning ch-2. Fasten off.

Use yarn or tapestry needle to weave in loose ends.

ABBREVIATIONS	
ch	chain
dc(s)	double crochet(s)
hdc(s)	half double crochet(s)
hk	hook
lp(s)	loop(s)
sc(s)	single crochet(s)
sk	skip
sl st	slip stitch
st(s)	stitch(es)
yo	yarn over
* [ ]	Instructions following asterisk or within brackets are repeated as directed.

FIG. 1

Whipstitch

Countin' Sheep Crocheted Slippers

CRAFT LEVEL: INTERMEDIATE

FINISHED SIZE: Directions are for adult size small slippers with a sole length of 7-3/4 inches. Changes for adult size medium with a sole length of 9-3/4 inches and adult size large with a sole length of 10-3/4 inches are in parentheses.

Both kids and adults get a kick out of my sleepy sheep. I designed them with our 10-year-old daughter in mind. She enjoys the furry look, which I created using the loop stitch. Now I plan to make more pairs of the slippers as gifts and one pair for myself, too.

Kathleen Stuart ★ San Jose, California

MATERIALS:

7(8,9) ounces of off-white 2-ply brushed acrylic mohair-like yarn (Lion Brand Jiffy yarn in Fisherman shown)

Small amount of 4-ply worsted-weight black yarn for sheep heads and ears

Size G/6 (4.25mm) crochet hook or size needed to obtain correct gauge

Six-strand embroidery floss—blue for eyes and pink for mouths

Polyester stuffing

Tapestry or yarn needle

Scissors

GAUGE: 16 dcs and 7 rows = 4 inches. To save time, take time to check gauge.

SPECIAL STITCHES:

lp st = loop stitch: With yarn wrapped from front to back over your left forefinger, insert crochet hk in next st as directed as if to make a sc; to form the lp of yarn, swing crochet hk behind both strands on your forefinger, draw both strands through first lp on the hk, yo and draw yarn through all lps on hk, remove your finger from lp, leaving a lp of yarn about 1 inch long.

fpdc = double crochet in front post: yo, insert hk from front to back between next two sts, then working from right to left, come up from back to front between the following two sts, yo, draw through a lp and complete the dc as usual.

DIRECTIONS:

Slipper (make 2):

Row 1: With off-white yarn, ch 40(44,48), join with a sl st in first ch made to form a ring for the ankle opening. For the instep (top of slipper), ch 16(18,20), sc in second ch from hk and in each of next 14(16,18) chs, sc in each ch of the ankle opening; working on opposite side of starting ch for the instep, sc in last 15(17,19) chs, turn: 70(78,86) scs.

Row 2: Ch 1; working in back lps only, work 1 lp st in each st, turn: 70(78,86) lp sts.

Row 3: Ch 1, working in back lps only, sc in each st, turn: 70(78,86) scs.

Rows 4, 6, 8, 10, 12 and 14: Repeat Row 2: 70(78,86) lp sts.

Rows 5, 7, 9, 11, 13 and 15: Repeat Row 3: 70(78,86) scs.

Rows 16-19: Repeat Row 3: 70(78,86) scs.

Row 20: For sole, fold piece so that lp sts face each other, ends of rows match and sts of Row 19 match. Working through sts of Row 19, ch 1, sl st in each of next 35(39,43) sts. Fasten off. Turn right side out.

Ankle Edging:

Round 1: With RS facing and working on opposite side of starting ch of ankle opening, join off-white with a sl st in first ch, ch 3 for first dc, dc in each remaining ch around, join with a sl st in third ch of beginning ch-3. Do not turn: 40(44,48) dcs.

Round 2: Ch 3, fpdc in each st around, join with a sl st in third ch of beginning ch-3: 40(44,48) fpdcs.

Round 3: Ch 3, fpdc in next 2 sts, fpdc next 2 sts tog, * fpdc in each of next 3 sts, fpdc next 2 sts tog; repeat from * around, join with a sl st in third ch of beginning ch-3: 32(35,39) sts. Fasten off.

Finishing:

1. Thread tapestry or yarn needle with off-white.

2. Stitch through ends of rows along opening (toe) of slipper. Draw up yarn to close opening and fasten off.

3. Weave in all loose ends.

Sheep: Head (make 2):

Round 1: With black, ch 2, work 6 scs in second ch from hk, do not join: 6 scs. Pull the beginning tail of yarn to close center of circle just made.

Round 2: * Sc in next st, work 2 scs in next st; repeat from * around, do not join: 9 scs.

Round 3: * Sc in next 2 sts, work 2 scs in next st; repeat from * around, do not join: 12 scs.

Round 4: * Sc in next st, work 2 scs in next st; repeat from * around, do not join: 18 scs.

Round 5: * Sc in next 2 sts, work 2 scs in next st; repeat from * around, do not join: 24 scs.

Round 6: * Sc in next 3 sts, work 2 scs in next st; repeat from * around, do not join: 30 scs.

Rounds 7-8: Sc in each st around: 30 scs. Fasten off, leaving an 8-in. length of yarn for sewing head to slipper.

Ears (make 2):

With black, ch 6, sc in second ch from hk and in each remaining ch across: 4 scs. Fasten off, leaving a 4-in. length of yarn for sewing ears to head.

Finishing:

1. Referring to photo at far left and Fig. 1 at right for position and stitch illustrations, use tapestry or yarn needle and unseparated blue floss to satin-stitch two eyes on the right side of each head.

2. In same way, use pink floss to satin-stitch a nose and to backstitch a mouth on each head.

3. Use tails of black yarn and tapestry or yarn needle to sew two ears to the top of each head.

4. Use tails of black yarn and tapestry or yarn needle to sew a head to the instep (top) of each slipper, stuffing head before fastening off.

5. Weave in all loose ends.

Teddy Bear Crocheted Slippers

Replace the black and off-white yarn with a single shade of brown to create a cute teddy bear look.

ABBREVIATIONS

ch(s)	chain(s)
dc(s)	double crochet(s)
fpdc(s)	front post double crochet(s)
hk	hook
lp(s)	loop(s)
RS	right side
sc(s)	single crochet(s)
sl st	slip stitch
st(s)	stitch(es)
tog	together
yo	yarn over
*	Instructions following asterisk are repeated as directed.

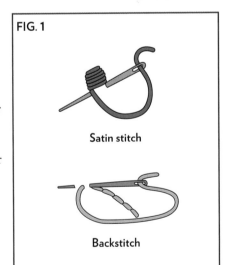

FIG. 1

Satin stitch

Backstitch

RECIPE & CRAFT INDEXES

There are three indexes for your convenience. The first is a complete alphabetical listing of all the recipes in this book. When you know the name of the recipe you need, simply turn to this index. The second index, General Recipe Index, lists every recipe by food category, major ingredient and/or cooking method. For example, if you're looking for an appetizer recipe or one that uses beef, use this index. The last index is all you need to find a craft... they're listed by title and type of craft.

Alphabetical Recipe Index

A
Alfredo Rice Casserole 105
Almond-Cheese Coffee Cake 110
Almond Pillow Cookies 139
Amaretto-Peach Preserves 130
Apple & Walnut Salad 47
Apple Brandy 133
Apple-Cinnamon Gelatin 89
Apple Cinnamon Rolls 113
Apple Rice Salad 105
Apple Sweet Potato Bake 101
Apricot Caramel Tart 33
Apricot-Raspberry Angel Torte 155
Artichoke & Mushroom Toasts 6

B
Bacon & Cheddar Strata 78
Bacon Caesar Salad 26
Baked Sweet Onions 24
Banana-Hazelnut Cake 174
Basil & Oregano Dinner Rolls 55
Beef & Roasted Pepper Pinwheels 9
Beef Fondue with Mustard-Mayonnaise
   Sauce 73
Beet Salad with Orange Vinaigrette 37
Best Chocolate Cake 56
Best Chocolate Raspberry Torte 57
Blue Cheese-Stuffed Shrimp 7
Brined Pork Roast with Port Wine Sauce ... 51
Broccoli Rabe with Tuscan Crumbs 53
Broccoli Romano Pasta 97
Burnt-Sugar Chiffon Cake 165
Butterscotch Peanut Butter Fudge 129

C
Caramel Apple Trifle Delight 173
Caramel Crispy Pops 123
Cheese Tortellini Salad 74
Cherry-Cheese Tea Ring 115
Cherry Syrup 134

Chicago-Style Beef Sandwiches 87
Chicken Artichoke Pizzas 16
Chocolate Almond Pie 161
Chocolate-Caramel Candy Bars 127
Chocolate-Caramel Dream Pie 154
Chocolate Cran-Raspberry
   Cheesecake Bars 162
Chocolate-Dipped Orange Cookies 143
Chocolate Hazelnut Tassies 142
Chocolate Macaroon Bars 152
Chocolate Mousse Cakes 71
Chocolate Reindeer 140
Christmas Cauliflower Casserole 97
Christmas Jam 122
Christmas Stollen 121
Cinnamon Pumpkin Truffles 169
Cinnamon Spritz 148
Cinnamon Stir Sticks 133
Citrus Fennel Salad 73
Citrus Spiced Olives 122
Coconut-Pecan Brownies 67
Coconut Pecan Joys 141
Crab Dip in a Bread Bowl 66
Cranberry & Port Wine Chutney 43
Cranberry-Champagne Granita 27
Cranberry Chutney Crostini 6
Cranberry Crunch Coffee Cake 117
Cranberry-Gorgonzola Stuffed
   Chicken 40
Cranberry Lime Sparkler 73
Cranberry-Orange Cream Pie 68
Cranberry-Orange Relish 92
Cranberry-Orange Spinach Salad 95
Cranberry-Orange Tartlets 16
Cranberry Orange Vinaigrette 129
Cranberry Orange Vinegar 129
Cranberry Tea 82
Cranberry Walnut Biscotti 120
Cranberry-White Chocolate Trifle 159

Cream Cheese Slice-and-Bake
   Cookies 145
Creamy Corn Casserole 92
Creamy Cranberry Dip 13
Creamy Garlic & Mushroom Soup 48
Creamy Garlic & Mushroom Soup with
   Pastry Caps 49
Creamy Rosemary Potatoes 95
Crumb-Topped Carrot Casserole 98
Curried Sweet Potato Soup 31

D
Decadent Broccoli Souffle 41
Dinner Rolls 54
Double Chocolate Espresso
   Cheesecake 171
Dutch Speculaas 89

E
Easy Cheese Danish 77
Eggnog 13
Eggnog Bavarian 102
Eggnog Cookies 138
Elegant Roasted Potatoes 41

F
Fabulous Fruit Salad 78
Fontina-Vegetable Crab Soup 42
French Onion Casserole 67
Fresh Herb Dinner Rolls 55
Frozen Strawberry Dessert 157
Fruit & Nut Bread 118

G
Garlic Roasted Broccoli 25
Garlic Roasted Winter Vegetables 101
German Almond Cookies 151
Ginger Apritinis 68
Gingerbread Waffles with Cream
   Cheese Topping 77
Glazed Orange Chicken Wings 11

Glittered Snowflake Cookies.......................151
Goat Cheese & Pear Stuffed Tenderloin ... 23
Golden Roasted Turkey 29
Gourmet Stuffed Mushrooms......................11
Greek Veggie Tartlets................................ 13
Grouper with Crabmeat Sauce 35

H

Hazelnut Chocolate Chip Pizzelle 141
Heavenly Praline Cake............................. 173
Herb Butter Cut-Outs...............................108
Herb-Buttered Green Beans 36
Herb-Rubbed Pork Loin 50
Herbed Cheesecake.................................. 15
Herbed Chestnut Stuffing......................... 30
Herbed Dinner Rolls.................................55
Holiday Pumpkin Pie................................170
Holiday Spirits 166
Horseradish-Celery Deviled Eggs 70
Hot Crab & Artichoke Dip 12

I

Italian Cheese Wontons 10

J

Jeweled Fruitcake 109
Jumbo Banana-Pecan Muffins 115

L

Layered Spinach & Orange Salad..............87
Lemon Bread... 111
Lemon Fruit Dip....................................... 14
Lemon Poppy Seed Cake......................... 157
Lime Tartlets..161
Lobster-Shrimp Salad Croissants 81
Lump of Coal Candy..................................88

M

Maple-Dijon Glazed Brussels Sprouts 92
Maple Peanut Mix.................................... 68
Maple Pecan Cake................................. 163
Maple-Walnut Ice Cream 169
Maple Wheat Bread.................................108
Mini Pumpkin Custards............................159
Minty Cocoa Mix..................................... 123
Mushroom Bread Dressing.......................105
Mushroom-Swiss Mac & Cheese...............99

N

Northwoods Beef Stew 62
Nutty Shortbread Cookies........................151

O

Olive Bread...117
Onion-Stuffed Portobellos 95

Orange-Cheesecake Breakfast Rolls......... 111
Orange-Cranberry Bars........................... 147
Orange-Scented Leeks & Mushrooms..... 101
Outrageous Peanut Butter Sauce............. 126

P

Pancetta Scallops on Potato Rounds......... 20
Pasta Puttanesca 98
Peach-Filled Muffins 125
Peachy Navel...70
Peanut Butter Cup Cookies..................... 123
Peanut Butter Custard Blast 167
Peppermint Meringue Clouds.................. 147
Pepperoncini Poppers 9
Pesto Bread...39
Petite Apricot Pastries..............................82
Petite Chocolate-Hazelnut Cakes.............83
Pickled Shrimp 61
Pineapple Orange Trifle 70
Pistachio Buttons 146
Poached Pears with Cheddar 9
Pomegranate Creme Brulee.....................166
Poppy Seed Cheese Bread.......................112
Poppy Seed-Filled Scones with Lemon
     Curd...85
Pork & Mozzarella Crostini 71
Pork Medallions in Green Peppercorn
     Sauce..62
Portobello Pizzas.....................................63
Pumpkin Bread Pudding 163
Pumpkin Cookies with Cream Cheese
     Frosting 139
Pumpkin Pecan Sundaes.......................... 69
Pumpkin Pie Martinis 19

R

Raspberry Fizz... 12
Raspberry Pear Salad with Glazed
     Walnuts 30
Raspberry Ribbons..................................116
Raspberry Sachertorte..............................39
Raspberry Sandwich Cookies................... 137
Red Velvet Cookies 149
Roasted Apple & Candied Walnut
     Salad..47
Roasted Red Pepper Bread 109
Romaine Salad with Vanilla Bean
     Dressing..63
Ruby Grapefruit and Shortcakes...............155
Rum Balls 125
Rustic Autumn Soup 94

S

Savory Mediterranean Orzo.......................93
Scrumptious Sugar Cookies 136
Seafood Brochettes..................................65
Sesame Chicken with Ginger Shiitake
     Cream Sauce......................................65
Simple Syrup..19
Smoked Sausages with Mustard Sauce...... 17
Sour Cream Date Drops............................141
Southwest Spinach Dip 14
Spearmint Thins....................................... 66
Spectacular Dirty Martini Salad 61
Spice-Brined Pork Roast 43
Spiced Caramel Corn...............................131
Spiced Cider Bundles 133
Spiced Cranberry-Chutney Gelatin
     Salad...103
Spiced Peanuts 17
Spicy Garlic Broccoli Rabe 52
Spicy Peppers & Corn...............................97
Spicy Praline Cashews............................ 126
Spinach Amandine Stuffing......................102
Strawberry Chocolate Truffles 164
Sunrise Sipper..79
Sweet Potatoes with Pecan-Cinnamon
     Crunch 106

T

T-Bones with Sun-Dried Tomato Butter ... 60
Taco Chili Mix 120
Tiramisu Snack Mix..................................131
Toasted Beer Bread with Asiago Dip......... 69
Triple-Tasty Cloverleaf Rolls 33
Turkey, Gouda & Apple Tea
     Sandwiches..83
Turkey Spinach Amandine Stuffing..........102

V

Vanilla Chai Tea....................................... 84
Vanilla Crescent Cookies.........................145
Veal Saltimbocca..................................... 44
Vegetable Couscous.................................43
Vienna Triangles...................................... 81
Virgin Sunrise Sipper 79
Vodka Peachy Navel.................................70

W

Waffle Mix 134
Warm Chicken Fiesta Dip............................7
White Chocolate Raspberry Cookies 138
White Sangria...36
Winter Squash Casserole.........................105

General Recipe Index

APPETIZERS & SNACKS

Cold Appetizers

Beef & Roasted Pepper Pinwheels 9

Blue Cheese-Stuffed Shrimp 7

Citrus Spiced Olives 122

Cranberry-Orange Tartlets 16

Greek Veggie Tartlets 13

Horseradish-Celery Deviled Eggs 70

Pepperoncini Poppers 9

Pickled Shrimp 61

Dips

Crab Dip in a Bread Bowl 66

Creamy Cranberry Dip 13

Hot Crab & Artichoke Dip 12

Lemon Fruit Dip 14

Southwest Spinach Dip 14

Toasted Beer Bread with Asiago Dip 69

Warm Chicken Fiesta Dip 7

Hot Appetizers

Artichoke & Mushroom Toasts 6

Beef Fondue with Mustard-Mayonnaise Sauce 73

Chicken Artichoke Pizzas 16

Cranberry Chutney Crostini 6

Glazed Orange Chicken Wings 11

Gourmet Stuffed Mushrooms 11

Italian Cheese Wontons 10

Pancetta Scallops on Potato Rounds 20

Poached Pears with Cheddar 9

Pork & Mozzarella Crostini 71

Smoked Sausages with Mustard Sauce 17

Snacks

Caramel Crispy Pops 123

Maple Peanut Mix 68

Spiced Caramel Corn 131

Spiced Peanuts 17

Spicy Praline Cashews 126

Tiramisu Snack Mix 131

APPLES

Apple & Walnut Salad 47

Apple Brandy 133

Apple-Cinnamon Gelatin 89

Apple Cinnamon Rolls 113

Apple Rice Salad 105

Apple Sweet Potato Bake 101

Caramel Apple Trifle Delight 173

Roasted Apple & Candied Walnut Salad 47

Spiced Cider Bundles 133

Turkey, Gouda & Apple Tea Sandwiches 83

APRICOTS

Apricot Caramel Tart 33

Apricot-Raspberry Angel Torte 155

Petite Apricot Pastries 82

ARTICHOKES

Artichoke & Mushroom Toasts 6

Chicken Artichoke Pizzas 16

Hot Crab & Artichoke Dip 12

BANANAS

Banana-Hazelnut Cake 174

Jumbo Banana-Pecan Muffins 115

BARS & BROWNIES

Chocolate Cran-Raspberry Cheesecake Bars 162

Chocolate Macaroon Bars 152

Coconut-Pecan Brownies 67

Orange-Cranberry Bars 147

BEANS

Herb-Buttered Green Beans 36

Taco Chili Mix 120

BEEF & GROUND BEEF

Beef & Roasted Pepper Pinwheels 9

Beef Fondue with Mustard-Mayonnaise Sauce 73

Chicago-Style Beef Sandwiches 87

Goat Cheese & Pear Stuffed Tenderloin 23

Northwoods Beef Stew 62

T-Bones with Sun-Dried Tomato Butter 60

Taco Chili Mix 120

Veal Saltimbocca 44

BEETS

Beet Salad with Orange Vinaigrette... 37

BEVERAGES

Apple Brandy 133

Cranberry Lime Sparkler 73

Cranberry Tea 82

Eggnog 13

Ginger Apritinis 68

Minty Cocoa Mix 123

Peachy Navel 70

Pumpkin Pie Martinis 19

Raspberry Fizz 12

Simple Syrup 19

Sunrise Sipper 79

Vanilla Chai Tea 84

Virgin Sunrise Sipper 79

Vodka Peachy Navel......................70

White Sangria................................36

BREADS (also see Coffee Cakes; Pastries; Rolls)

Christmas Stollen.........................121

Fruit & Nut Bread.........................118

Jeweled Fruitcake 109

Jumbo Banana-Pecan Muffins..........115

Lemon Bread 111

Maple Wheat Bread 108

Olive Bread..................................117

Peach-Filled Muffins 125

Pesto Bread...................................39

Poppy Seed Cheese Bread.............112

Poppy Seed-Filled Scones with Lemon Curd...................................85

Raspberry Ribbons.......................116

Roasted Red Pepper Bread 109

Toasted Beer Bread with Asiago Dip...69

BROCCOLI

Broccoli Rabe with Tuscan Crumbs....53

Broccoli Romano Pasta 97

Decadent Broccoli Souffle..................41

Garlic Roasted Broccoli.....................25

Spicy Garlic Broccoli Rabe 52

BRUSSELS SPROUTS

Maple-Dijon Glazed Brussels Sprouts.......................................92

CAKES & TORTES (also see Coffee Cakes)

Apricot-Raspberry Angel Torte 155

Banana-Hazelnut Cake 174

Best Chocolate Cake 56

Best Chocolate Raspberry Torte.........57

Burnt-Sugar Chiffon Cake.................165

Chocolate Mousse Cakes....................71

Heavenly Praline Cake 173

Lemon Poppy Seed Cake...................157

Maple Pecan Cake............................163

Petite Chocolate-Hazelnut Cakes......83

Raspberry Sachertorte.......................39

CANDIES

Butterscotch Peanut Butter Fudge ...129

Chocolate-Caramel Candy Bars........127

Cinnamon Pumpkin Truffles..............169

Lump of Coal Candy...........................88

Rum Balls 125

Strawberry Chocolate Truffles 164

CARAMEL

Apricot Caramel Tart.......................... 33

Caramel Apple Trifle Delight.............173

Caramel Crispy Pops.........................123

Chocolate-Caramel Candy Bars........127

Chocolate-Caramel Dream Pie........154

Lump of Coal Candy...........................88

Spiced Caramel Corn.........................131

CARROTS

Crumb-Topped Carrot Casserole.......98

CAULIFLOWER

Christmas Cauliflower Casserole........97

CHEESE & CREAM CHEESE

Appetizers

Blue Cheese-Stuffed Shrimp 7

Herbed Cheesecake 15

Italian Cheese Wontons...................10

Poached Pears with Cheddar...........9

Pork & Mozzarella Crostini...............71

Breads

Almond-Cheese Coffee Cake 110

Cherry-Cheese Tea Ring................115

Easy Cheese Danish......................... 77

Gingerbread Waffles with Cream Cheese Topping......................77

Orange-Cheesecake Breakfast Rolls..66

Poppy Seed Cheese Bread 112

Toasted Beer Bread with Asiago Dip 69

Desserts

Chocolate Cran-Raspberry Cheesecake Bars..................... 162

Cream Cheese Slice-and-Bake Cookies 145

Double Chocolate Espresso Cheesecake 171

Pumpkin Cookies with Cream Cheese Frosting 139

Main Dishes

Bacon & Cheddar Strata.................78

Cranberry-Gorgonzola Stuffed Chicken 40

Goat Cheese & Pear Stuffed Tenderloin 23

Salad & Side Dishes

Cheese Tortellini Salad 74

Broccoli Romano Pasta...................97

Mushroom-Swiss Mac & Cheese....99

Soup & Sandwiches

Fontina-Vegetable Crab Soup 42

Turkey, Gouda & Apple Tea Sandwiches 83

CHERRIES

Cherry-Cheese Tea Ring 115

Cherry Syrup 134

Christmas Jam 122

CHICKEN

Chicken Artichoke Pizzas 16

Cranberry-Gorgonzola Stuffed Chicken................................... 40

Glazed Orange Chicken Wings..........11

CHICKEN (continued)

Sesame Chicken with Ginger Shiitake Cream Sauce 65

Warm Chicken Fiesta Dip.....................7

CHOCOLATE

Cakes & Tortes

Best Chocolate Cake 56

Best Chocolate Raspberry Torte 57

Chocolate Mousse Cakes 71

Petite Chocolate-Hazelnut Cakes..83

Raspberry Sachertorte 39

Candies

Chocolate-Caramel Candy Bars ...127

Strawberry Chocolate Truffles 164

Cookies & Bars

Chocolate Cran-Raspberry Cheesecake Bars 162

Chocolate-Dipped Orange Cookies 143

Chocolate Hazelnut Tassies 142

Chocolate Macaroon Bars 152

Chocolate Reindeer 140

Coconut-Pecan Brownies 67

Hazelnut Chocolate Chip Pizzelle 141

White Chocolate Raspberry Cookies 138

Desserts

Chocolate Almond Pie...................161

Chocolate-Caramel Dream Pie ...154

Cranberry-White Chocolate Trifle159

Double Chocolate Espresso Cheesecake 171

Snacks & Beverages

Minty Cocoa Mix 123

Tiramisu Snack Mix 131

COCONUT

Chocolate Macaroon Bars 152

Coconut-Pecan Brownies....................67

Coconut Pecan Joys...........................141

COFFEE CAKES

Almond-Cheese Coffee Cake...........110

Cherry-Cheese Tea Ring 115

Cranberry Crunch Coffee Cake........117

CONDIMENTS

Amaretto-Peach Preserves 130

Cherry Syrup 134

Christmas Jam 122

Cranberry & Port Wine Chutney 43

Cranberry-Orange Relish 92

Cranberry Orange Vinaigrette..........129

Cranberry Orange Vinegar 129

Herb Butter Cut-Outs.......................108

COOKIES (also see Bars & Brownies)

Cutout Cookies

Almond Pillow Cookies 139

Chocolate Reindeer 140

Dutch Speculaas...........................89

Glittered Snowflake Cookies 151

Raspberry Sandwich Cookies.........137

Scrumptious Sugar Cookies 136

Drop Cookies

Coconut Pecan Joys 141

Pumpkin Cookies with Cream Cheese Frosting 139

Red Velvet Cookies........................149

Sour Cream Date Drops 141

No-Bake Cookies

Holiday Spirits................................166

Spearmint Thins.............................66

Refrigerator Cookies

Cream Cheese Slice-and-Bake Cookies 145

Eggnog Cookies............................138

Pistachio Buttons...........................146

Shaped Cookies

Chocolate-Dipped Orange Cookies 143

Chocolate Hazelnut Tassies 142

Cinnamon Spritz............................148

Cranberry Walnut Biscotti.............120

German Almond Cookies 151

Hazelnut Chocolate Chip Pizzelle 141

Nutty Shortbread Cookies 151

Peanut Butter Cup Cookies 123

Peppermint Meringue Clouds 147

Vanilla Crescent Cookies 145

White Chocolate Raspberry Cookies 138

CORN

Creamy Corn Casserole 92

Spicy Peppers & Corn 97

CRANBERRIES

Chocolate Cran-Raspberry Cheesecake Bars 162

Cranberry & Port Wine Chutney 43

Cranberry-Champagne Granita 27

Cranberry Chutney Crostini.................6

Cranberry Crunch Coffee Cake........117

Cranberry-Gorgonzola Stuffed Chicken.. 40

Cranberry Lime Sparkler.....................73

Cranberry-Orange Cream Pie...........68

Cranberry-Orange Relish 92

Cranberry-Orange Spinach Salad 95

Cranberry-Orange Tartlets.................16

Cranberry Orange Vinaigrette..........129

Cranberry Orange Vinegar 129

Cranberry Tea.....................................82

Cranberry Walnut Biscotti 120

Cranberry-White Chocolate Trifle....159

Creamy Cranberry Dip 13

Orange-Cranberry Bars 147

Spiced Cranberry-Chutney Gelatin
  Salad.. 103

DESSERTS (also see Bars & Brownies; Cakes & Tortes; Candies; Cookies; Ice Cream & Toppings; Pies & Tarts; Trifles)

Cranberry-Champagne Granita 27

Double Chocolate Espresso
  Cheesecake..................................... 171

Frozen Strawberry Dessert 157

Mini Pumpkin Custards...................... 159

Peanut Butter Custard Blast 167

Pomegranate Creme Brulee.............. 166

Pumpkin Bread Pudding 163

Ruby Grapefruit and Shortcakes....... 155

DIPS

Crab Dip in a Bread Bowl 66

Creamy Cranberry Dip 13

Hot Crab & Artichoke Dip 12

Lemon Fruit Dip................................... 14

Southwest Spinach Dip 14

Toasted Beer Bread with Asiago Dip..69

Warm Chicken Fiesta Dip...................... 7

EGGS

Bacon & Cheddar Strata 78

Eggnog...13

Eggnog Bavarian................................ 102

Eggnog Cookies 138

Horseradish-Celery Deviled Eggs 70

FISH & SEAFOOD

Blue Cheese-Stuffed Shrimp................ 7

Crab Dip in a Bread Bowl 66

Fontina-Vegetable Crab Soup............ 42

Grouper with Crabmeat Sauce 35

Hot Crab & Artichoke Dip 12

Lobster-Shrimp Salad Croissants........ 81

Pancetta Scallops on Potato Rounds..20

Pickled Shrimp 61

Seafood Brochettes 65

FRUIT (also see specific kinds)

Fabulous Fruit Salad 78

Fruit & Nut Bread................................118

Jeweled Fruitcake 109

Ruby Grapefruit and Shortcakes....... 155

GARLIC

Creamy Garlic & Mushroom Soup.....48

Creamy Garlic & Mushroom Soup with
  Pastry Caps 49

Garlic Roasted Broccoli....................... 25

Garlic Roasted Winter Vegetables 101

Spicy Garlic Broccoli Rabe 52

GRILLED RECIPES

Seafood Brochettes 65

Spice-Brined Pork Roast 43

T-Bones with Sun-Dried Tomato
  Butter 60

GROUND BEEF (see Beef & Ground Beef)

ICE CREAM & TOPPINGS

Maple-Walnut Ice Cream 169

Outrageous Peanut Butter Sauce 126

Pumpkin Pecan Sundaes 69

LEMON

Citrus Fennel Salad.............................. 73

Citrus Spiced Olives............................122

Lemon Bread 111

Lemon Fruit Dip.................................. 14

Lemon Poppy Seed Cake 157

Poppy Seed-Filled Scones with Lemon
  Curd 85

LIME

Citrus Spiced Olives............................122

Cranberry Lime Sparkler 73

Lime Tartlets 161

MAIN DISHES

Bacon & Cheddar Strata 78

Brined Pork Roast with Port Wine
  Sauce 51

Cranberry-Gorgonzola Stuffed
  Chicken... 40

Goat Cheese & Pear Stuffed
  Tenderloin.. 23

Golden Roasted Turkey 29

Grouper with Crabmeat Sauce 35

Herb-Rubbed Pork Loin 50

Northwoods Beef Stew 62

Pork Medallions in Green Peppercorn
  Sauce 62

Portobello Pizzas................................. 63

Seafood Brochettes 65

Sesame Chicken with Ginger Shiitake
  Cream Sauce..................................... 65

Spice-Brined Pork Roast 43

T-Bones with Sun-Dried Tomato
  Butter 60

Veal Saltimbocca................................. 44

MAPLE

Maple-Dijon Glazed Brussels Sprouts.....92

Maple Peanut Mix................................68

Maple Pecan Cake.............................. 163

Maple-Walnut Ice Cream 169

Maple Wheat Bread 108

MINT

Holiday Spirits 166

Minty Cocoa Mix.................................123

Peppermint Meringue Clouds........... 147

Spearmint Thins 66

MIXES

Minty Cocoa Mix..................................123

Taco Chili Mix 120

Waffle Mix 134

MUSHROOMS

Artichoke & Mushroom Toasts.............. 6

Creamy Garlic & Mushroom Soup.....48

Creamy Garlic & Mushroom Soup
    with Pastry Caps 49

Gourmet Stuffed Mushrooms.............. 11

Mushroom Bread Dressing...............105

Mushroom-Swiss Mac & Cheese........99

Onion-Stuffed Portobellos 95

Orange-Scented Leeks &
    Mushrooms 101

Portobello Pizzas..................................63

Sesame Chicken with Ginger
    Shiitake Cream Sauce....................65

NUTS & PEANUT BUTTER

Breads

Almond-Cheese Coffee Cake 110

Fruit & Nut Bread 118

Jumbo Banana-Pecan Muffins.......115

Cookies & Bars

Almond Pillow Cookies 139

Chocolate Hazelnut Tassies 142

Coconut-Pecan Brownies 67

Coconut Pecan Joys 141

Cranberry Walnut Biscotti.............120

German Almond Cookies 151

Hazelnut Chocolate Chip Pizzelle....141

Nutty Shortbread Cookies 151

Peanut Butter Cup Cookies 123

Pistachio Buttons...........................146

Desserts

Banana-Hazelnut Cake..................174

Butterscotch Peanut Butter
    Fudge 129

Chocolate Almond Pie................161

Heavenly Praline Cake...................173

Maple Pecan Cake 163

Maple-Walnut Ice Cream.............. 169

Outrageous Peanut Butter Sauce.... 126

Peanut Butter Custard Blast.......... 167

Petite Chocolate-Hazelnut Cakes..83

Pumpkin Pecan Sundaes...................69

Vienna Triangles 81

Salads & Side Dishes

Apple & Walnut Salad.....................47

Herbed Chestnut Stuffing..............30

Raspberry Pear Salad with Glazed
    Walnuts.......................................30

Roasted Apple & Candied Walnut
    Salad 47

Spinach Amandine Stuffing 102

Sweet Potatoes with Pecan-
    Cinnamon Crunch 106

Turkey Spinach Amandine
    Stuffing.......................................102

Snacks

Maple Peanut Mix 68

Spiced Peanuts................................17

Spicy Praline Cashews 126

OLIVES

Citrus Spiced Olives..........................122

Olive Bread...117

Spectacular Dirty Martini Salad 61

ONIONS

Baked Sweet Onions 24

French Onion Casserole 67

Onion-Stuffed Portobellos 95

ORANGE

Beet Salad with Orange Vinaigrette... 37

Chocolate-Dipped Orange
    Cookies....................................... 143

Citrus Fennel Salad............................. 73

Citrus Spiced Olives...........................122

Cranberry-Orange Cream Pie............68

Cranberry-Orange Relish 92

Cranberry-Orange Spinach Salad 95

Cranberry-Orange Tartlets 16

Cranberry Orange Vinaigrette..........129

Cranberry Orange Vinegar 129

Glazed Orange Chicken Wings...........11

Layered Spinach & Orange Salad.......87

Orange-Cheesecake Breakfast
    Rolls 111

Orange-Cranberry Bars 147

Orange-Scented Leeks
    & Mushrooms...............................101

Pineapple Orange Trifle 70

OVEN ENTREES

Bacon & Cheddar Strata 78

Brined Pork Roast with Port Wine
    Sauce 51

Cranberry-Gorgonzola Stuffed
    Chicken.. 40

Goat Cheese & Pear Stuffed
    Tenderloin...................................... 23

Golden Roasted Turkey 29

Grouper with Crabmeat Sauce 35

Herb-Rubbed Pork Loin 50

Portobello Pizzas..................................63

PASTA & NOODLES

Broccoli Romano Pasta 97

Cheese Tortellini Salad........................74

Mushroom-Swiss Mac & Cheese........99

Pasta Puttanesca.................................98

Savory Mediterranean Orzo...............93

Vegetable Couscous............................43

PASTRIES

Easy Cheese Danish 77

Petite Apricot Pastries........................82

Vienna Triangles.................................. 81

PEACHES

Amaretto-Peach Preserves 130

Peach-Filled Muffins 125

Peachy Navel 70

Vodka Peachy Navel 70

PEARS

Goat Cheese & Pear Stuffed
  Tenderloin....................................... 23

Poached Pears with Cheddar 9

Raspberry Pear Salad with Glazed
  Walnuts 30

PEPPERS & CHILIES

Beef & Roasted Pepper Pinwheels 9

Pepperoncini Poppers 9

Roasted Red Pepper Bread 109

Spicy Peppers & Corn 97

PIES & TARTS

Apricot Caramel Tart......................... 33

Chocolate Almond Pie 161

Chocolate-Caramel Dream Pie 154

Cranberry-Orange Cream Pie............68

Holiday Pumpkin Pie......................... 170

Lime Tartlets....................................161

PINEAPPLE

Pineapple Orange Trifle 70

POMEGRANATE

Pomegranate Creme Brulee............. 166

PORK, BACON & SAUSAGE

Bacon & Cheddar Strata..................... 78

Bacon Caesar Salad............................ 26

Brined Pork Roast with Port Wine
  Sauce... 51

Gourmet Stuffed Mushrooms.............11

Herb-Rubbed Pork Loin 50

Pancetta Scallops on Potato
  Rounds...20

Pork & Mozzarella Crostini 71

Pork Medallions in Green
  Peppercorn Sauce 62

Portobello Pizzas.............................. 63

Smoked Sausages with Mustard
  Sauce...17

Spice-Brined Pork Roast 43

POTATOES & SWEET POTATOES

Apple Sweet Potato Bake 101

Creamy Rosemary Potatoes...............95

Curried Sweet Potato Soup.................31

Elegant Roasted Potatoes................... 41

Pancetta Scallops on Potato
  Rounds...20

Sweet Potatoes with Pecan-
  Cinnamon Crunch........................106

PUMPKIN

Cinnamon Pumpkin Truffles............. 169

Holiday Pumpkin Pie......................... 170

Mini Pumpkin Custards..................... 159

Pumpkin Bread Pudding 163

Pumpkin Cookies with Cream
  Cheese Frosting 139

Pumpkin Pecan Sundaes.....................69

Pumpkin Pie Martinis 19

RASPBERRIES

Apricot-Raspberry Angel Torte 155

Best Chocolate Raspberry Torte.........57

Chocolate Cran-Raspberry
  Cheesecake Bars 162

Raspberry Fizz...................................12

Raspberry Pear Salad with Glazed
  Walnuts 30

Raspberry Ribbons............................116

Raspberry Sachertorte....................... 39

Raspberry Sandwich Cookies............137

White Chocolate Raspberry
  Cookies 138

RICE

Alfredo Rice Casserole 105

Apple Rice Salad................................ 105

ROLLS

Apple Cinnamon Rolls 113

Basil & Oregano Dinner Rolls 55

Dinner Rolls.......................................54

Fresh Herb Dinner Rolls..................... 55

Herbed Dinner Rolls........................... 55

Orange-Cheesecake Breakfast
  Rolls 111

Triple-Tasty Cloverleaf Rolls 33

SALADS

Apple & Walnut Salad 47

Apple-Cinnamon Gelatin................... 89

Apple Rice Salad................................ 105

Bacon Caesar Salad............................ 26

Beet Salad with Orange
  Vinaigrette....................................... 37

Cheese Tortellini Salad....................... 74

Citrus Fennel Salad............................ 73

Cranberry-Orange Spinach Salad 95

Eggnog Bavarian............................... 102

Fabulous Fruit Salad 78

Layered Spinach & Orange Salad....... 87

Lobster-Shrimp Salad Croissants........ 81

Raspberry Pear Salad with Glazed
  Walnuts...30

Roasted Apple & Candied Walnut
  Salad.. 47

Romaine Salad with Vanilla Bean
  Dressing... 63

Spectacular Dirty Martini Salad 61

Spiced Cranberry-Chutney Gelatin
  Salad.. 103

SANDWICHES

Chicago-Style Beef Sandwiches 87

Lobster-Shrimp Salad Croissants........ 81

SANDWICHES (continued)

Turkey, Gouda & Apple Tea
Sandwiches.........................83

SEAFOOD (see Fish & Seafood)

SIDE DISHES (also see Condiments; Salads; Soups)

Alfredo Rice Casserole 105

Apple Sweet Potato Bake 101

Baked Sweet Onions 24

Broccoli Rabe with Tuscan Crumbs 53

Broccoli Romano Pasta 97

Christmas Cauliflower Casserole........97

Creamy Corn Casserole 92

Creamy Rosemary Potatoes...............95

Crumb-Topped Carrot Casserole 98

Decadent Broccoli Souffle 41

Elegant Roasted Potatoes................... 41

French Onion Casserole 67

Garlic Roasted Broccoli......................25

Garlic Roasted Winter Vegetables 101

Herb-Buttered Green Beans 36

Herbed Chestnut Stuffing 30

Maple-Dijon Glazed Brussels
Sprouts 92

Mushroom Bread Dressing..............105

Mushroom-Swiss Mac & Cheese.......99

Onion-Stuffed Portobellos 95

Orange-Scented Leeks &
Mushrooms 101

Pasta Puttanesca 98

Savory Mediterranean Orzo...............93

Spicy Garlic Broccoli Rabe 52

Spicy Peppers & Corn 97

Spinach Amandine Stuffing..............102

Sweet Potatoes with Pecan-
Cinnamon Crunch.....................106

Turkey Spinach Amandine
Stuffing 102

Vegetable Couscous...........................43

Winter Squash Casserole 105

STOVETOP ENTREES

Pork Medallions in Green Peppercorn
Sauce..62

Sesame Chicken with Ginger
Shiitake Cream Sauce 65

Veal Saltimbocca.................................44

SLOW COOKER RECIPES

Chicago-Style Beef Sandwiches 87

Northwoods Beef Stew 62

SOUPS

Creamy Garlic & Mushroom Soup.....48

Creamy Garlic & Mushroom
Soup with Pastry Caps...................49

Curried Sweet Potato Soup.................31

Fontina-Vegetable Crab Soup.............42

Rustic Autumn Soup 94

SPINACH

Cranberry-Orange Spinach Salad 95

Layered Spinach & Orange Salad.......87

Southwest Spinach Dip 14

Spinach Amandine Stuffing...............102

Turkey Spinach Amandine
Stuffing 102

SQUASH

Winter Squash Casserole 105

STRAWBERRIES

Frozen Strawberry Dessert 157

Strawberry Chocolate Truffles 164

TIPS

A refreshing ice 27

About crystallized ginger 155

Balsamic vinegar 25

Butter bliss 108

Chocolate stars 154

Citrus loop garnish.............................161

Cleaning leeks 12

Cooked chicken...................................17

Coring pears like a pro 9

Enjoy your party 19

Flattening chicken breasts 65

Forming fan rolls 54

Grinding nuts......................................151

Mile-high chiffon 165

Piping creates new spritz designs 148

Reheating coffee cakes 110

Salad add-ins 87

Scraping a vanilla bean......................145

Second life for tortilla chips 14

Splitting cakes into layers...................56

Tart tampers make it easy 142

Teatime done right...............................84

Testing fish for doneness.....................35

TRIFLES

Caramel Apple Trifle Delight.............173

Cranberry-White Chocolate Trifle.... 159

Pineapple Orange Trifle 70

TURKEY

Golden Roasted Turkey 29

Turkey, Gouda & Apple Tea
Sandwiches.....................................83

Turkey Spinach Amandine
Stuffing 102

VEGETABLES (also see specific kinds)

Fontina-Vegetable Crab Soup............42

Garlic Roasted Winter Vegetables 101

Greek Veggie Tartlets..........................13

Rustic Autumn Soup 94

Vegetable Couscous...........................43

YEAST BREADS (see Breads)

Craft Index

A

A Forest of Trees..................................219
Add Your Own Touch 223

B

Barbed Star 187
Beaded Crafts
    Beads & Chain Necklace 208
    Three-Tiered Beaded Necklace 221
    Twinkling Star Ornament....................201
Beads & Chain Necklace.........................208
Bow Place Cards 29

C

"C" is for Christmas Wreath....................189
Candles
    Ice Candles 214
    Scented Ice Candles..........................214
Centerpieces & Table Toppers
    Charming Napkin Bows 79
    Classy Frosted Hurricane Vase 58
    Gift Bag Flower Centerpiece 60
    No-Sew Table Runner 185
    Poinsettia Candleholders....................178
    Retro Christmas Scene.......................177
    Ribbon Revelry...................................113
    Ribboned Serving Dish 93
    Simply Stunning Hurricane Vase...........58
    Snowy Candle Centerpiece...................23
    Stocking Utensil Holders 89
Chandelier Christmas Wreath...................183
Charming Napkin Bows 79
Checkerboard Tree Skirt 182
Christmas Cards & Gift Tags
    A Forest of Trees...............................219
    Gingerbread Boy Invitations 136
    Festive Package Tags.........................216
    Stamped Christmas Tree Card............219
    3-in-1 Greeting Cards.........................207
Christmas Cookie Poppers......................125
Christmas Countdown Chalkboard..........191
Christmas Tree Floor Mat........................195
Classy Coupon Holder.............................215
Classy Frosted Hurricane Vase 58
Clay Crafts
    Poinsettia Candleholders 178
Cloth Silverware Holder............................197
Countdown to Christmas.........................180

Countin' Sheep Crochet Slippers 228
Cozy Gift Sacks 225
Craft Stick Nativity 194
Crocheting
    Add Your Own Touch 223
    Countin' Sheep Crochet Slippers 228
    Flying Geese Crochet Pillow 220
    Lacy Christmas Balls..........................222
    Peppermint Twist Afghan 226
    Teddy Bear Crocheted Slippers..........229
Cross-Stitched Santa...............................190
Cross-Stitching
    Cross-Stitched Santa..........................190
    St. Nick Finger Towel 217

D

Decorating
    Chandelier Christmas Wreath............ 183
    Christmas Tree Floor Mat...................195
    Cloth Silverware Holder.....................197
    Countdown to Christmas 180
    Dried Flower Angel 192
    Felt Christmas Coasters......................19
    Frosted Snowman 188
    Hide a Picture 193
    Let it Snow Wall Hanging 202
    Making a Multi-Loop Bow..................184
    Standout Seasonal Seating.................184
    Tabletop Tree Boughs 193
Dried Flower Angel 192

F

Fabric Gift Bag....................................... 134
Felt Christmas Coasters........................... 19
Festive Felt Stocking 198
Festive Package Tags..............................216
Fluffy Sheep Ornament...........................181
Flying Geese Crochet Pillow 220
Frosted Snowman 188

G

Gift Bag Flower Centerpiece 60
Gift Giving
    Beads & Chain Necklace 208
    Classy Coupon Holder.......................215
    Countin' Sheep Crochet Slippers 228
    Cozy Gift Sacks 225
    Flying Geese Crochet Pillow 220
    Ice Candles 214

Lacy Christmas Balls..............................222
Painted Angel Christmas Bulb 224
Peppermint Twist Afghan 226
Polar Bear Money Holder 218
Pretty Painted Soap............................206
Purple Bead & Chain Necklace............208
Reindeer Pull-Toy 211
St. Nick Finger Towel 217
Scented Ice Candles 214
Skyline Purse......................................209
Teddy Bear Crocheted Slippers..........229
Three-Tiered Beaded Necklace 221
Votive Trim Kits..................................226
Wine Bottle Gift Sacks 225
Gingerbread Boy Invitations....................136

H

Hide a Picture..193

I

Ice Candles 214
It's a Wrap 213

L

Lacy Christmas Balls................................222
Let it Snow Wall Hanging 202

M

Making a Multi-Loop Bow........................184
Merry Mitten Ornaments 176

N

No-Sew Table Runner 185

O

Ornaments
    Add Your Own Touch 223
    Barbed Star..187
    Craft Stick Nativity 194
    Cross-Stitched Santa..........................190
    Fluffy Sheep Ornament......................181
    Lacy Christmas Balls..........................222
    Merry Mitten Ornaments 176
    Painted Angel Christmas Bulb............224
    Paper Globe Ornaments 186
    Twinkling Star Ornament....................201

P

"P" is for Personalizing...........................189
Painted Angel Christmas Bulb 224
Paper Candy Dish Party Favors 169

Paper Crafts
A Forest of Trees.................................219
Bow Place Cards....................................29
"C" is for Christmas Wreath 189
Festive Package Tags...........................216
Hide a Picture 193
"P" is for Personalizing.......................189
Paper Candy Dish Party Favors 169
Paper Globe Ornaments 186
Stamped Christmas Tree Card............219
3-in-1 Greeting Cards.........................207
Paper Globe Ornaments 186
Party Favors
Christmas Cookie Poppers..................125
Gift Bag Flower Centerpiece 60
Paper Candy Dish Party Favors 169
Peppermint Twist Afghan 226
Place Cards
Bow Place Cards....................................29
Poinsettia Candleholders 178
Polar Bear Money Holder 218
Pretty Painted Soap.................................206
Purple Bead & Chain Necklace...............208

R
Reindeer Pull-Toy 211

Retro Christmas Scene...........................177
Ribbon Revelry.......................................113
Ribboned Serving Dish 93

S
St. Nick Finger Towel................................217
Santa Tree Topper......................................200
Scented Ice Candles..................................214
Sewing
Classy Coupon Holder.........................215
Cozy Gift Sacks...................................225
Fabric Gift Bag....................................134
Festive Felt Stocking 198
Let it Snow Wall Hanging 202
Merry Mitten Ornaments 176
Reindeer Pull-Toy................................211
Skyline Purse.......................................209
Stocking Utensil Holders 89
Wine Bottle Gift Sacks........................225
Simple Snowflake Wreath 177
Simply Stunning Hurricane Vase..............58
Skyline Purse...209
Snowy Candle Centerpiece......................23
Stamped Christmas Tree Card.................219
Standout Seasonal Seating.......................184
Stocking Utensil Holders 89

Stockings
Festive Felt Stocking 198
Stocking Utensil Holders 89

T
Tabletop Tree Boughs 193
Teddy Bear Crocheted Slippers 229
3-in-1 Greeting Cards..............................207
Three-Tiered Beaded Necklace 221
Tree Skirts
Checkerboard Tree Skirt.....................182
Tree Toppers
Santa Tree Topper...............................200
Twinkling Star Ornament..........................201

V
Votive Trim Kits.......................................226

W
Wine Bottle Gift Sacks.............................225
Wreaths
"C" is for Christmas Wreath 189
Chandelier Christmas Wreath.............183
"P" is for Personalizing........................189
Simple Snowflake Wreath 177

Share in the Magic of Christmas

Do you have a unique recipe that has become part of your family's Christmas tradition? Do you have unique for decorating on a budget or make the most superb original gifts? Those are the type of recipes, ideas and crafts we'd like to include in future editions of **Taste of Home Christmas.**

To submit a recipe, craft or decorating idea, print or type the information on a standard sheet of paper. Please be thorough and include directions, measurements and sizes of materials or equipment. Also include your name, address and daytime phone number, photo if available and add a few words about yourself and your submission.

Send to "Taste of Home Christmas Annual," 5400 S. 60th Street, Greendale WI 53129 (include a self-addressed stamped enveloped if you'd like your materials returned). Or E-mail your submission and photos to bookeditors@reimanpub.com (write "Taste of Home Christmas Annual" on the subject line).